DAVID O. McKAY LIBRARY

P9-DUK-290

OCT 29 2004

WITHDRAWN

JUN 24 2004
PROPERTY OF:
DAVID O. McKAY LIBRARY
BYU-IDAHO
REXBURG ID 83460-0405

THE
AGREEMENT

OF THE

CUSTOMS

OF THE

EAST-INDIANS

With Those of the JEWS

(1705)

JOHN TOLAND AND DE LA CRÉQUINIÈRE

TOGETHER WITH

AN
ESSAY

UPON

LITERATURE

(1726)

DANIEL DEFOE

INTRODUCTION

BY

JOEL REED

Publication Numbers 271-276

Published for
The William Andrews Clark Memorial Library and the
UCLA Center for Seventeenth- and Eighteenth-Century Studies

by

AMS Press, Inc., New York
1999

EDITOR

Maximillian E. Novak, *University of California, Los Angeles*

ADVISORY EDITORS

Paula R. Backscheider, *Auburn University*

Charles L. Batten, *University of California, Los Angeles*

John Bender, *Stanford University*

Ralph Cohen, *University of Virginia*

Vinton A. Dearing, *University of California, Los Angeles*

Viscountess Eccles, *Somerville, New Jersey*

George Robert Guffey, *University of California, Los Angeles*

Phillip Harth, *University of Wisconsin, Madison*

Robert D. Hume, *Pennsylvania State University*

Jayne Lewis, *University of California, Los Angeles*

John Loftis, *Stanford University*

Earl Miner, *Princeton University*

Peter H. Reill, *University of California, Los Angeles*

Introduction © 1999 by The Regents of the University of California

Library of Congress Cataloging-in-Publication Data

La C***, Mr. de.

[Conformité des coutumes des Indiens orientaux, avec celles des Juifs & des autres peuples de l'antiquité. English]

The agreement of the customs of the East Indians with those of the Jews, and other ancient people : being the first essay of this kind towards the explaining of several difficult passages in Scripture, etc. / translated from the French of De La Créquinière by John Toland. Together with, An essay upon literature, or, An enquiry into the antiquity and original of letters, proving that the two tables written by the finger of God in Mount Sinai was the first writing in the world, and that all other alphabets derive from the Hebrew, etc. / by Daniel Defoe. Introduction by Joel Reed.

(The Augustan reprints; no. 271-276)

First work originally published: London: W. Davis, 1705. 2nd work originally published: London : T. Bowles, 1726.

"Published for the William Andrews Clark Memorial Library and the UCLA Center for Seventeenth- and Eighteenth-Century Studies."

ISBN 0-404-70271-6

1. Bible—Evidences, authority, etc.—Early works to 1800. 2. Deism—Early works to 1800. 3. India—Social life and customs—Early works to 1800. I. Toland, John, 1670-1722. II. Defoe, Daniel, 1661?-1731. Essay upon literature. III. Title. IV. Title: Essay upon literature. V. Series: Publication (Augustan Reprint Society) ; no. 271-276.

BT89.L1913   1999

220. 1—dc21

97-35902

CIP

All AMS Books are printed on acid free paper that meets the guidelines for performance and durability of the Committee on Production Guidelines for Book Longevity of the Council on Library Resources.

AMS Press, Inc.

56 East 13th Street, New York, NY 10003-4686 U.S.A.

MANUFACTURED IN THE UNITED STATES OF AMERICA

Introduction

Daniel Defoe and John Toland would have bristled at finding themselves between the same covers, though their concerns bound them together in an antagonism over religion, politics, and history that began a few years before Toland published *The Agreement of the Customs of the East Indians and the Jews* (London, 1705); Defoe had the last word (if only because he lived longer than Toland) in the *Essay Upon Literature* (London, 1726) and other anti-deist works of the late 1720s. Though superficially addressing different topics, *The Agreement* and the *Essay* share a concern with the validity of biblical information about the world's cultural history. Toland's text proclaims its intention to use what we would call cultural anthropology or comparative ethnography to explicate the Bible, though it in fact casts doubt on the Bible as an absolute historical source. Defoe, on the other hand, maintains an unshakable faith in scriptural authority while working within the terms of scholarly and rational investigation established by Toland and other deists. Tracing the debate between Toland and Defoe reveals the extent to which the conflicts between deists and Christians (both Anglicans and Non-Conformers could agree on their dislike for deists) extended beyond relatively narrow confines of theology into more encompassing concerns with state policy, cultural history, and even the very nature of knowledge itself. Following their conversations also contributes to our understanding of the reach of Defoe's eclecticism, and demonstrates that Toland, who already holds secure positions in the histories of philosophy and religion, might deserve a chair in literary history as well.

iii

Conflict between Defoe and Toland began soon after Toland published his *Christianity Not Mysterious* (London, 1696); their debates first became public when Defoe mentioned Toland in *Reformation of Manners* (London, 1702), where he appears as *"Socinian T   d"* who "poyson[s] Souls with his infected Breath" (12, 21). Some years later, while writing to gain continued support for official toleration, Defoe insists on the fundamental principles which unite Anglicans and Protestant dissenters by distinguishing the latter from deists like "Mr. *Toland*," who promote *"an unlimited Toleration"*:

> no *Dissenter* will be for tolerating Blasphemy, Atheism, Deism, Socinianism, or any Errors inconsistent with, or invading the Being and Attributes of God, the Doctrines of the Trinity, Redemption by a Mediator, or any essential Point of the Christian Religion.[1]

Defoe's criticism is both doctrinal and political. He rejects the religious views of Toland and other anti-Trinitarians, and he feels that they harm the cause of Presbyterians by giving all dissent a bad name. As High-Church polemicists would merge all dissenters in a single gesture of intolerance, Defoe felt it was expedient to reject Toland's extremity in favor of a limited toleration, in order to give moderate dissenters the appearance of only minor differences with the Church.

Defoe named Toland again some years later, in his *Argument Proving that the Design of Employing and Enobling Foreigners, Is a Treasonable Conspiracy* . . . (London, 1717), though this time Toland fought back. The *Argument* rebuts Toland's *State-Anatomy of Great Britain* (London, 1717), which functioned for many years as a Whig-party bible, and covers a range of issues, from the standing army debate, to Toleration and the naturalization of Europeans who serve the Crown. *The State-Anatomy* appeared when Defoe was writing for the Tory Nathaniel Mist's *Weekly Journal* and defending Harley in his "secret histories."[2] It is no surprise then that in the *Argument* Defoe draws from his long-standing distaste for Toland's religious views to slander his political pamphlets:

> It is meet to unmask this Writer effectually; and we shall find him
> as heterodox in Politicks, as he is in Religion. Nor can Mr. *T* ____ ;
> for that's the Man, forbear acting the *Jesuit* in every Thing he
> appears in. . . . a Man, whose Life has been to act in a Mask, to
> pretend true Religion, and yet profess Heresy; to talk as a Protes-
> tant, and yet worship as a *Socinian.* (50–51)

In *The Second Part of the State Anatomy* (London, 1717), Toland plays
on "D.F." 's inconsistencies, particularly emphasizing the contrast between the *Argument*'s stance against naturalization and the famously
unchauvinistic *True-Born Englishman* (London, 1701). Defoe's *Farther
Argument* (London, 1717) argues in turn that "*De Foe*" could not have
written the *Argument* for "he has been sick in his Bed all the while"
(4–5), then defends "De Foe" by claiming that either he was wrong
in *The True-Born Englishman,* but now is right, or that he has merely
contradicted himself, "a fault which Modesty should have taught
Toland to have pass'd over in silence" (5–6), and finally suggesting
that Toland's "wrangling and unseemly Language upon *De Foe,* are
worth no Notice at all" (43). This dismissal notwithstanding, Defoe
has given Toland a great deal of "notice," and promises that he "shall
have a farther occasion to talk with him" (43).

Though Defoe never again addressed Toland by name, he returned to their conversation in the many works of the 1720s with
which he counters what Maximillian Novak called the "deist offensive" of the early eighteenth century.[3] In *Mere Nature Delineated*
(London, 1726), Defoe turns a story about a "wild child" found in
the Black Forest into a treatise on the nature of the soul and on
proper education, mixing satire with seriousness as when he snips
at the "Skeptical, Deistical" or "Anti-Enthusiastick" readers who
"place so little Weight upon Religion in general, that they never are
at the Pains to make Pretensions to Inspirations or Revelations of
any kind whatsoever" (83). In *The New Family Instructor* (London,
1727) Defoe is even more direct in his criticism of the deists. The
sentiment of the "daughter" and "father" is typical of the tone of
the entire work:

Daugh. O! Sir, they despise all *Revelation* and all *Scripture.*
Fa. Then I think all they say merits to be despised, and themselves
to be despised too, only that we pity and pray for them. (256)

Defoe's own generalizations about deists need to be taken with a
grain of salt; though it appeared to him that a rejection of revelation is
the definitive feature of deism, as Frank Manuel warns, it is difficult
to generalize too much about a very disparate group of thinkers who
held only related tenets.[4] Toland took less of an absolute position
against revealed religion, arguing in *Christianity Not Mysterious* that
for revelation to be divine, it must be based in reason, but he does not
dismiss revelation *per se*.[5] Toland's chapter on the immortality of the
soul in *Letters to Serena* (London, 1704) goes a bit further in allowing
a purely reasonable spiritual belief. Here Toland argues that the con-
cept of the soul's immortality has a history which precedes divine
revelation and which can be traced through scholarly study: it "had
a Beginning at a certain time, or from a certain Author who was the
Inventor thereof, and which was favour'd or oppos'd as Peoples Per-
suasion, Interest, or Inclination led 'em" (21). His philosophical history follows two branches of the immortal soul's progress: first, from
the Egyptians to Greece and its colonies, and from there to Rome and
through Europe, and second, from Egypt to the Chaldeans and further East to India (53). Nowhere does Toland question the immortality of the soul—he was no atheist—but he undermines the foundations of Judeo-Christian exclusivity by substituting secular history
for biblical claims about revelation. One does not need divine revelation to arrive at Christianity's conceptual foundation.

Toland argues in both the *Letters to Serena* and in the later *Nazarenus:
or, Jewish, Gentile, and Mahometan Christianity* (London, 1718) that prejudice and bigotry prevent people from rationally and historically considering concepts such as that of the soul's immortality. The first
"letter" in the earlier work is devoted to understanding the sources of
prejudice, criticizing the nurses and maids who fill their wards with
false and frightening stories, and suggesting that priests also contribute
to the belief in superstition. In *Nazarenus* he more forcefully returns to
this theme, arguing that corrupt priests and princes actively encourage

bigotry to keep their subjects historically ignorant as a way to enslave them under the absolute power of Church and State. Bigotry prevents people from the disinterested inquiry into the history of religion which would demonstrate that Judaism, Christianity, and Islam not only descend from the same source, but that the primitive Church allowed the coexistence of Jewish and heathen practices from respective converts, and that Muslims respect the same rules and patriarchs as "true and original Christianity." In *Nazarenus*, Toland uses his research in ancient cultures and texts to revise the Scriptural canon, questioning the validity and importance of some of the Gospels and substituting others in their stead, and to merge non-Christian cultures into a spiritual coalition which he describes as "Union without Uniformity" (v).

Toland achieves this balance of identity and difference through an essentially scholarly reading of canonical and non-canonical Scripture, though the "Queries to be sent to Christians residing in Mahometan Countries" he appended to the end of the text demonstrate the importance of world travel and exploration to religious investigation.[6] *The Agreement of the Customs of the East Indians with those of the Jews*, a translation of La Créquinière's *Conformité des coutumes des Indiens orientaux, avec celles des Juifs et des autres peuples de l'antiquité* (Brussels, 1704), achieves similar syncretic goals by splitting its attention between scholarship and travel narrative, though it privileges the firsthand observations of the traveller.[7] *The Agreement* proposes to "illustrate many Places of *Ancient Authors*, and particularly of *Holy Scripture*" (iv), a purpose that would seem to ground the text firmly within a Judeo-Christian basis of knowledge.

Demonstrating a similar intention, John Chardin wrote that during his travels in the East he drew up "certain Notes upon very many Passages of the Holy Scriptures, whereof the Explication depends on the Knowledge of the Customs of the *Eastern Countries*;" Toland writes that "the Knowledg of the *Customs* of the *Indians*, is no ways useful in itself . . . only to justify what is told us of the *Ancients*" (viii).[8] But a doubleness in purpose emerges which belies Toland's absolute claim: by asserting the necessity of studying the "*Oriental Customs*" for an accurate understanding of the Bible, Toland suggests that only through the kind of comparative cultural studies he later returned to in *Nazarenus* can a true sense of religion be found (iv.). And as in *Nazarenus* and in *Letters to Serena*, Toland opens *The Agreement* by observing that bigotry and preconceived ideas of religion and culture have traditionally prevented his kind of enquiry, for "it is dangerous to write of Foreign Countries, upon the Account of the Prejudice which many People have against every thing that comes from far" (i); in the final "article" of the text he reaffirms the need to "lay aside all Prejudices" (141).

Certainly the biggest prejudice *The Agreement* faced was that against deism itself. Toland gave his contemporaries cause to link travel literature and deism when he provocatively asks in the preface "whether *God* in giving a *Law* to his people, did not prescribe to them many things which other Nations observ'd before" (vi–vii). This question suggests similarities between *The Agreement* and Toland's consideration of the immortality of the soul in *Letters to Serena*, for it hints that the Jews were not the exclusive recipients of divine revelation; indeed, it rhetorically suggests that God was the recipient of human knowledge. The printer Joseph Marshall must have heard the deist undertones within Toland's rhetoric, for he brought out a second edition of *The Agreement* in 1724, perhaps to capitalize on the controversy created that year by Toland's friend, Anthony Collins. In his *A Discourse of the Grounds and Reasons of the Christian Religion* (London, 1724), Collins argued that

> the mission of MOSES to the *Israelites* suppos'd a former revelation of God (who from the beginning seems to have been constantly giving a succession of dispensations and revelations) to their ancestors: and many of the religious precepts of MOSES were borrowed, or had an agreement with the religious rites of the heathens, with whom the *Israelites* had correspondence. (22)

Collins further claims that religious comparison demonstrates the universality of revelation, and that the history of religion would show a succession from one revealed religion to another (23). Within "Of the Transmigration of Souls," Article X of *The Agreement*, Toland similarly undermines Judeo-Christian priority and exclusivity, stating—while maintaining that he does "not intend" to affirm—that the Indians maintained a steady belief in monotheism and the soul's immortality "while the *Jews* were continually falling into *Idolatry*" (57–58). These rhetorical tricks were not uncommon for Toland, whose works include the Ciceronian *Clito: A Poem on the Force of Eloquence* (London, 1700), and who claimed in *Christianity Not Mysterious* that a philosopher who wanted to engage controversial issues had to choose between "perpetual Silence" and "Paradox."⁹ Other places which question Jewish priority are seen in *The Agreement*'s discussion of the "Worship and Adoration" of fire (25–26), and in its section on the location of temples (32–36), where Toland places the Jews within a broad cultural and religious context; elsewhere, however, as in the long chapter on circumcision, he affirms Judaic priority.¹⁰ Contrary, then, to *The Agreement*'s stated purpose of explaining Scripture (and thus maintaining its status as a privileged document), the text represents the kind of comparative religious and cultural study that would allow Toland to assert the presence of transcultural religious concepts and practices. The presence of religious fundamentals across many cultures and regions would suggest that at one time a single, true religion existed that was gradually corrupted by priestcraft; this comparative study affirms religious belief, though it diminishes the relative importance of any particular religion, including Judaism and its own offshoot, Christianity.

It is therefore at first puzzling to find that Toland warns his readers away from deism. He advises that a traveller needs "a solid Foundation of *Religion*," for the exposure to many different religious practices "is very dangerous, lest by this Means he fall into a kind of Indifference about Religion, which borders upon *Deism*" (152–53). A statement like this, at the end of a text which delighted in relating religious practices from different cultures to one another, might seem like one of those paradoxes which so intrigued Toland, or even like a necessary lie inserted to avoid the censure of anti-deists. It is worth noting here that La Créquinière (or his printer) closed the *Conformité* with an "Extrait du Privilege du Roi" granting permission to publish, though Toland's text ends with a list of related travel literature available from the publisher (thus paying tribute to a different absolute authority: the market). It was perhaps more crucial for La Créquinière to satisfy church and state than Toland, who nonetheless had his own reasons to fear pushing too far the limits of a free press.[11] But perhaps the anti-deist statements are not merely the leftovers of La Cré-quinière's or Toland's self-protection. *The Agreement* is of course far from "indifferent" toward religion, and we should keep in mind that not only did Toland never refer to himself as a deist, but he coined "pantheist" to avoid doing so.[12]

As *The Agreement* amply demonstrates, to become a pantheist demands knowledge of foreign cultures that only comes with travel, or from travel books. The traces of travel literature surface in this text's blend of the history of religion with the exotica which was a seemingly necessary feature of the eighteenth-century's production of knowledge about the East.[13] Article XXVI's discussion of the Fakir's acts of mortification and penance (87–89), Article XXVIII on the snake-charmers (93–95), and most significantly the section on wife-burning (84–87), contain details that stray from the strict purpose of religious syncretism and instead titillate with visions of exotic foreignness. Rather than allowing the "Union without Uniformity" that Toland encourages in *Nazarenus,* these sections suggest that Eastern cultural difference is inassimilable to the West. This suggestion is reinforced further in *The Agreement*'s occasional reliance on stereotypical depictions of Eastern character, as when, attempting to account for the contentious relationship between Eastern rulers and their subjects, Toland writes that "the *Eastern* People are generally more Effeminate, and more addicted to Pleasures than other Nations are, and consequently they are less capable of a true and solid Vertue" (8).

The presence of these stereotypes in a text which urges its readers to "lay aside all Prejudices," like the rhetorical paradoxes within the *Agreement*, formally reinforce a more fundamental dualism that runs through Toland's work. Frank Manuel discusses the "twofold philosophy" within much English deism, which held that a true religion of enlightened, tolerant monotheism coexisted throughout history with a more popular, debased religion reliant on superstition and senseless rituals.[14] In the *Agreement* Toland repeatedly cites the distance between priestly knowledge and popular belief, writing, for example, that the "Common People are fully persuaded of the Vertue and Innocence of the *Fakirs*" (88), or distinguishing between the philosopher Phoe's "Internal, or Secret" doctrine of the "Annihilation of the *Soul* after death . . . [which] is nothing else but *Atheism*" and his "External, or Publick" doctrine of the transmigration of the soul (56–57; see also 99–100). Toland consistently criticized priestly and political manipulation of belief, but nonetheless held that a distinction between "internal" and "external" doctrines was necessary to ensure the ability of a relatively restricted avant garde to pursue the truth free from prejudice and persecution.[15] The practical politics implied by this "twofold philosophy" are evident in Toland's *Pantheisticon* ([London], 1720), which draws a clear distinction between the members of a secret society devoted to rational religion and the servants who wait on them. For Toland, exoteric discussion of controversial issues was the ideal toward which philosophers strive, but might not be able to achieve, and the ability to refute public prejudice was their constant challenge. Thus, with an elitism which plagues even twentieth-century heirs of what Margaret Jacob calls the "Radical Enlightenment," republican ideals are thought to trickle down to the "mob."[16]

Defoe's *Essay Upon Literature* reveals a few contradictions of its own, though it remains consistently anti-deist. Paula Backscheider notes that in the *Essay* Defoe develops a theme he first articulated in his *History of Discoveries:* "the first knowledge of Letters was from Heaven itself, and that immediately by the Finger of God writing the *Hebrew* Law, which we call the Decalogue or Ten Commandments, and putting it into the Hand of *Moses* to teach the *Hebrews*."[17] By reinforcing the biblical version of cultural history to demonstrate its truth and priority, the *Essay* is directed against the methodology of deist writers who disseminate non-Judeo-Christian cultural history as a means of casting doubt on the absolute truth of the Scripture. If Defoe can prove that the Bible is correct about the history of writing, then, by association, it is also true on matters of religious doctrine. Repeating the thesis from the *History of Discoveries*, but emphasizing more strongly its relevance to the deist controversy, Defoe writes in the *Essay:*

> as to *Writing,* and the knowledge of Letters, the first we meet with
> in Scripture, and *Scripture is the oldest as well as the truest Account of*
> *these Things in the World;* was the two *Tables of Stone,* written by
> the Finger of GOD himself. (3)

This thesis of writing's origins directly contradicts statements made
in Article XXXII of *The Agreement,* "Of the Manner in which the Indians WRITE, and of what they make use of instead of PAPER," where
Toland considers attributing the alphabet to Enoch, Moses, and the
Egyptians, before concluding: "I think that 'tis very possible, that the
Phoenicians were truly Inventers of *Letters*" (120). Most of the *Essay* dis-
credits that proposition, in part by borrowing from predecessors who
refuted the first generation of English deists, though Defoe includes
less controversial digressions, and ultimately channels his concern
with the theory and history of religion to the politics of the nation.

While Toland's work is related to that of Collins, Matthew Tindal,
and other deists, Defoe is working within an opposing tradition. He
cites Thomas Godwin (on 27–28) and Theophilus Gale (on 39–40),
and is surely familiar with Edward Stillingfleet's work. Godwin's
Moses and Aaron: Civil and Ecclesiastical Rites, Used by the ancient
Hebrews was a blockbuster of comparative religion, appearing in thir-
teen editions between 1625 and 1686; the early editions include a
chapter on writing which concludes that *"Moses first taught the use of*
letters to the Jewes, and that the Phenicians learned them from the Jewes,
and the *Grecians* from the *Phenicians."*[18] Like *The Agreement,* this work
examines the "conformities" between Jewish and pagan customs, but
without indulging in the paradoxes or ambiguities which help Toland
diminish Judaic, and biblical, priority. In *The Court of the Gentiles: or*
A Discourse touching on the Original of Human Literature Part I: *Of*
Philologie (Oxford, 1669), Gale sets as his first purpose *"to confirme*
the Authoritie, and demonstrate the Perfection, of the Sacred Scrip-
tures," noting *"how much will their Divine Majestie, Perfection, and*
Precellence *beyond all human books and Records, be enhansed hereby"*
(sig. *3v). Gale made this argument in part by combining the biblical
version of alphabetic history with studies of cultural "agreements,"
noting first that Plato includes the Phoenicians, Egyptians, Chaldeans,

and Syrians under the broad category of the Jews (12–13), and then that the Phoenician language is "but a *Dialect* of the *Hebrew*," which shows "the great *Affinity*, and *Correspondence* 'twixt these two *Nations*" (27); Defoe echoes this last point within the *Essay* (on 25). Christian Raue's *A Discourse of the orientall tongues, viz. Ebrew, Samaritan, Calde, Syriac, Arabic, and Ethiopic* (London, 1648) argues that Hebrew was the Adamic language, and that Moses' tablets were the first writing, but does so by combining all of the "orientall" languages into one. With this combination, Raue, and to a lesser extent Gale, slide past the historical difficulties of determining alphabetic priority while maintaining the authority of the Scripture.

Defoe's approach however is closer to that of Stillingfleet, who, in *Origines Sacrae; or A Rational Account of the Grounds of Christian Faith* (London, 1662), seeks to demonstrate "the defectiveness and insufficiency of the Eastern histories as to the giving any full account of themselves and their own original" (45). Stillingfleet devotes more attention to a critique of non-scriptural authorities than does Gale, explaining this focus by arguing that those who contradict the Old Testament's version of ancient history do so in order to question biblical claims for Divine revelation (14). While Christian believers have the certainty of their faith, deists use reason and research to undermine that certainty. For example, in *Letters to Serena* Toland uses the Bible to exploit the contradictions between reported fact and logical conclusions:

> the Jews and a world of Christians pretend that the Egyptians had all their Learning from ABRAHAM . . . . The Pentateuch makes no mention of his Learning; or if he understood Astronomy or any other Science, why did he not take the same pains to instruct his own Nation as he did the Egyptians? . . . it is recorded in the Acts of the Apostles for the Honor of MOSES, not that he follow'd the Doctrins of ABRAHAM, but that he was educated and had excell'd in all the Learning of the Egyptians. The Pentateuch it self makes mention of their Religion and Sciences long before the Law was deliver'd to MOSES, which is an indisputable Testimony of their Antiquity before any Nation in the World. (39–40)

Toland casts doubt on the absolute certainty of the Bible's version of events, and thus on the Bible's absolute authority in matters of religious practice as well. Stillingfleet writes that defending the Mosaic origins of the alphabet is important because if one "take[s] away but any one of the main foundations of the *Mosaical history*, all the *superstructure* will be exceedingly weakened, if it doth not fall quite to the ground" (108).

At many places Defoe follows Gale, Stillingfleet and others by combining antiquarianism with Christian defense. In this way he too is able to confront the deists in a rational debate in their own terms; in fact, by moderating the rhetoric of certainty with one of probability, the *Essay* is steeped in the language of early eighteenth-century epistemology.[19] Rather than assert the truth of the Bible as a matter of faith, Defoe constructs a scholarly and logical argument for scriptural authority. Interrogating, for example, the story that Memnon the Egyptian invented the alphabet, Defoe asks his readers to decide whether it "was more probable" that Memnon taught God to write, or that Memnon learned from the Jews after God's instruction (32). He argues that the case for Memnon's existence before Moses is made "*without any certainty*," and concludes that "all argument from Probability seems to be against them" (33). On the other hand, Defoe argues "from Reason, and the Nature of things" for the alphabet's Mosaic origins (39).[20]

Nonetheless, Defoe does not completely abandon the mystical and mysterious bases of revelation which distinguish Christians from deists, and finds letters themselves evidence of divine inspiration (34). The very workings of the written alphabet, its ability to take the form of diverse languages and to combine into complex words, is miraculous in itself, and as such can only be viewed as evidence of God's supernatural power:

> The writing Words, in all Languages . . . is a surprising Thing in the Nature of it, and if fully and seriously consider'd, carries us beyond Nature it self, ending only in Astonishment and an unresolv'd Wonder. (93–94)

Here then is Defoe's own two-pronged argument: evidence of the alphabet's divine origin is found not only in the Bible, but also in the very unknowability of how the Bible's letters work. The *Essay Upon Literature* refutes both the syncretic argument against the exclusive validity of Scriptural claims for revelation, and the position that one can know God only through reason. While Toland held that many miracles recounted in the Bible are merely hyperbolic stories, and that those which remain could not violate rational, natural law, Defoe counters by claiming that the very letters in which an argument against miracles is written disprove it, and in this way the alphabet becomes an important foundation of scriptural revelation.[21] Thus when Defoe traces the course of the alphabet from God to Moses and the Israelites along two paths, one branching through the Egyptians to the Ethiopians, and the other following Cadmus the Phoenician to the Greeks (29), he slightly but significantly redirects the historical trail of the soul's immortality Toland traveled in *Letters to Serena* (on 53), a slippage from the spirit to the letter which suggests that the two are in some ways comparable developments.

While Defoe's insistence on the mysteries of written language help remind readers of the stakes in the deists' rejection of revelation, it also indicates a strain of anti-intellectualism within the *Essay*. Writing is "incomprehensible" (34), and "Tis hardly to be conceiv'd" how people could invent it on their own (35). These statements illustrate how Defoe is playing to two audiences; in addition to writing for the scholars who would recognize the over three dozen authorities he cites within the text, Defoe is popularizing academic debates for a lay audience. Therefore he chooses not to explain the philosophy of language as it was developed in the work of John Locke and others, though the theory of the arbitrary linguistic sign they provide would have demystified some of Defoe's professed wonder.[22] Accordingly, though Defoe's argument for Hebrew as the original script continued to be made into the eighteenth century, the *Essay* itself appeared to have little direct influence on subsequent histories and theories of writing.[23]

This more popular format also allows Defoe room for the digressions typical of his other prose. His comments on the importance of the book business (114, 120) connect with those in the *Essay* on Egyptian and Phoenician commerce (7–12), to remind us that mercantile concerns were always present for the author of *The Complete English Tradesman* (London, 1726–27) and *A Plan of English Commerce* (London, 1728). Another parallel between the *Essay* and Defoe's other work is seen in his references to the changes language undergoes over time: "having no settled Rule of Speech . . . Custom and ordinary Usage, without any other Authority, as it does to this Day, brought them to differing Dialects and differing Pronunciation of Speech" (61). Later, Defoe shifts this observation from variations in speech to those in writing, specifically criticizing the instability of "Assumption, legitimated only by Custom" in Britain (95, see also 110–11). Here Defoe is returning to a theme from one of his first publications, for the language academy proposed in the *Essay Upon Projects* (London, 1697) would stabilize linguistic change "with a Sort of Judicature over the Learning of the Age. . . . *Custom,* which is now our best Authority for Words, wou'd always have its Original here" (236).

The language academy Defoe proposed would have functioned specifically to increase the glory of English nation and king at the expense of the French. I have argued elsewhere that a more sublimated nationalism exists in Defoe's emphasis on the biblical version of the alphabet's history.[24] Many eighteenth-century "Hebraizers" of English and British culture attempted to draw a direct line of descent from the biblical Jews to inhabitants of Great Britain, and often did so by finding signs of the ancient Hebrew in the history of English.[25] In the *Vindication of the Press* (London, 1718), Defoe complained that the "Infidels possess such Vast Regions, and Religion in its Purity shines in a small Quarter of the Globe" (4), concluding "Tis owing to Writing, that we enjoy the purest Religion in the World" (5). He goes even further, surprisingly praising the official church in a rhetorical flourish which suggests that the English have taken on the mantle of a chosen people, passed on to them with the letters of the sacred text:

> how infinitely happy are we by the Use of our Sacred Writings . . . besides the Satisfaction we of the Church of *England* have in this felicitous Contemplation, that our Religion . . . is the nearest that of our Saviour and his Apostles of any Profession of Faith upon Earth. (5).

Claims such as this one respond to the ways Toland's attribution of the alphabet to the Gentiles challenges the line of descent which depends on writing's Judeo-Christian lineage, just as dispersing the history of ancient Jewish customs throughout the East diminishes any Christian nation's claim as the exclusive recipient of revelation. Defoe's earlier nationalistic claims for a religion of the book are bolstered by the *Essay's* historical work; revelation shines not on the land of the Muslims, nor did it illuminate the ancients who once occupied their present territories. In fact, according to Defoe, Hebrew writing itself has suffered a "miserable Degeneracy . . . occasioned, principly, by . . . the *Turks*," but a substitute for Hebrew has been chosen "in *England*, where the Art of Writing is carried to the highest Perfection of any part of the world" (*Essay*, 105). The biblical history of writing Defoe affirmed against the deists' rational use of secular sources to question the Scripture doubles back, as sacred history writes a tale of secular geo-politics and national self-glorification.

Subsequent research in the history of the alphabet eventually vindicated Toland; scholars today agree that the Phoenicians invented the first alphabetic writing system, while the rediscovery of Sanskrit, the Indo-European language families, and the subsequent reevaluation of the development of both Semitic and Indo-European languages has led to a much more complex view of language and writing than what Defoe could find in the Bible.[26] *The Agreement*, a text described by Basil Guy as "pansophist," is itself not innocent of being too clever in the connections it draws between world cultures.[27] Both of these works are ultimately less significant as accurate cultural history than they are for revealing the tensions comparative cultural studies produced in the early eighteenth century. I am not suggesting, however, that we are "beyond" these tensions. Today's cultural critics and anthropologists grapple no less than those of the eighteenth century with the interrelations of knowledge and prejudice, and have so far been unable to remain completely untainted by the metaphysics of both faith and reason.

Syracuse University

Notes

1. Defoe, *A Review of the State of the British Nation* VI (London, 1709): 410

2. On the *State-Anatomy*'s importance for the Whigs, see Stephen H. Daniel, *John Toland: His Methods, Manners, and Mind* (Kingston: McGill-Queen's University Press, 1984), 31, 12. On Defoe's support for Harley in his *Minutes of the Negotiations of Monsr. Mesnager* (1717), and on his work for the "extreme Tory" Mist, see Paula Backscheider, *Daniel Defoe: His Life* (Baltimore: Johns Hopkins University Press, 1989), 406–08, 430–32.

3. Maximillian E. Novak, "Defoe, the Occult, and the Deist Offensive during the Reign of George I," *Deism, Masonry, and the Enlightenment: Essays Honoring Alfred Owen Aldridge,* ed. J. A. Leo Lemay (Newark: University of Delaware Press, 1987), 93–108.

4. Frank Manuel, *The Eighteenth Century Confronts the Gods* (Cambridge, Mass.: Harvard University Press, 1959), 57.

5. See Daniel, *John Toland,* 41; also see Joel C. Weinsheimer, *Eighteenth-Century Hermeneutics: Philosophy of Interpretation in England from Locke to Burke* (New Haven: Yale University Press, 1993), 46–71.

6. On connections between travel and new knowledge about religion in the early eighteenth century, see P. J. Marshall and Glyndwr Williams, *The Great Map of Mankind: Perceptions of New Worlds in the Age of Enlightenment* (Cambridge, Mass.: Harvard University Press, 1982); R. W. Frantz, *The English Traveller and the Movement of Ideas, 1660–1732* (Lincoln: University of Nebraska Press, 1967); and David A. Pailin, *Attitudes to Other Religions: Comparative Religion in Seventeenth- and Eighteenth-Century Britain* (Manchester: Manchester University Press, 1984).

7. Despite some debate over *The Agreement*'s authorship, the most recent bibliographer attributes the work to Toland; see Giancarlo Carabelli, *Tolandiana: materiali bibliografici per lo studio dell'opera e della fortuna di John Toland (1670–1722)* (Florence: La Nuova Italia, 1975), 114–15. Robert E. Sullivan also discusses the work as Toland's in *John Toland and the Deist Controversy: A Study in Adaptations* (Cambridge, Mass.: Harvard University Press, 1982), 21–22, 45, 159–60, 184, 185, 187, 209, 337.

8. *The Travels of Sir John Chardin into the East-Indies* (London, 1686), sig. C1; Marshall and Williams relate Chardin to *The Agreement* in *The Great Map of Mankind,* 10.

9. Cf. Sullivan, *John Toland and the Deist Controversy,* 45–46, on Toland's use of paradox and rhetorical questions.

10. Though "Of Circumcision" (9–22) ultimately reinforces Judaic pri-

ority and the attribution of custom to revelation, Defoe nonetheless apparently created a pastiche of this chapter and Toland's *Nazarenus* in his *History of Pyrates* (London, 1728), where the deist Caraccioli relates the circumcision of the Jews to what "other Nations do, who inhabit the Southern Climes," as a way to prove that "all Religion was no other than human Policy":

> In short, he ran through all the Ceremonies of the *Jewish*, Christian and *Mahometan* Religion, and convinced him these were, as might be observed by the Absurdity of many, far being Institutions of Men inspired. (8–9)

11. Toland's radical religious views led to his exile from Oxford in 1695, and *Christianity Not Mysterious* was condemned by the Irish Commons and ordered burnt by the public hangman, leading Toland to flee Ireland in 1697; see Sullivan, *John Toland and the Deist Controversy*, 5–9.

12. See Sullivan, *John Toland and the Deist Controversy*, 204.

13. On the interrelated production of knowledge and exotica in the eighteenth century, see the essays included in G. S. Rousseau and Roy Porter, eds., *Exoticism in the Enlightenment* (Manchester: Manchester University Press, 1990).

14. Manuel, *The Eighteenth Century Confronts the Gods*, 65–69. On the "twofold philosophy" also see J. A. I. Champion, *The Pillars of Priestcraft Shaken: The Church of England and its Enemies, 1660–1730* (Cambridge: Cambridge University Press, 1992), 165–69; Peter Harrison, *'Religion' and the Religions in the English Enlightenment* (Cambridge: Cambridge University Press, 1990), 85–98.

15. Cf. Sullivan, *John Toland and the Deist Controversy,* 173–204; and Daniel, *John Toland,* 164–85.

16. Margaret C. Jacob, *The Radical Enlightenment: Pantheists, Freemasons and Republicans* (London: George Allen & Unwin, 1981).

17. Backscheider, *Daniel Defoe: Ambition and Innovation* (Lexington: University Press of Kentucky, 1986), 115–16; *The History of the Principal Discoveries and Improvements* (London, 1727), 84. *The History* collects Defoe's *A General History of Discoveries and Improvements*, released periodically from 1725 to 1727.

18. Godwin, *Moses and Aaron* (London, 1625), 304.

19. On the rhetoric of probability and the epistemological shifts it signals, see Ian Hacking, *The Emergence of Probability* (Cambridge: Cambridge University Press, 1975); Richard W. F. Kroll, *The Material Word: Literate Culture in the Restoration and Early Eighteenth Century* (Baltimore: Johns Hopkins University Press, 1991); Barbara Shapiro, *Probability and Certainty in*

Seventeenth-Century England (Princeton: Princeton University Press, 1983); and Henry G. Van Leeuwen, *The Problem of Certainty in English Thought 1630–1690* (The Hague: Martinus Nijhoff, 1963).

20. Other instances of the *Essay's* rhetoric of probability can be found on 48, 49, 64, 78–79.

21. On Toland and miracles, see Sullivan, *John Toland and the Deist Controversy*, 127–28.

22. On seventeenth- and eighteenth-century language theory, see Hans Aarsleff, *From Locke to Saussure: Essays on the Study of Language and Intellectual History* (Minneapolis: University of Minnesota Press, 1982); Murray Cohen, *Sensible Words: Linguistic Practice in England 1640–1785* (Baltimore: Johns Hopkins University Press, 1977); and M. M. Slaughter, *Universal Languages and Scientific Taxonomy in the Seventeenth Century* (Cambridge: Cambridge University Press, 1982).

23. For example, Francis Wise, *Some Enquiries Concerning the First Inhabitants Language Religion Learning and Letters of Europe. By a Member of the Society of Antiquaries in London.* (Oxford, 1758), 99–101, attributes the first alphabet to Moses' tablets, as does William Stukeley, in *Stonehenge, a Temple Restor'd to the British Druids* (London, 1740).

24. See my "Nationalism and Geoculture in Defoe's History of Writing," *Modern Language Quarterly* 56.1 (1995): 31–53.

25. See Howard D. Weinbrot, *Britannia's Issue: The Rise of British Literature from Dryden to Ossian* (Cambridge: Cambridge University Press, 1993), 403–31, 482–91.

26. See the essays by Frank Moore Cross and Ronald S. Stroud in *The Origins of Writing,* ed. Wayne M. Senner (Lincoln and London: University of Nebraska Press, 1989). Also see Julia Kristeva, *Language: The Unknown; An Initiation into Linguistics,* trans. Anne M. Menke (New York: Columbia University Press, 1989), 93–97.

27. See Basil Guy, "*Ad majorem Societas gloriam:* Jesuit perspectives on Chinese mores in the seventeenth and eighteenth centuries," *Exoticism in the Enlightenment,* 76.

Bibliographical Note

Because of the difficulty in attaining a reproducible microfilm of a complete copy of *The Agreement of the Customs of the East-Indians With those of the Jews and other Ancient People,* we have compiled a working copy of the first edition based on the texts held by the Syracuse University Library, Department of Special Collections (Shelf Mark: DS421.L14) and the British Library (Shelf Mark: 220.e.18). A typical page (17) of the Syracuse University copy measures 185 x 113 mm, and of the British Library copy measures 178 x 108 mm. Reproduction by permission of the Syracuse University Library and the British Library Board. *An Essay Upon Literature* is reproduced from a copy in the William Andrews Clark Memorial Library (Shelf Mark: *PR3401.D10). A typical page (B4) measures 195 x 116 mm.

THE
AGREEMENT
OF THE
CUSTOMS
OF THE
EAST-INDIANS
With thofe of the JEWS,

And other Ancient PEOPLE:

Being the firſt ESSAY of this kind towards the Explaining of ſeveral difficult Paſſages in *Scripture*,

And ſome of the moſt *Ancient Writers*

By the preſent ORIENTAL CUSTOMS, With CUTS.

To which are Added

Inſtructions to Young Gentlemen that intend to Travel.

L O N D O N:

Printed for *W. Davis*, at the *Black Bull*, next the *Fleece-Tavern*, in *Cornhill*, 1705.

A
GENERAL *IDEA*
Of the following
TREATISE.

AS it is dangerous to write of Foreign Countries, upon the Account of the Prejudice which many People have againſt every thing that comes from far, and appears ſurprizing ; ſo 'tis no leſs dangerous to paſs over in ſilence thoſe Countries a Man has ſeen, becauſe many others imagine, that if one does but go out of his own Country, he muſt find every moment wonderful things ; That among Foreigners every thing is extraordinary, and that a Traveller needs only open his Eyes to perceive them. Thus what way ſoever a Man takes, he runs the hazard of being accus'd either of Inſincerity or Negligence.

To ſatisfie the former, a Man muſt relate nothing but what is very common, becauſe every thing that is extraordinary is ſuſpected by them ; and to pleaſe the latter, a Man muſt al ways write of *Prodigies* and *Wonders*, for if a thing be but agreeable to the ordinary *Laws* of *Nature*, it appears to them infipid and defpicable.

I am fully perfwaded that the following *Treatife* will pleafe neither of thefe two forts of *Readers :* For as I have been long enough in the *Indies* to fpeak pertinently about certain Matters which may appear furprizing, fo on the other hand, I ftay'd there too fhort a time, to be able to fpeak confidently about every thing that is there, or to flatter myfelf, that I perfectly underftand the *Politicks* and *Cuftoms* of the *Indians ;* and that I acquir'd in three or four Years fuch a clear and full Knowledg of them, as a Man can hardly have who has liv'd there twenty Years. But if my way of writing of the *Indians,* do not pleafe either of thefe two forts of People ; yet perhaps it will not difpleafe thofe who know how to frame a juft *Idea* of things, altho' they are far diftant, and judg of them without Prejudice : And if they perceive that I am fo unhappy as not to hit always exactly, in the Parallel I have drawn between the *Cuftoms* of the *Indians,* and thofe of the *Ancients ;* yet at leaft I dare flatter myfelf, that they will not diflike the Defire I have fhown of opening a way for the Knowledg of *Antiquity ,* by ftudying the *Cuftoms* of thefe People.

I have gone quite out of the common Road, which is ufually taken by almoft all thofe who write Relations; for he that writes the fame things which others have faid before him,

and

and agrees with them in every thing, is only their *Transcriber*; and this a Man may easily do, without giving himself the trouble of going so far off: but if one writes other things than what has been said before, he does but increase the Confusion which is already too great among the greatest part of the *Writers* upon this Subject; and yet he cannot flatter himself that he shall meet with better Entertainment than others, and find more Credit with his *Readers*, who will think (as they may certainly do) that in process of time, there will appear new *Writers*, who will still publish different *Accounts*.

I did at first resolve to apply myself only to the Study of the *Religion* of the *Indians*, and the first *Discoveries* I made confirm'd me in this *Resolution*, having observ'd such a *Connexion* between their *Principles* and their *System* of a triple *Divinity*, viz. *Barhama, Bisnou* and *Roudre*, as is not to be found in that Rabble of *Gods*, whom the *Greeks* and *Romans* ador'd, and of whom *Hesiod* has describ'd the *Genealogy*. But since Error is always Error, and cannot possibly have such a Concatenation of Proofs and Reasons as Truth has, but is always attended with Contradiction and Confusion, when I came to descend more particularly into the Detail of the different *Sects* among the *Pagans*, and to penetrate further into their *Mysteries*, I found in them so many and great *Absurdities*, that I thought I could not reasonably apply my Mind to them; especially considering, that there is scarce any thing to be observ'd that is common

to

to their *Theology,* and that of the Ancient *Pagans.*

I had not the same Opinion of their peculiar *Customs,* which I look'd upon as precious Remains of Antiquity, which may serve to illustrate many Places of *Ancient Authors,* and particularly of *Holy Scripture,* these Notices being absolutely necessary for giving a Literal Explication of certain Passages to which the most Learned Interpreters have often given only an Allegorical Sense, for want of being well inform'd of the *Oriental Customs.*

Besides, we find in the *Scripture,* many Places, and also many Terms, which at first hearing, appear to us harsh: But after we have a little frequented the *Eastern Nations,* they grow familiar to us, because among them we may still see all these Characters of *Antiquity,* which are observ'd in the *Bible,* and generally in the Books which speak of the *Jews,* or any other Ancient *People.*

St. *Jerom* knew very well the Usefulness of this Knowledg, for he travell'd all over the *East* to learn their *Customs,* and notwithstanding all the Reports that have been spread against his Reputation, 'tis certain that he study'd under a *Doctor* of the *School* of *Tiberias,* who taught him the Ancient *Customs* of the *Jews,* and afforded him great Assistance in his *Translation* and his *Commentaries.*

My Design was to travel over *Asia,* if I could have done it with any Convenience, and to
                                                        have

have obferv'd in it exactly the fmalleft things, fuch as, for Inftance, the old *Cuftoms* of the Common People, their *Feftivals*, their *Proverbs*, their manner of *Building*, of *Feeding*, *Cloathing* themfelves, and of *Cultivating* the *Ground*: For I am very certain, that if any Footfteps of *Antiquity* are to be found there, they are to be met with among the fimpleft and plaineft fort of *People*, among them who dwell in *Defarts*, and in general among thofe who are leaft civiliz'd, who have neither Ambition nor Riches, to invent new Fafhions, or to follow thofe which the great Lords invent, and confequently never alter from the *Fafhions* of their *Anceftors*.

All *Travellers* almoft have hitherto neglected this kind of Obfervation, which they look'd upon as Trifles and things unworthy of their Confideration. And indeed 'tis true, that taken by themfelves they are nothing worth; but if one does but a little reflect upon the Advantages that may be drawn from them, for the Underftanding of *Ancient Authors*, he will eafily grant, that 'tis very well worth our Pains to fearch after them and write them down.

I neglected nothing that might conduce to inftruct me fully in the *Cuftoms* of the *Indians*, and I obferv'd even thofe that are moft common, as exactly as poffibly I could: But if a Man would fee them in all their Purity, he fhould go farther up into the Country than I did; becaufe by the Sea-fide, the continual *Commerce* they have with the *Europeans*, makes

A 4   them

them, remiſs in the Obſervation of their Rules, and negligent as to many things which formerly they were oblig'd to do by a ſevere Law. Whence it comes to paſs that they are commonly neither *Chriſtians*, nor religious Obſervers of *Paganiſm*; and this makes it more difficult to make Diſcoveries there : Beſides that one muſt learn their Cuſtoms by himſelf, for it is almoſt impoſſible to draw any thing out of them upon this Subject, the greateſt part of them being too buſie about *Traffick*, to think of any thing elſe, and the Learn'd Men among their *Brahmans* being perſwaded, that their *Doctrines* and *Rules* are prophan'd, whenever they are communicated to *Foreigners*.

I was therefore oblig'd to make Inquiry into their moſt ordinary *Actions* and *Cuſtoms*, and from them to draw almoſt all the *Remarks* I have made, whence you may eaſily conclude that they could not be very numerous.

I have made it my Buſineſs to inquire only after that which the *Indians* have in common with other *Ancient People*, but more particularly with the *Jews*, without entring upon that great Queſtion, *viz.* Whether thoſe who in the Days of *Pekah* the Son of *Remaliah* the King of *Iſrael*, were carry'd into *Aſſyria* by *Tiglethpileſer*, or thoſe whom *Shalmaneſer* tranſported thither under the Reign of *Hoſeah*, did not ſo far penetrate into the *Indies*, that they communicated to the People there, thoſe things wherein we obſerve them now to reſemble the *Jews* ? Or, whether *God* in giving a *Law* to his People,

ple, did not prefcribe to them many things which other Nations obferv'd before, as being good in themfelves?

Many things may be alleg'd in favour of each of thefe Opinions, but becaufe they are only probable Reafons, and demonftrative Proof cannot be given upon fuch an Article as this, I have thought fit to wave them.

Some perhaps will think it ftrange, that this Work confifts only of Remarks independent upon one another, that have no Connexion together: But this way I made choice of, becaufe in effect each *Article* treats of a particular Matter which has no Relation to the preceding and following *Articles*; befides, that thefe *Articles* could not have been connected together, but only by long *Digreffions*, which would have been very impertinent, and would certainly have difgufted thofe, who defire to fee nothing in a Book but what fhould be there, *i. e.* what the Title promifes, or at leaft has fome Relation to it.

I have cited fome Paffages of *Scripture* in *Latin*, efpecially when they treat of any difficult Matter, wherein 'tis hard to find out the true Sentiment of the Author. And as to fome Places of *Greek* Authors I have alleg'd, I have given their Senfe in the Words of the beft Tranflators, becaufe there are many who are otherwife very Learned, that do not underftand the *Greek Tongue*. I know that thefe Citations will not relifh well with many People; but then on the other fide, I believe they will

be

be very grateful to others; and thofe who are acquainted with the Matter treated of will rejoice to find that they can judg of them by themfelves, without having Recourfe to the Authors I quote, provided I have given the true Senfe of the Paffages I relate, and rightly inferr'd the Conclufions I have made.

Perhaps fome will wonder, that I have faid much more of the *Ancients* than of the *Indians*, particularly in my firft *Remarks*, wherein having related fuccinctly enough what concerns the *Indians*, I have treated very largely of *Antiquity*: But they will not think it ftrange, if they well confider what I have already faid, *viz.* That the Knowledg of the *Cuftoms* of the *Indians*, is no ways ufeful in itfelf, That I thought my felf oblig'd to make ufe of it, only to juftify what is told us of the *Ancients*, and to explain it whenever an Occafion offers, and in a word that *Antiquity* was my only Aim.

Since in all the Places where I have difcours'd of the *Indians*, and of their Agreement with the *Ancients*, I have not always explain'd fome Paffages of *Ancient Writers*; perhaps it may be ask'd, why I have mention'd that Agreement, fince the *Indian Cuftoms* afford us no Light, in fome Cafes, for explaining the *Scripture* and the *Writers* of the firft Ages. To which I anfwer, That the chief end which I propos'd to myfelf in making thefe Remarks, was indeed to explain fome Places in the *Ancient Writers* which appear to be difficult; but this was not my only End, for I defign'd alfo by this means

to

to fatisfie thofe, who cannot imagine that there ever were People fo blind, as the *Pagans* are reprefented to have been in ancient Times; and to fhow them, that fince there are People, who are fo unhappy now at this day, as to live in thefe monftrous Superftitions, 'tis not to be wondred at, if there have been fuch in former times.

I muft entreat the Reader to obferve, that the greateft part of the Conclufions I have drawn, from the Agreement there is between the *Cuftoms* of the *Indians*, and thofe of the *Jews*, or generally of any other *Ancient People*, are propos'd only as Conjectures, and that I do not blindly efpoufe any of the Opinions, that are fcatter'd here and there in this fmall Tract.

I muft alfo defire the Reader to take notice, that when in *Article* 29, I give an Account from the Teftimonies of *Quintus Curtius*, and *Chares* of *Mitylene*, of the *Drunkennefs* of the *Indians*, and that famous *Bacchanale* which was kept after the Death of *Calanus*, to honour his *Funerals*; and when I fay, that the Conqueror at that Drinking-Match, drunk 192 Pints of Wine, according to the Account that *Athenæus* gives of four *Congiufes*, I did rather regard the Reputation of the great Drinkers, whom the Author fuppofes to be among this People, than the manner in which the Word *Congius* is commonly explain'd, which in ftrictnefs ought not to contain more than 4 Pints and an half, and fo 4 of them would be no more than 18 Pints, which

which would not have been a thing so extraordinary. *Novellius Torquatus,* as *Pliny* relates, *l.* 14. *c.* 22. drunk 3 *Congiuses* at one Draught, *i. e.* 13 Pints and a half; whereupon the Name of *Tricongiarius* was given him. And *Julius Capitolinus,* in the Life of *Maximinus,* says, that he drunk in one day an *Amphora,* which contain'd 8 *Congiuses,* that amount to 36 Pints, according to the common way of reckoning. And therefore, the Reason why I assign'd to 4 *Congiuses* the Measure of 192 Pints, was only, because I believ'd, that the way in which Authors speak of this famous Drinking-Match requir'd no less a Quantity: But moreover I suppose a *Congius* to contain 6 *Sextariuses,* as all Men do, and each *Sextarius* to contain 8 Pints; and herein I have follow'd the way of Measuring us'd by the Gagers, because I knew not how I could better accommodate myself to the Description which *Chares* of *Mitylene* has given us of this Debauch. The Reader may judge if he pleases, whether I am in the right or no.

E R R A T A.

PAge 8. line 15. dele *to.* p. 21. l. 1. r. *quamobrem.* p. 28. l. 28. f. *understands,* r. *explains.* p. 33. l. 30. after *Half-tribe,* r. *of.* p. 38. before *what,* r. *for.* p. 39. l. 3. after *of,* r. 520. p. 41. l. 27. f. *we,* r. *were.* p. 45. l. 1. f. *from,* r. *for.* p. 51. l. 8. r. *Huetius.* 69. l. 25. d. *is.* p. 72. l. 2. r. *Church.* p. 73. after *House,* r. *of.* p. 75. l. 16. after *punishing,* r. *them for.* p. 98. l. 9. after *Silver,* d. *that.* p. 99. l. 25. f. *to,* r. *in.* p. 111. l. 16. d. *unto.* p. 119. l. 30. d. *that.* p. 120. l. 16. after *if,* r. *it.* p. 121. l. 13. r. *veloci.* p. 133. l. 14. after *have,* r. *to.* p. 142. l. 25. d. *that.* p. 143. l. 25. f. *higher,* r. *thicker.*

A Table of the ARTICLES.

ARTI-

A Table of the Articles.

ARTI-

A Table of the Articles.

ARTI-

A Table of the Articles.

THE

The Agreement of the

CUSTOMS

Of the Oriental

INDIANS,

With thofe of the *Jews*, and other Ancient *Nations*.

ARTICLE. I.

Of the Dominions of the Great Mogol.

ALtho' I am refolv'd to relate nothing in my Remarks, but what I found the *Indians* retain ftill in common with the Ancients; yet fince the People of whom I treat, live under the Dominion of the *Great Mogol,* I thought it indifpenfably neceffary to fay fomething of that *Empire,* and to give at leaft a General *Idea* of its Commencement and Extent.

Temur-lengue, which fignifies the *Lame Prince,* and whom we corruptly call *Tamerlan,* was the firft that Founded the *Empire* of the *Great Mogol,* whom fome Authors pretend to be defcended from an Ancient and Noble Family of the *Tartars;* but in this they

B　　　　　are

are singular, for almost all other Historians, who have wrote of him, do confess, that he was descended of the dregs of the People, and ow'd his Advancement purely to his own Merits.

He Married the Daughter of the Prince, who had the Sovereign Command in all the *Great Tartary*, and who was one of the Successors to the Famous *Gingius-Can*, who had been the first *Emperor* of it. About the Year of *Jesus Christ*, 1400. he put himself at the Head of the *Mogols*, who were the People that inhabited the *Eastern* Part of *Great Tartary*, and march'd with them into the *Indies* ; where having Subdued many of the petty Princes of *Indostan* and the Neighbouring Provinces, at last he laid the Foundation of that vast *Empire*, which at this Day is call d, the *Empire* of the *Great Mogol*.

'Tis very well known, that it was he who took Prisoner the Famous *Bajazet*, *Emperor* of the *Turks* ; and who having try'd all possible means of making him more easy in his Captivity, and even of coming to some Accommodation with him, was at last oblig'd, by the fierce Temper and continual Menaces of this *Sultan*, to shut him up in an *Iron-Cage* ; which so enrag'd him, that he broke his Head against one of its Bars. *Tamerlan* had a vast Soul, was of an undaunted and enterprizing Spirit, and would have been unreproachable, if he had had a little more Humanity.

The *Empire* lost much of its Lustre under his Posterity, who for the most part neglected the Profession of War, and wholly addicted themselves to their Pleasures, leading an Idle and Luxurious Life ; but in the last Age, a Prince ascended the Throne, who had nothing of the Effeminate Softness of many of his Predecessors, and did no less resemble *Tamerlan* in his Courage and great Exploits, than in the severity of his Temper : He it was, that did not only

restore

reſtore to the *Empire* the Glory it had loſt, but alſo enlarg'd its Bounds much further than ever they were before.

Aurenge-Zeb is the Prince I mean; but before I proceed to ſay any thing more of him, I think it will be neceſſary to begin a little higher with the Hiſtory, and to give an Account after what manner his Father aſcended the Throne, and how he was driven away from it.

Chab-Jehan, who before his Advancement to the *Empire* was call'd *Sultan Corom*, was the Father of *Aurenge-Zeb*; He was the Son of *Jehan Guire*, *Great Mogol*, and might expect to Succeed him without difficulty: But either from an impatient Deſire of Dominion, or ſome Private Diſcontent, he Rebell'd againſt his Father, and it happen'd luckily for him, that his Father Dy'd during the time of his Rebellion; for thoſe who under *Jehan Guire* had Govern'd the *Empire*, knowing that *Sultan-Corom* was no Friend of theirs, had procur'd *Bulloqui* the Grand-ſon of *Jehan Guire* to be Proclaim'd *Emperor*. This News was ſo far from Humbling *Sultan-Corom*, that it did only irritate him the more; for he purſu'd *Bulloqui*, and found means to Apprehend him, and caus'd him to be Strangled after he had Reign'd three Months: Whereupon he was generally acknowledg'd for *Great Mogol*, under the Name of *Chab-Jehan*.

This Prince continued only ſo long in the quiet Poſſeſſion of his Dominions, while his four Sons were ſo Young, that they were not capable of diſturbing his Repoſe; for aſſoon as they came to Years of Diſcretion, and could underſtand what it was to bear Rule and Command over others, they all pretended to the Supreme Power. *Dara* by the Right, which the Title of Eldeſt Son to *Chab-Jehan*, gave him, and the reſt being mov'd meerly by their own Ambition.

Of thefe four Brethren *Dara* was the Eldeft, *Sultan Sujah* the fecond, *Aurenge-Zeb* the third, and *Morad-backche* the youngeft. *Chah-Jehan* had alfo befides them two Daughters, whereof the Eldeft was call'd *Begum-Saheb*, who was no lefs Witty than Cruel, and the other was *Banchenara-Begum*, one of the fineft Princeffes of her Age.

Dara, *Sultan Sujah* and *Morad-backche*, fufficiently difcover'd their Defign to throw off all Subjection to one another, and to live free and independent; but *Aurenge-Zeb*, who was a more fubtle and excellent Wit, but more referv'd, and was no lefs Ambitious than the reft, thought fit to appear unconcern'd as to the pretenfions of *Empire*, that he might the better compafs his Defigns, by which means he obtain'd all the good Succefs he defir'd. To remove therefore all kind of Sufpicion, and to prevent any Diftruft his Brethren might entertain of him, he embrac'd the Life of a *Faquir*, *i. e.* of a poor *Monk*, and a Man who had wholly renounc'd all the Pomps and Pretenfions of this World; and being difguis'd under this Mask, he knew fo well how to provoke his Brethren againft one another, that they all took Arms, and fcarce one of them knew why they did it.

Aurenge-Zeb, during thefe Divifions, fided always with the weaker Party, and publickly declar'd, that for his Part, having renounc'd all kind of Pretenfions, he labour'd for nothing but the Publick Good, and to procure his Father's Repofe; yet in Private he fpar'd for nothing, to make Friends under-hand, and to draw to his Party the Principal Heads of the *Empire*. When he faw that he had fufficient Force to Support him, and that the moft confiderable *Omrah's*, who are Generals of the *Moors*, were joyn'd to his Intereft; at laft he pull'd off the Mask, and his Brethren knew, but too late, that by Rifing one againft another, they had only labour'd to procure

cure their own Ruin, and the Advancement of *Aurenge-Zeb.*

He first discover'd himself, by detaining his Father *Chah-Jehan* Prisoner, in a Fortress to which he had fled, where he Dy'd six Years after. This Prince, under his Misfortune, never appear'd to complain; for he had formerly Rebell'd against his Father, and now his Children Rebell'd against him. After *Aurenge-Zeb* had secur'd his Father, he endeavour'd to seize his Brethren, and to render them uncapable of disturbing him in his *Empire*: And this he did, without much trouble, accomplish; for *Dara*, who was the Eldest, was taken and Poison'd, and he easily found means to set his Heart at ease, as to any Danger from the rest of his Brethren. In the Year 1660. he was Proclaim'd the *Great Mogol.* Every one may read in Monsieur *Bernier*, and many other Authors, who have wrote of the *Indies*, all the particular Passages of the Wars between *Aurenge-Zeb* and his Brethren, and the means he made use of to ascend the Throne. He was still alive when I left the Kingdom of *Bengala*, which was the 10th. of *February*, in the Year 1702. but the common report was, that he was become a Child again.

It cannot be deny'd, but this Prince was one of the greatest Politicians, and one of the greatest Monarchs in his time, and any that reads the History of his Reign, will be fully satisfy'd of it. Tis true indeed, he is accus'd of causing great Confusions in his Family, and of using it with great hardship, particularly his Father and his Brother *Dara*; yet in all this, he did nothing but follow the Maxims of the greatest part of the *Eastern* People, among whom, whoever pretends to a Throne, must run the hazard of losing all, that he may gain all:

If any Man has a mind to compare *Aurenge-Zeb* to one of the Princes, who has appear'd very glorious in *Europe*, I think he cannot make choice of a

fitter

fitter Perſon for that end than *Pope Sixtus* the 5*th*. For if *Aurenge-Zeb* was not Advanc'd to the Throne, but by giving Publick Teſtimony that he had renounc'd it, and by leading a retir'd Life for a long time : So neither was *Sixtus* promoted to the Pontifical Dignity, but by his affected Speeches, that he was nowiſe fit for it, and by paſſing the time of his Cardinalſhip in a ſtrict Solitude, tho' he liv'd in the middle of *Rome*. *Aurenge-Zeb*, did not appear to be in truth what he was, until after his advancement to the Throne, or at leaſt until his Brethren could but weakly conteſt the Crown with him, and he was ſure to obtain it : So *Sixtus* did not appear to be what really he was, until the Triple-Crown was plac'd upon his Head ; for the World was aſtoniſh'd to ſee ſo great a change in him, all on a ſudden. Both of them made the Dominions they Poſſeſs'd to flouriſh, both of them procur'd Fear and Reſpect from their own People, and the Neighbouring Princes ; and tho' both of them were too ſevere, and did many things, which being conſider'd in themſelves, ought not to be commended ; yet both of them acquired to themſelves Immortal Glory. *Aurenge-Zeb* indeed made great Conqueſts, which *Sixtus* did not. But then 'tis to be conſider'd, that the firſt Reign'd Forty two Years, whereas the other held his Pontificat only Five ; which was a great happineſs to many of the Princes of *Italy*, but more particularly for the King of *Spain*, who perhaps could not have kept the Kingdom of *Naples* if he had Reign'd much longer ; for he had as great a deſire to make himſelf Maſter of it, as *Aurenge Zeb* had to join the Kingdom of *Golgonda* to his own *Empire*, upon the account of the rich Mines of Diamonds that are there. And if he had liv'd ſome Years longer, perhaps he might have Succeeded as well in his Enterprize, as *Aurenge-Zeb* did in his.

'Tis

'Tis hard to determine, whether the Refolution to Die or Reign, wherewith almoft all the *Eaftern* Princes are poffeffed, who have any Pretenfions to a Crown, be the confequence of the Cruelty and Fiercenefs of the Kings, under whofe Government they are oblig'd to live ; or whether the Inhumanity and Cruelty which the Kings difcover, be a confequence of that infatiable Defire of Reigning which poffeffes the Princes that are fubject to them : Neither is it certainly known whether the Princes are Cruel and Sanguinary upon the account of the Inconftancy of their Subjects, and the little Love they have for them, or whether their Subjects are fo inconftant, and have fo little Love for them, becaufe they are Cruel and Sanguinary : For in fine, fome will fay, for inftance, how can any be Mild and Gentle, who has to do with fuch Subjects : With a People who are continually inclin'd to Rebellion ? But others again will fay, who would not endeavour to be deliver'd from the Tyranny of fuch Princes, who breath nothing but Fire and Sword ; and how can any Subject love them, and be faithful unto them?

But as to this difficulty, it may probably be alleg'd, that the little Love which the *Eaftern* People have commonly for their Kings, is an effect of the Inhumanity and Cruelty of the firft Kings that Reign'd there, whofe Tyranny made fo ftrong an Impreffion upon the Minds of the People, that in the following Times, they look'd upon all their Princes as Tyrants ; whereupon the Succeffors of thefe fame Princes were oblig'd, for preventing the deadly confequences which fuch bad Impreffions as the Conduct of their Anceftors had made upon their Minds might produce, to continue the fame Methods, *i. e.* to treat their Subjects as Slaves, to keep them always in Fear, and to be cruel Tyrants to them as their Predeceffors had been. Thus the Cruelty of the firft Sovereigns produc'd, at firft, this

Diftruft

Diftruft and Fear in the Minds of the Subjects ; and this Diftruft and Fear of the Subjects, produc'd in the following Times, the fame Cruelty in the Sovereigns.

Befides, the *Eaftern* People are generally more Effeminate, and more addicted to Pleafures than other Nations are, and confequently they are lefs capable of a true and folid Vertue, which is no lefs neceffary for a good Subject than it is for a great Prince : For if it requires much Knowledge and Sharpnefs of Wit, to know how to Command, and to Rule with Difcretion ; both thefe Qualifications are no lefs neceffary to know how to Obey as we fhould ; and it requires at leaft as much Greatnefs of Soul, to be a good Subject as to to be a good Sovereign.

But tho' there were no occafion to fear any thing from the evil Temper of Subjects, yet many Princes would ftill be oblig'd, if I may fo fay, to be Cruel to them : For the People are fo inconftant, that they cannot long continue in that Reverence they owe to their Kings, either becaufe they know them to be truly Good, and confequently grow too bold ; or becaufe they know that they are Cruel, and confequently dread them : So that many *Eaftern* Princes, being devoid of thofe good Qualities which fhould retain their Subjects in their Duty, muft be in a manner forc'd, for this end to make ufe of Tyranny and Cruelty.

The Dominions of the *Great Mogol* extend on the Eaft fide, juft beyond the River *Ganges* ; on the South they are bounded on the Ocean ; on the Weft by *Macran* and *Candabar*, and on the North, by the *Tartars*. The two chief Cities of this *Empire*, are *Agra* and *Delli*, which are both called *Capital*.

I think it may be affirm'd, without any danger of miftaking, that the Dominions of the *Great Mogol* are the Richeft in the World ; for not only all the Nations of *Europe*, but alfo thofe of *Afia*, carry thither

ther Gold and Silver, and bring nothing thence but Merchandize : So that this *Empire* is a kind of Gulf, into which all the Riches of the World are thrown, and from which nothing of them ever comes out again.

ARTICLE. II.

Of Circumcision.

THE *Pagan Indians* (at leaſt ſo far I have had any knowledge of them) do not uſe Circumciſion at all; and yet I have thought fit to ſay ſomething of Circumciſion, with reſpect to the People of *Guinea*, among whom it is in uſe, and to thoſe Countries of it thro' which I have Travelled ; becauſe ſome Cricks have pretended to prove by this and other Examples, which I am now to relate, that Circumciſion was not a thing peculiar to the *Jews* ; and that without any relation to the Precept of God to *Abraham*, it was practis'd by other Nations, and look'd upon as a natural means of facilitating Generation to them.

But before I examine the Paſſages they allege, and the Examples they relate to ſupport their Opinion, I think it will be convenient to ſay ſomething in general of Circumciſion, to give an account of the Time in which it was inſtituted, and to conſider the Terms which the Scripture uſes upon this occaſion.

We hear nothing of Circumciſion in Scripture before *Abraham*, to whom God appointed this Ceremony, as a token of the Covenant, which ſhould hereafter be made between him and the Poſterity of this Holy Patriarch. *And ye ſhall circumciſe the fleſh of your foreskin, that it may be for a ſign of the Covenant between me and you,* Gen. 17. 11. This then was the reaſon, why God appointed Circumciſion to

the

the *Jews, viz.* to be a Sign and Token of the Covenant which he had made with *Abraham*, and the Nations which should Descend from him; and here is no mention of any peculiar advantage by it.   In the same Chapter, God threatens in his Fury, him that shall not be Circumcised, and says, that he shall be cut off from his People.   *And the uncircumcised Man-child, whose flesh of his foreskin shall not be circumcised, that Soul shall be cut off from his People*, Gen. 17. 14.   In effect, when *Moses*, by God's command, left the Country of the *Midianites*, to go and deliver his People from the hard Bondage under which they groan'd in *Egypt*, the Angel of the Lord would have kill'd his Son by the way, because he was not Circumcis'd, and *Sephora* could not otherwise pacify the just Anger of Heaven, but by taking quickly a sharp Stone, with which she Circumcis'd him.

The *Midianites* in all probability did not use Circumcision at all, for if they had observ'd this Ceremony, 'tis very probable that *Jethro*, who was a Priest of *Midian*, would not have suffer'd his Son-in-law; contrary to the Custom of the Country, to remain uncircumcis'd: Besides that *Moses*, if he had been in a Country where Circumcision was us'd, would not have fail'd to Circumcise him, being so zealous as he was for the Religion of his Fathers: And therefore 'tis very probable, that he was hinder'd by the contrary Custom of the Country in which he was.

The *Sichemites*, who were a People of the Land of *Canaan*, were not at all subject to the Law of Circumcision, neither did they all undergo it, until they were willing to comply with the Family of *Jacob*, that *Sichem* who was the Son of *Hemor*, the Prince of the Country, might marry *Dina*, Gen. 34. The *Philistines* at that time were not circumcis'd, and they were no less known to the Jews, by the title of the Uncircumcis'd, than by that of their own Coun-

Country: Thus *Saul* having loft the Battel, bid his Armour-bearer kill him, for fear left he fhould fall alive into the Hands of the *Philiftines*, and be made a May-game and a Laughing-ftock to thefe uncircumcifed People. *Then faid* Saul *unto his Armour-bearer, draw thy fword, and thruft me thorough therewith, left thefe uncircumcis'd come and thruft me thorough, and abufe me,* 1 Sam. 31. 4. In fine, it feems that the word *Uncircumcis'd*, was ufed by the Jews to fignify all the other Nations, or at leaft all thofe that were not defcended from *Abraham*. Neverthelefs, I do not pretend to affirm, that none but the Jews were circumcifed, but only that Circumcifion was eftablifh'd among them as a Sign to diftinguifh them from other People; and that if any other Nation made ufe of it, the Ufage was only deriv'd from them, and obferv'd only in imitation of them, as I fhall now endeavour to prove.

Some indeed pretend, that Circumcifion was not peculiar to the *Jews, i. e.* that without any relation to the Command which God gave to *Abraham*, many other People have practis'd it. Thofe of this Opinion, endeavour to fupport it by fome Paffages of the Ancients, and befides allege the Example of many Nations, among whom this Ceremony is ftill in ufe; nay they pretend further, that it is even neceffary to fome People, who without it cannot perform the act of Generation.

Herodotus fpeaking of Circumcifion, tells us, *lib.* 2. that thofe of *Colchos, Egypt* and *Ethiopia*, were the only People that were Circumcis'd at firft. This Author adds afterwards, that he dare not affirm which of thefe People it was that firft had Circumcifion, becaufe it appears to be very ancient among all of them: But neverthelefs, fince the *Ethiopians* and thofe of *Colchos*, had much Commerce and Correfpondence with the *Egyptians*, he thinks it may very well be deriv'd from them, and confequently that it came

in

in the first place from *Egypt* : And this Conjecture he builds upon this Remark, that none but the *Phœnicians*, who held some Correspondence with the *Egyptians*, made use of Circumcision, during the time it was not used by those who had no Commerce but with the *Grecians*. *Herodot. Ib.*

Diodorus Siculus lib. 4. *c.* 2. speaking of the *Troglodites* says, That they circumcis'd themselves as the *Egyptians* did. These *Troglodites* were the People that inhabited that Part of *Africa*, which we now call the Coast of *Abex* or *Abexim*, which is the *Eastern* Part of *Abyssinia*. And moreover, it is reported that the Famous *Thales* caus'd himself to be circumcis'd, that he might appear the less Barbarous and Strange to the Learned Men of *Egypt*, and be more easily admitted into their Conversation by complying with them in this Custom, and so put himself in a Capacity to penetrate further into their Mysteries. *Clem. Alex. Strom. l.* 1.

Upon these and some other such-like Passages, some Learned *Criticks* in our Days have endeavour'd to prove (as I have already told you) that *Circumcision* was in use among many other People, who never receiv'd it from the *Jews*, and from the Precept which *God* gave them about it : And they pretend likewise that among certain Natives, it was absolutely necessary to Generation. Let us now see what may be answer'd to the Arguments which may be drawn from these Authorities.

There are but Three Reasons that can oblige Men to circumcise themselves, *viz.* The Command of that Religion which they profess ; The Impossibility of having Children without that Operation ; or lastly, The Example of People with whom they live, and the Idea they frame of that Ceremony.

We have no ground at all to believe, That the *Egyptians* were oblig'd to *Circumcision* by any Commandment of their Law, and what we know at present

of

of their Religion and Cuſtoms, can give us no In-
ſight into this Matter. Neither could the Impoſſi-
bility of having Children without this Operation,
oblige them to circumciſe themſelves; for in effect
their Bodies were not otherwiſe fram'd at that time,
than they are at preſent; and 'tis very certain,
that at this day they do not ſtand in need of this
Ceremony to give them Succeſſors; ſince there is at
preſent in *Egypt* a multitude of *Chriſtians* who are
not now circumcis'd, and yet their Land is no more
a Deſert than it was in former times, when they
were circumcis'd; or if it be, it is only by the great
number of Young People that are educated there to
be made Slaves, and not becauſe the Men are im-
potent. And hence it follows, that the *Egyptians*
were not circumcis'd, but in Complyance with the
Example of the People with whom they liv'd, *viz.*
Of the *Jews*: And indeed this laſt Account of the
Matter is much more probable than any of the other
two.

To prove therefore that the *Egyptians* receiv'd
Circumciſion from the *Jews*, or at leaſt that this Opinion is preferable to the other two, it will be ſufficient to make ſome Reflexions upon their ſeveral
Characters, and upon the ſtrong Impreſſions which
the Notable Events, that befel them upon the Account of the *Iſraelites*, might make upon them.

The *Egyptians* were at all times the moſt Superſti-
tious, and withal the moſt Myſterious of all Mankind, and conſequently the moſt unfit to receive new
Impreſſions in matters of Religion. On the other
ſide, there was never any thing ſeen ſo aſtoniſhing
and terrible, as what happen'd to them in the time
of *Moſes*; from whence we may conclude that the
ſurprizing Conduct of this great Law-giver, and generally every thing that had any Relation to him,
left deep and laſting Impreſſions upon the Minds
of this People.

The

The Miracles wrought by the Hand of this Great Man, that Army of *Pharaoh* which was drown'd in *Red-Sea*, the Death of all the First-born, the Darkness which cover'd the Land of *Egypt*; and in fine, all the Means he us'd to deliver the People of *Israel* from their Bondage : All this, I say, could not but strike great Terror into the common People, and give their Learned Men a great Idea of him, who did such Miracles. And since all the Ancient *Pagans* make no scruple of admitting into the number of their Deities, the Gods of Foreigners which they believ'd to be powerful, and to embrace any thing in the Religion of other People ; I think we may hence conclude, that the *Egyptians* being astonish'd with so many wonderful Works as the *Israelites* did before their Eyes, did espouse some of their principal Ceremonies, and more particularly did embrace those, which do chiefly distinguish the Children of *Israel* from other Nations ; and since *Circumcision* is the most essential Mark of *Judaism*, there is all the probability in the World, that they chiefly adopted *Circumcision*, and observ'd it.

To all this we may still add, that it appears very probable, that before the Children of *Israel* departed out of *Egypt*, the *Egyptians* did not Circumcise themselves ; which Conjecture may be grounded upon a Passage in the Book of *Joshua*. The Scriptures inform us, that after the Passage over *Jordan*, *Joshua* caus'd all the *Israelites* to be Circumcis'd, because this Ceremony had not been observ'd in the *Wilderness*, and that after they were Circumcis'd, the Lord said to this worthy Successor of *Moses*, that he had this Day taken from among them the reproach of *Egypt*. *And it came to pass when they had done circumcising all the People, that they abode in their Places in the Camp, till they were whole. And the Lord said unto* Joshua, *This day have I roll'd away the reproach of* Egypt *from off you*, Josh. 5. 8, 9. It seems to me,

that

that by this reproach of *Egypt* which was taken away by *Circumcifion*, nothing elfe can be underftood but the *Prepuce* ; and if this part was look'd upon by the *Jews* as the reproach of the *Egyptians*, probably the *Egyptians* had it then, and confequently were not Circumcis'd at that time : But if they were not Circumcis'd when the Children of *Ifrael* went out of their Country, and yet there are fufficient Proofs that they were Circumcis'd afterwards ; from hence I think it may be concluded, as we have already obferv'd, that all the Miracles which *Mofes* wrought among them, gave them fo great an Idea of him and his Religion, that they were thereby oblig'd to embrace what was moft peculiar in that Religion, and to adopt that which diftinguifh'd them moft manifeftly from all others ; which without all queftion was *Circumcifion*.

It may at firft view be objected to what I have been faying, that thefe are only probable Reafons, and confequently do not certainly conclude, that the *Egyptians* did receive *Circumcifion* from the *Jews*, and that their Practice of it was derived from the Precept which was given to *Abraham*. I know very well that the Reafons I have alleg'd, are not certain and demonftrative Proofs ; but I think when we cannot have Phyfical Certainty about any matter, we ought always to adhere to that which is moft probable ; and it appears to me much more probable, that the *Egyptians* deriv'd *Circumcifion* from the *Jews* with whom they liv'd, and by whom they had feen fo many great things done, which infinitely furpafs'd all that their Priefts and Enchanters could do, than to admit that the *Egyptians* had the ufe of it without deriving it from the *Jews*, efpecially where there is no ftrong Reafon for this Affertion : For if any one pretends to build it upon the forecited Paffage of *Herodotus*, which is the moft ancient and moft authentical Proof which thofe can

allege

allege who maintain the last Opinion, nothing can be concluded from the Passage, but that the *Egyptians* did Circumcise themselves, and he does not say that they had this Ceremony of themselves, and that it was not deriv'd from the *Jews*. If there were any Example or Passage, which mention'd the *Circumcision* of the *Egyptians*, before the Arrival of the Children of *Jacob* in *Egypt*, then we might justly conclude, that this People being Circumcis'd before they had any Correspondence, or Commerce with the *Israelites*, did not derive this Ceremony from them. But now we meet with nothing like this, and *Herodotus* who wrote about 240 Years after the Foundation of *Rome*, and consequently about 1018 Years after the departure of the *Israelites* out of *Egypt*, says nothing else of the *Egyptians*, but that they us'd *Circumcision*, without telling us the time when they first began to use this Ceremony, or the Persons from whom they first receiv'd it: And therefore I cannot see how the forecited Passage of this Author, can prove the Proposition now contested, or conclude any thing in favour of this Opinion.

But still it may be objected, that not only the *Egyptians*, but also those of *Colchos* and *Ethiopia* Circumcis'd themselves, as *Herodotus* relates; which Argument is of no more Force than the former, for this Author himself adds, that he does not know certainly whether the *Egyptians* or *Ethiopians* first began this Ceremony; tho' he thinks it very probable, that the *Egyptians* first begun it, and that the *Ethiopians* deriv'd it from them, because none but they had Commerce with the *Egyptians*, among whom *Circumcision* was in use. Now if *Ethiopia* receiv'd it from *Egypt*, we must not allege the Example of that People to prove that the Practice of *Circumcision* was not deriv'd from the *Jews*; since it will always be suppos'd, that the *Egyptians*, from whom other Nations deriv'd it, receiv'd it themselves from the *Jews*.

Diodorus

Diodorus Siculus indeed speaks of the Circumcision of the *Troglodites*; but he adds, that they did in this imitate the *Egyptians*, from whom 'tis very probable that they deriv'd it, being not far distant from them.

'Tis true, the *Negroes* do also circumcise themselves; but they hold the Circumcision of *Mahomet*, and we have no manner of Proof, that they us'd to do so before this false Prophet appear'd. 'Tis very certain that they embrac'd, at least imperfectly, *Mahometism*; for I have seen among them two kinds of Phylacteries about the Neck, and about the Arms, which are written in very good *Arabic* Characters, and which contain'd certain Invocations, which are to be found in the *Alcoran*: I say, That they embrac'd it imperfectly, because 'tis certain that they have still among them some Reliques of *Paganism*; as for instance, they offer Sacrifices to their Evil Demons for fear they should hurt them, and use many other Ceremonies not unlike this.

We have therefore no reason, or proof, for admitting Circumcision among the *Negroes* before *Mahomet*; and granting that they had us'd it before him, still this would not prove, that is was not deriv'd from the Precept given to *Abraham*, for they might receive it from the *Ethiopians* who lie most *Easterly*, and had commerce with the *Jews*. There are also many in that Nation who make open Profession of *Judaism*, and go constantly to Worship at *Jerusalem*; as we find in the *Acts* of the Apostles, that some Persons of great Quality among them were wont to do, *Acts* 8. 27. *And behold a man of* Ethiopia, *an Eunuch of great Authority, under* Candace *Queen of the* Ethiopians, *who had the charge of all her treasure, and had come to* Jerusalem *to Worship.* The *Ethiopians* therefore, having among them some People that read the Scriptures, and the Law of the *Jews*, and who did not only frequent the Temples

C   they

they could have in their own Country, but also went to Worship at that in *Jerusalem*, must in all appearance have a great Opinion of *Judaism*, and Reverence for its Ceremonies; and since Men commonly seek to imitate what they esteem and admire, 'tis very probable that they observ'd the Precept of Circumcision, which is so often repeated in the Scriptures and in the Books of the Law, for which they had so great an Esteem and Veneration.

It were impertinent to object against this, That *Herodotus* does not say, that the *Ethiopians* receiv'd Circumcision from the *Jews*, but from the *Egyptians*; for I am willing to believe, that my Readers will prefer the consequences drawn from passages of Scripture, before the Account given by this Author, who, altho' he be commonly call'd the Father of History, yet he is not always very exact, and has been often guilty of such Errors in the description of Times, People and Empires, as *Pliny* committed in the History of Nature. Besides, without Examining which of these two Authorities is to be preferr'd, it is not difficult to reconcile them: For it may very well be, that at first the *Ethiopians* receiv'd Circumcision from the *Egyptians*; but understanding afterwards that the *Egyptians* themselves deriv'd it from the *Jews*, they set up a correspondence with the latter, that they might fetch that from them in all its purity, which they could find but obscurely among the *Egyptians*, who probably had mingled it with their Follies, making one Compound of the two Religions.

To prove that the *Negroes* did not receive Circumcision from the *Jews*; some have affirm'd, that it was absolutely necessary for them to circumcise themselves, and that unless they did it, they could have no Children, because with them, *Præputium tegit ab integro glandem, excepto minusculo foramine*: But those who have related this of them, do not certainly
know

know them, for they are not otherwiſe made as to theſe Parts than we are, and not only in *Guinea*, but alſo in thoſe places of *America* and *Aſia* where I have been, and where I took great care to inform my ſelf about this matter, I could never hear of any ſuch thing, but on the contrary I learn'd that in the hot Countries, *Præputium erat ſemper maxime dilatatum.* As to what concerns *Egypt* and the Country of the Ancient *Troglodites*, ſince I was never there, I cannot ſpeak of them ſo poſitively ; but this at leaſt I can ſay, that I have known ſome Perſons of good Credit, who have travell'd thro' theſe Countries, and they have told me, that they never heard of any ſuch thing.

Others have proceeded ſo far as to ſay, that Circumciſion was no leſs neceſſary to the *Jews* than to the *Negroes* ; but if this were ſo, there muſt be a ſtrange multiplication of Miracles, which muſt laſt for the ſpace of 40 Years ; for during all that time that the *Iſraelites* were in the *Wilderneſs*, they were not circumciſed, and yet this did not hinder them from having Children : Beſides many *Jews*, after they have embrac'd Chriſtianity, have had Children ; and theſe Children, tho' they were never circumcis'd, have had Children in their turn whenever they came to Age : And therefore Circumciſion was not neceſſary to render them capable of begetting Children, ſince they could beget them without it.

If ever there was occaſion to ſay, that the Ceremonies of the *Jews* were only Figures appointed by God to ſignify ſomething more Sublime than what they naturally import, or Preſages of ſome things that were to come to paſs, without all queſtion we have reaſon to ſay ſo of Circumciſion, which was a Ceremony by which God gave his People to underſtand, that they ought to cut off from their Heart, whatſoever is contrary to their laſt end, and to thoſe things for which they were deſign'd. And this

C 2 is

is not a Figurative Explication of any private Person, or the bold Effort of some Interpreter, who sometimes wrests the Sense of Scripture according to his Fancy, and accommodates it to his own Opinion; for it is God himself who speaks thus by the Mouth of *Moses, Circumcise therefore the foreskin of your Heart, and be no more stiff-necked,* Deut. 10. 16. 'Tis true, some may say, that 'tis very possible, for Circumcision to be at once a necessary means to procure Generation, and at the same time a Figure of what is to be done in the Heart of Man. But since it has been prov'd, that Circumcision was not necessary to Generation, and it appears evidently, that the *Jews* could live and propagate for a long time without it, I think we may safely conclude, that it was nothing in Truth, but a Figure, which was to instruct a Man, as we have already said, to cut off from his Heart, whatever was not agreeable to his last end, *i. e.* to God.

Some perhaps will say, that tho' Circumcision was not absolutely necessary to the *Jews* in order to Generation, yet it was a convenient means to facilitate it, and *Philo* at the end of his Book, *of special Laws,* seems to be of this Opinion; where he says, that *some mock'd at the Circumcision of our Ancestors, altho' other Nations,* and *chiefly the* Egyptians *did highly honour it.* Where we may observe by the by, that from this place of *Philo* it may be also prov'd, that the *Egyptians* deriv'd Circumcision from the *Jews,* since he says expresly, that the Circumcision of our Ancestors, was honour'd by the *Egyptians.*

This Author gives many natural Reasons for Circumcision, to prove to Foreign Nations, that it ought not to appear to them so very extraordinary; and he says, that, besides that it was a sign of the Covenant between God and the *Jews,* it was also instituted, *ut caveatur morbus curatu difficilis, vocatus carbunculus——— ut totum corpus sit purius, ne impediat officia Sacerdotalis ordinis;*

ordinis; quamorbem etiam radunt corpora Ægyptii Sacri-
fici, ne quid ſordium vel ſub pilis, vel ſub præputiis hære-
at, quod poſſit obeſſe puritati ſacris debitæ: And laſtly he
adds, that this Operation, *eſt cura fœcunditatis & nu-*
meroſæ ſobolis, —— & idcirco circumciſas gentes fœ-
cunditate pollere, eſſeque populoſiſſimas.

To anſwer the paſſages of this Author, we muſt
obſerve, that he had a mind to reconcile the Minds
of many Strangers to Circumciſion, who were very
averſe to it ; and therefore without inſiſting much
on the reaſons of its Inſtitution, which would not
have been well-reliſh'd by thoſe who maintain'd a
Syſtem of Religion quite different from his, he was
oblig'd to produce ſome natural Reaſons for it ; and
in the greateſt part of them, he appears to be much
miſtaken.   As to the firſt Reaſon he gives, that it is
a means to avoid certain Diſeaſes, which are hard to
be Cur'd, I can by no means admit it to be true,
and am rather inclin'd to believe the contrary ; but
this is a matter that muſt be left to the Examination
of Phyſicians : And beſides, ſuppoſing it were ſo, this
is only putting a Man to a great deal of trouble, by
uſing many precautions beforehand, to Cure a Di-
ſeaſe more ſpeedily, from which any Man may eaſily ſecure himſelf, and which no Man can catch,
except he be very willing.

His ſecond Reaſon appears to be more probable,
becauſe the *Eaſtern* Nations, and among the reſt
the *Jews* and *Egyptians*, had great Scruples as to the
Purity and Qualifications of their Prieſts ; but ſince
they carried their Scruples ſo far, it ſeems to me
wonderful, that they did not puſh them yet further,
and imitate the Prieſts of *Arcadia*, or thoſe of the
Gauls.   As to his laſt Reaſon, it is of no force, and
to diſcover its Falſhood, we need only reflect a little
upon the pretended Fecundity of the circumciſed Nations.   The *Jews, Turks, Arabians*, and generally all
People among whom Circumciſion is us'd, are not

C 3   more

more fruitful than others; and on the contrary, I am persuaded, that if the matter were well Examin'd, it would appear that they are less Populous. But *Philo* wanted some Reasons, either good or bad, to oppose against those who did not approve this Usage, and would admit none that were deduc'd from Religion, and the Covenant which God made with *Abraham* and his Posterity, which the *Gentiles*, and particularly the *Romans*, derided; and therefore it is not to be wondred, if all the Reasons he alleges are not very exact.

ARTICLE III.

Of the Principal Causes of Paganism *and* Idolatry.

Since the Remarks I have made upon the *Indies*, are all concerning the Customs of the *Pagans*, and that the greatest part of these Customs are founded upon *Paganism*, and are indeed the consequents of it, I think it will not be improper to say something in general of *Idolatry*, and to give an account of the principal causes of that pernicious Institution.

There are few bad things in matters of Religion, which did not proceed from a Cause in some measure good, and few Errors which had not their beginning from some Truth that was misunderstood, or corrupted by length of time: Thus the Fables of the Gods, their Generation, Divisions and Victories, and all the Fictions which the Poets sing to us; all this, I say, took its rise from the Truth, for the source of it was the Religion which we profess at this Day; yet the Truth is so disfigur'd among the *Pagans*, by all the Follies and Fables in which they have wrapt it up, and its Features are hereby so far alter'd, that it is almost impossible to discover it among them.

It

It may appear very furprizing, that fo great a change fhould be made in Religion, and that from the Truth wholly pure and fimple, Men fhould fall into an Abyfs of Errors, and into a Chaos of all forts of Fables: Yet if any would reflect a little upon the Character of the greateft part of Men, and the Power of time, it would not any more appear fo very ftrange.

The little care which Men take to judge of things by their Mind alone, and the ftrong Inclination they have always had to their Senfes, was the firft caufe of all their Errors. They muft have fomething to affect them externally and fenfibly, and therefore when the Truth could not be difcover'd by external Signs, they chofe rather to embrace a Fiction, than to abandon their Senfes, and judge without them: And this may be the reafon why God, who knows the fecret windings of the Heart of Man, even to the fmalleft Inclinations that are in it, inftituted in the *Jewifh* Religion fo vaft a number of Ceremonies, which to us feem ufelefs, for fear, left if their Senfes were not fix'd by fomething that's good, and might lead them to the Truth, they fhould give themfelves up to fomething that was bad, and might occafion their falling into Error.

The Idea which Men had always of the Deity, was one of the Caufes of *Idolatry*: They wanted a God, and they were perfuaded there was one, for all things Preach'd to them this Truth, the Heavens, the Earth, the regular Motion of the Stars, and the fettled order of the Univerfe, which never changes, were as fo many Witneffes of the Exiftence of a God; but the ftrongeft and moft convincing Proof they had, was the fecret Motions of their own Heart, which carried them, as it were againft their Will, towards fomething more fublime and great than the Creatures, which they perceiv'd to have a beginning,

ginning, to encreaſe and periſh before their Eyes :
For *Idolatry* did not commence with the Adoration
of theſe Creatures which Men knew to be corruptible, they did not at firſt fall into ſuch groſs Stupidi-
ty, which was begun by the *Egyptians*, and perfected
afterwards by the *Greeks* and *Romans* ; neither did
they Worſhip in the firſt Ages, any thing but that
which (next to the Divinity) appear'd moſt Ado-
rable.

At firſt the Sun, Moon and the other Stars were
ador'd ; but becauſe Men could not always ſee theſe
Luminous Bodies, they ſought after ſomething,
which might in ſome manner ſecure them, for
theſe Moments in which they were depriv'd of the
ſight of them, and which was a Hieroglyphic of
theſe pretended Divinities. And they could find
nothing that came nearer to them than Fire, which
was a moſt ſenſible ſign of the Brightneſs of the Stars,
and particularly that of the Sun, and they firſt devoted themſelves to Fire. Neither did they Worſhip it at firſt, but as a Repreſentation of the Star
which they ador'd, but by degrees they ador'd alſo
the thing it ſelf. This Worſhip firſt commenc'd
among the *Chaldeans*, and *Ur* of the *Chaldees*, where
Abraham was Born, was the Place where this Worſhip was firſt paid, whence it came to paſs, that the
Name of *Ur* was given to it, which ſignifies Fire.

I ſhall here relate a very pleaſant Hiſtory, which
Euſebius has given us, *Hiſt. Eccl. lib.* ii. *cap.* 26.
upon the occaſion of Fire, which the *Chaldeans* look
upon as a Deity. Theſe People pretended that their
God was the ſtrongeſt and moſt powerful of all the
Gods, neither could any one be found that was able to
reſiſt him ; for aſſoon as they brought any God of
other Nations, they threw him into the Fire, which
never fail'd to conſume him, ſo that the God of the
Chaldeans was publickly eſteem'd the Conqueror of
all other Gods : But a Prieſt of *Canops*, who was
one

one of the Gods of *Egypt*, where there was alſo a
City of the ſame Name, found out a way to deſtroy
the great Reputation he had got. He caus'd for this
end, an Idol to be made of a very porous Earth, of
which the Pots were commonly made, that ſerv'd
to purify the water of *Nile*. This Statue which had
a very great Belly, was fill'd with water, and the
Prieſt ſtopt with Wax a multitude of little holes that
were in it ; and then he offer'd his God *Canops* to
enter the Liſts againſt *Fire*, the God of the *Chaldeans*:
Who therefore prepar'd one, into which the *Egyptian* put his Statue ; but the Wax melting with the
Heat, the holes were open'd, and the water guſh'd
out, and at laſt extinguiſh'd the Fire. Whereupon
it was immediately publiſh'd, that the God *Canops*
had overcome the God of the *Chaldeans*, and had deſtroy'd him ; and as a Monument of this famous
Victory, the *Egyptians* made their Idols always for the
future with a great Belly and little Feet, becauſe
that which overcame the *Fire*, was ſhap'd after this
manner ; and this is exactly the Figure of the greateſt part of the Idols now made by the *Indians*.

The *Perſians* alſo ador'd the Fire, which they
commonly caus'd to be carried before their Kings,
and at the Head of their Armies, and to be attended
by 360 Prieſts. There are ſtill ſome at this Day
in that *Empire*, which obſerve the Ancient Religion
of the Nation, but they are a ſort of Savages which
dwell in the Mountains, and would never receive
the *Alcoran*. The *Athenians* kept a perpetual Fire in
the *Prytaneum*, which was a kind of Fortreſs, and
was to them what the *Town-Houſe* is with us, beſides
that, it was the Place where old Officers were entertain'd, and ſuch as had done ſome notable Service
to the *Republick*. This Fire was kept by the Wi-
dows, whereas that of the *Romans* was kept by the
Virgins that were call'd *Veſtal*. It is well known
alſo, that the *Jews* were to keep a Fire which burnt
con-

continually, as they were commanded in the sixth Chapter of *Leviticus*.

Some have affirm'd, that this Worship and Adoration which so many Nations have paid to Fire, was founded upon that passage of *Deuteronomy, Chap.* 4. *Verse* 24. *The Lord your God, O Israel; is a consuming Fire* ; but this is no-wise probable, since, as we have just now shown, the *Chaldeans* Ador'd the Fire a long time before the written Law.

In process of time, the Statue of a Man was Ador'd, but in the Article of Houshold-Gods, we shall discourse of the first Causes of that Superstition. Lastly, by degrees Men proceeded so far as to Worship *Beasts*, and such as are vilest among them, and even that which is most infamous in Nature.

All these *Idolatries* into which Men fell, are also owing in some Measure to the ordinary Stile of the Oriental Languages, to the Scrupulosity of the People, and to the Veneration they had for every thing that was deliver'd to them by their Priests, and their Ancient Predecessors. At all times the Stile of the Orientalists, but more particularly that of the Priests, and of those whom they call'd Philosophers, was full of Figures and Comparisons ; they affected Pompous Words, and Metaphorical Expressions, and the common People believ'd them to be so much the abler Men, and the more Spiritual the less they understood them : Afterwards the first Poets improv'd this Hotch-potch with great swelling Words and Hyperbole's, until at last it appear'd, that what they said, was perfectly opposite to what they intended to signify. *Lactantius* speaks sharply of the Mischiefs that were produc'd by the Poets, and says, that when one is not upon his Guard, he is easily Surpriz'd by the soft, pleasant and insinuating Stile they make use of. *Poetæ perniciosi sunt, qui incautos animos facile irretire possunt suavitate sermonis, & carminum dulci modulatione currentium, Lactant. lib.* 1. *cap.* 11.

The

The common People, without diving into the sense of the Figure, and inquiring into the thing Represented by it, stops at the Figure it self, and then one may easily judge, what kind of Idea's they frame of the Deity, and of Mysteries: For this is just as if we, for instance, should Explain literally what the Scripture tells us of God, and so we should attribute to him a sharp Sword, a Buckler, Bow and Arrows, we should-make him lye in wait to kill some body, we should sometimes think him Merry and Joyful, and sometimes Angry or Melancholy; In fine, by degrees we should make a Man of him, and oftentimes even a Man that was not very wise: And yet this is what the *Gentiles* do, for they have attributed to God in reality, what is spoken of him only Figuratively: And thus they begun with assigning him a Body, which Error was founded first upon the Portraiture which their Priests and Poets gave them of him; and secondly, upon the Inclination they had to judge of all things by their Senses, and to frame no Idea's but such only as are material

After that Men had once proceeded so far as to attribute a Body to a Deity, we must not wonder at these odd and uncouth Figures under which they Represent him, and the different Offices they assign unto him. 'Tis very well known, that they had Gods of all sorts, and that there was no corner in the House which had not for its Safe-guard a God or a Goddess; they Plac'd one even in their Houses of Office, and call'd her the Goddess *Cloacina*. In fine, they push'd this extravagant Humour as far as it would go. *Tertullian*, *Lactantius*, and many, even of the Heathen Authors, have given us the detail of all these Follies and Superstitions

In the Article of Tutelar Gods, we shall say something of the Veneration the People had for every thing that came from their Priests, and their Ancient Predecessors; which, as we have already obferv'd, observ'd, was one cause of their strict adherence to their Errors, and to the Fables they had receiv'd from their Fathers.   But this may suffice to be said of a matter, which the most Learned Writers of our times have search'd to the bottom ; and in their Works, any one may easily see the Absurdity and Ridiculousness of *Paganism*, and at the same time perceive the difference between the Belief of those who have a little Knowledge, and that of the common People.

ARTICLE IV.

Of the Sacrifices of the Indians, *and their manner of Honouring the Gods.*

MAnkind in all Ages have paid an External Worship to the Deity, which consisted in Offering to him the best and most precious things they had, as if it were on purpose to recognize him, as the great Landlord of whom they held all.   Thus *Cain* who till'd the Ground, offer'd of its Fruits to God, and *Abel* who kept the Flocks, Sacrific'd to him the fattest of his Lambs.

'Tis not certainly known, whether at first they had any fix'd Ceremonies in making their Oblations ; and there is great reason to believe that *Enos* was the first who begun to give them a regular Form, according to that passage in *Genesis, Chap. 4. Ver.* 26. *Then began men to call upon the name of the Lord.*   But Father *Petavius* understands these words in a different sense, and understands by them, that this Grandson of *Adam* restor'd the Worship of God, which the Children of *Cain* had abolish'd.

There was another kind of Sacrifice, call'd the Sacrifice of Drink-offering, which was made by pouring out some Liquor before the Lord ; and this was also in use under the Written Law.   As

As for inſtance, after the Return of the Ark of the Covenant, when the *Iſraelites* Aſſembled at *Mizpeh*, to thank God for delivering it out of the Hands of the *Philiſtines*, the Scripture obſerves that at their Thankſgiving, *they drew water and pour'd it out before the Lord*, 1 Sam. 7. 6.

The Water which *David* pour'd out when he was before *Bethlehem*, and which he refus'd to Drink of, becauſe they had drawn it with the hazard of their Lives, was no leſs a Sacrifice of Drink-offering than the former ; but the Liquor which was commonly made uſe of for this end, was Oyl. Thus *Jacob* intending to give Thanks to God for the Myſterious Dream wherein he ſaw that Ladder, on which the Angels were Aſcending and Deſcending, and looking upon the Place where Heaven had done him this favour, as a Place that was truly Holy, and as the Houſe of God, pour'd out Oyl upon the Stone on which he had laid his Head, during this Dream. *And* Jacob *roſe up early in the Morning, and took the Stone he had put for his Pillow, and ſet it up for a Pillar, and pour'd Oyl upon the top of it*, Gen. 28. 18.

We may obſerve, *en paſſant*, from this action of *Jacob*, that in his Days, Travellers that were Pious, were wont to take care before they ſet out from their Houſes, to put themſelves in a Condition, to Praiſe and Honour God during their Journey, and that the Sacrifice of *Libation* being of all others the moſt commodious, and that which required the leaſt Ceremony, they took care to carry Oyl along with them, to pour it out before God, and offer it up to him as an acknowledment of his Almighty Power, and to thank him for ſome Favour, or to obtain one of him.

The Sacrifices of *Libation*, were us'd alſo among the *Gentiles*, who offer'd up many other ſorts of Liquors. As for inſtance, Milk was offer'd to *Rumina*, who was the Goddeſs whom they invok'd for Children

dren at the Breast: The *Athenians* never offer'd Wine to the *Sun*, the *Moon*, to *Aurora*, *Urania*, who is one of the *Muses* that was suppos'd to have invented *Astrology*, or to *Mnemosyne*, by whom *Jupiter* had the 9 *Muses*, or to the *Nymphs*, but only Honey mixt with Water.

Some pretend that the first Sacrifices of *Libation* were made of Wine, and that the word *Libation* derives its Original from *Bacchus*, who was otherwise call'd *Liberus*: And to this purpose, *Ovid* tells us in his Third Book of *Fasti*. *Nomine ab Authoris ducunt Libamina nomen.*

This kind of Sacrifices which at first were instituted only to Honour the Gods, were quickly after us'd in Feasts and Debauches; where profane *Libations* were made, and Wine was poured out as a Ceremony, which in all probability was always done in Honour of *Bacchus*. *Macrob. lib. Saturnal. cap.* 11.

The Doctrine of Transmigration, hindred the *Indians* from Offering any Bloody Sacrifice to their Gods, whereof some, according to their Theology, had liv'd in the shape of those Animals which were most fit to be Sacrific'd: And therefore they only offer to their Idols, the Fruits of the Ground and Incense.

They do also pour out Oyl before them, and not only so, but they rub them over with it every time they make an Offering to them, whereby they are commonly Black, Smok'd, and all over Slippery with Oyl. This is what *Arnobius* relates of the Idols of his time; *Lubricatum lapidem & ex olivi unguine sordidatum, tanquam inesset vis præsens adulabar. Arnob. advers. Gent.* I flatter'd a Stone all over slippery, and durtied with Oyl, says the Author, as if it had had some Power.

Besides the Sacrifices, they agree also in many things with the *Jews*, as to the manner of Honouring the Gods, and Praying in their *Pagods*; they have

have Drums, Trumpets, and Quires, which Sing Hymns to their Honour; they fometimes carry their Idols in Proceffion, and walk thro' all the Streets of a City: And in thefe Publick Ceremonies, they have aways Women appointed to Sing and Dance before them, at the found of the Mufical Inftruments of the Country, as formerly *David* did before the Ark, playing upon his Harp, 2 *Sam.* 6. 14.

Thefe Dancers among the *Indians,* are always Publick Women, and tho' they Dance in the *Pagods,* and before their Gods, they are never the wifer for all that, nor of better Reputation.

It appears alfo, that the *Jews* had no great efteem of thofe, who did the fame Office among them, and that they were look'd upon, at leaft for the moft part, as vain Perfons, for *Michal* upbraids *David,* that he had acted the part of a *Buffoon,* when he was publickly difrob'd. *And he was uncovered as one of the vain fellows uncovereth himfelf,* 2 Sam. 6. verfe 20.

As to the Circumftances in which *David* was, when *Michal* upbraided him for Dancing before the Ark, *i. e.* for difrobing himfelf, we muft obferve, that the *Jews,* to remove every thing that might incommode them, and that they might Dance the more freely, put off their Upper-Garments, and kept on only thofe which were next their Body, that they might be the more light, and confequently the fitter to Dance, which did not at all become the Gravity, upon which the *Jews* and all the *Eaftern* People value themfelves.

The *Indian* Women that Dance, do alfo the fame, for when they have a mind to Dance, they throw off a fort of great Veil, that covers their Heads and wear nothing but a Linen Waftcoat, and a Petticoat about them.

The *Indians,* who embrace *Chriftianity,* take care to have in their Churches, little Trumpers, fome kind

kind of Hoboys, and Drums, at the sound of which they Sung *Psalms*; at least they use such things at *Pondicheri.* So that it might be said of them, that they Praise the Lord in his Temple, *in tympano & choro.*

ARTICLE V.

Of the Places they make choice of for paying their Devotions to the Deity, *and of the Building of their Temples.*

MAnkind have always made use of darkish Places, and the shadow of great Trees, for paying their Devotions to the *Deity*; and when the *Jews* put an Oak into the Sanctuary, under which *Joshua* plac'd the Stone, whereon was Engraven the Promise they had made unto him, that they would never forsake the Worship of the true God, they did nothing herein, but follow the Example of other Nations; *And set it up there under an Oak that was by the Sanctuary of the Lord,* Josh. 24. 26. Which nevertheless, was contrary to the Command of God, who forbad them to Plant any Grove or Tree near his Altar, *Deut.* 16. 21. Yet they still kept to this way, even in their *Idolatry,* and when they worship'd false Gods, they did it in Places cover'd with Trees, as the Scripture upbraids them in these words, *Sub omni ligno frondoso prosternebaris,* Jer. 2. 20. And when the Prophet *Hoseah* reproves them for this Crime, he says, they sought out for this end, those Trees that cast the largest shadow. *They Sacrifice upon the tops of the Mountains, and burn Incense upon the Hills, under Oaks, and Poplars, and Elms, because the shadow thereof is good,* Hos. 4. 13.

Before God order'd *Solomon* to Build him a Temple, Pious Men offer'd Sacrifices to the true God,

upon

upon Hills, and even under the shadow of great Trees, as *Gideon* did under the Oak, where *the Angel of the Lord touch'd the Sacrifice with the end of the Staff that was in his Hand, and made the Fire rise out of the Rock, which consum'd the Flesh and unleavened Cakes,* Judges 6. 21.

It seems, that at that time, it was allow'd to offer Sacrifices in the several places where any one happen'd to be, and yet without doubt those places were always to be excepted, which were cover'd with Trees, or which had any affinity with the sacred Groves of the *Pagans,* for it is expresly forbidden by the Law, *Deut.* 16. 21. *to plant any Grove of Trees by the Altar of the Lord,* as I have just now observ'd.   And this conjecture may be prov'd by the Example of some Pious Men, who, however zealous for the regular Observance of the *Jewish* Law, did nevertheless offer Sacrifices, as we have already said, in the first place they came to : Yet I think in this, they did not shew themselves zealous Observers of the Precepts of the Law, which was very express to the contrary : And therefore they cannot be excus'd, but by saying, that this Custom of offering Sacrifices every where to God, which was indeed a legal Fault, was nevertheless as it were Lawful, by reason of the number of those that Practis'd it.   But it was no Fault in it self, for in the days of *Joshua,* a Question was started upon that occasion, and all the Children of *Israel* were scandaliz'd, because the Tribes of *Reuben* and *Gad,* and the half Tribe *Manasseh,* who after the Conquest of the *Holy-land,* return'd to the place that *Moses* gave them beyond *Jordan,* and there erected a Monument, which the other Tribes believ'd to be an Altar: Whereupon the most violent among the *Jews,* were of Opinion, that to Punish this Crime, they should immediately take up Arms, and go and destroy their Country ; but the more Prudent, Thought fit to send an *Embassy,* to

enquire

enquire what Reafon they had to rear up an Altar, contrary to the Prohibition of the Law. This laft Opinion prevail'd, and fome Embaffadors were fent to them, to demand an account of this Action : And their only Excufe was, that they never defign'd to rear up an Altar, but only to raife a Monument, to put their Pofterity in mind, that they were really *Jews*, and confequently were fubject to the Law of God, which was given them by *Mofes*. But after the Temple of *Jerufalem* was built, it was more particularly forbidden, to offer Sacrifice any where elfe. This is what *Mofes* himfelf told them in the *Defart*, when he prefcrib'd to them what they fhould do after God had put them in poffeffion of the Land of Promife. *Take heed, that you do not offer your Burnt-offerings in every place that you fhall fee, but only in the place which the Lord fhall chufe*, Deut. 11. 18.

Neverthelefs, fome have ftill obferv'd the Ancient Cuftom of offering Sacrifices upon the Mountains, or under the thick Trees : Thus when it is faid of fome Kings of *Judah*, as of *Jehofhaphat*, and many others, that they did not demolifh the *High-places*, where the People Worfhipt, *Verum Excelfa non abftulit*, 2 Chron. 20. 33. We muft not always underftand by that Phrafe, that thefe Altars were built to falfe Gods, for they were often Dedicated to the true God, according to that Paffage, 2 *Chron*. 33. 17. *Yet the People ftill Sacrific'd to the Lord their God in the High-places*. And it was no Sin to Sacrifice in the firft place they came to, but only becaufe the Lord had forbidden to do it any where but at *Jerufalem*.

The *Indians* have many *Idols* which are difpers'd here and there in the Fields, and commonly plac'd in little Groves, or at the Foot of fome Tree that cafts a great fhadow; there Travellers make their Prayers and Oblations, to obtain of the Gods a happy Journey.

The

The *Jews* had alſo in the Fields, Altars which were deſign'd for Travellers, and upon which they offer'd Sacrifices to the Lord, which was likewiſe forbidden after the building of the Temple at *Jeruſalem*, and it is ſet down as one of the beſt actions in the Life of *Aſa*, that he demoliſh'd them : *Et ſubvertit altaria Peregrini cultus, & Excelſa*, 2 Chron. 14. 2.

The *Indian-Pagans* affected alſo a Shadow, and Darkneſs in their Temples, which they call'd *Pagods*, and they were very careful that no Light ſhould enter into them, but .only by the Door which was commonly very Strait and Low, or by ſome little Crevices that were left in the Windows : They had ſome alſo which had no open place, but only at the Gate.

Abraham no leſs affected a Dark place, wherein to pay his Devotions to God, and to Pray unto him, and the Scripture obſerves that *he Planted a Grove at* Beerſheba, *and called there upon the Name of the Lord, the everlaſting God,* Gen. 21. 33. The *Jews* in following times, had very near the ſame Idea of God, and thought that he delighted in ſhaded Places, in thick Clouds, and generally in Darkneſs. Thus when *Solomon* fetch'd the Ark of the Covenant into the Temple he had built, and ſaw the ſame Temple fill'd with ſo thick a Cloud, that the Prieſts could not perform their Office in it, he obſerv'd that *the Lord had ſaid, he would dwell in the Cloud,* 1 Sam. 12. and in 2 *Chron.* 6. 1, *The Lord hath ſaid that he would dwell in the thick Darkneſs. David*, in *Pſal.* 18. reckoning up all the attendance of the Divine Majeſty, ſays, Verſe 12. *that he made Darkneſs his ſecret Place.* In fine, almoſt all the Ancients had this Opinion of the *Deity,* which perhaps was deriv'd from our firſt Parents ; for 'tis ſaid, that God walk'd in the *Terreſtrial Paradiſe,* which was a place fill'd with Trees, and conſequently dark, *And when they heard the voice of the Lord God walking in the Garden,* Gen. 3. 8.   D 2   More-

Moreover, if one would give some natural Reason, why almost all Nations took so much care to find out shady Places for the Worship of the Gods, I think it may be said, that Darkness is the most proper place for that recollection of Modesty which ought to be observ'd in the Temples, and generally when we place our selves in the Presence of God, because the Sight is the Sense which is the chief cause of Distraction, therefore that Darkness which hinders our Eyes from receiving any object that may Distract us, is most convenient and agreeable to places design'd for Prayer and Religious Worship.

Besides, a shady and dark Place produces in us, whether we will or no, a certain Horror that is attended with such an awful Veneration as is due to the *Deity* : And I believe that upon this account, the *Latines* have given to God a Name which properly signifies Fear or Horror ; for the *Latin* word, *Deus*, seems plainly to be deriv'd from the *Greek* word *Deos*, *formido* ; from whence also the *Grecians* might well enough have deriv'd their *Theos*, altho' some have deriv'd it from *Theein*, *currere* ; because many believ'd in ancient Times, that the Stars, who (as one may say, are always running their course) were Gods.

ARTICLE VI.

Of the Temples Dedicated to Priapus.

WE find among the *Indians*, Temples Dedicated to *Priapus*, tho' under several different Names ; and we may say, that they are much refin'd above the infamous Postures, wherein the *Egyptians*, *Greeks* and *Romans*, have Represented him : Many also wear a little Figure of him about their Neck, but it is cover'd with a little Silver, and they
pretend

pretend by doing this to obtain Vigour and Fruitfulneſs.

'Tis certain, that this abominable *Idol* did formerly meet with Worſhippers among the *Jews*, for the
Scripture informs us, that *Aſa* drove away his Mother *Maacham* from Court, becauſe ſhe had erected
an Altar to *Priapus*, which he caus'd to be broken
in pieces, and burnt near the River *Kidron*. *Sed &*
Maacham *matrem* Aſæ *Regis ex auguſto depoſuit imperio,
eo quod feciſſet in luco ſimulachrum* Priapi : *quod omne con-
trivit, & in fruſta comminuens combuſſit in torrente Ce-
dron,* 2 Chron. 15. 16.

The *Jews* in all probability learn'd from the *Egyptians* to pay Divine Honours to *Priapus*, and to erect Statues to him, for *Egypt* perhaps was the place where this
pretended *Deity* was held in greateſt Veneration ; for
there it was look'd upon as the Cauſe of the moſt noble
Creature in the World, *i.e.* of Man, and his Generation;
and there were few publick Buildings erected, above
which were not plac'd the two Figures which are
moſt ſuitable to this *Idol*, and which were there
look'd upon as *Hieroglyphics* of the greateſt and moſt
perfect State that can be deſir'd in this World, as for
inſtance, of enjoying Honour, Abundance, Fertility, Strength, Vigour, and Health.

The *Romans* alſo did not only invoke *Priapus* for
the Propagation of Mankind, and for giving them
Children, but alſo for the Fruitfulneſs and Fertility
of their Lands. Every one commonly erected to
himſelf a Statue in his Garden, which if it could
contribute to nothing elſe that was expected from it,
in procuring them a plentiful Harveſt ; yet at leaſt
ſerv'd for a Scare-crow to fright away the Birds, as
Horace tells us, *Serm. lib.* 1.

*Olim truncus eram ficulneus, inutile lignum ;
Cum Faber incertus, ſcamnum faceretne* Priapum,
*Maluit eſſe Deum. Deus inde ego, furum aviumque
Maxima formido*　　　　D 3　　　　From

Long time I lay a useless piece of Wood
'Till Artists doubtful what the Log was good
A Stool or God ; resolv'd to make a God :
So I was, my Form the Log receives
A mighty Terror I to Birds and Thieves:

From this Place of *Horace* we may observe, how among the *Romans*, the Men of Wit, but more particularly the Poets, made bold with their Gods, and and treated them in a Drolling manner.

A R T I C L E   VII.

*Of their Houshold-*Gods, *and the Original of their Tutelar* Deities.

BEsides the *Gods* which the *Indians* have in their Temples, we find also among them, those which the Ancients call'd, *Lares, Manes,* and *Penates,* which are little Figures, plac'd in several parts of their Houses, whom they take great care to rub with Oyl, and encompass with Flowers, as thinking that by this means, they render them propitious. Some say that the *Manes* were the Infernal *Deities,* and distinguish them from the *Penates* and *Lares,* but all Authors almost do indifferently use these three words, to signify the Souls of the Deceas'd; and therefore I shall not enter upon a Discussion of the difference which those of the contrary Opinion pretend to find.

These Tutelar *Deities* are most Ancient, and the use of them commenc'd a long time before the *Grecians,* who probably deriv'd them, as well as the first Foundations of their fabulous History, from those who first form'd the *Assyrian Empire,* supposing the Origine of that Monarchy, to be laid in Building the City of *Niniveh,* and allowing it to have lasted

for

for the fpace of 1300 Years; for if we follow the Opinion of *Herodotus*, and allow to it only the fpace of   and make it commence about the time when *Deborah* judg'd the People of *Ifrael*, the *Affyrians* would be later than the *Grecians*, and confequently the later could not derive their Fables from the other. The moft Ancient *Grecian* King whom we know, is *Inachus*, who Reign'd at *Argos*, and who, according to the Calculation of the 70, was cotemporary with *Mofes*, altho' *Eufebius* thinks that this Holy *Law-Giver*, liv'd in the time of *Cecrops*, which was more then 300 Years after, and that he Founded the 12 Cities of which the Kingdom of *Athens* was compos'd; and thofe who follow this Opinion, fuppofe *Inachus* and *Abraham* to live at the fame time, and fo they have embroil'd the ancient Chronology. See *the Antiquities of time Reftor'd*, by Mr. *Boffuet*.

But to return to my fubject, we meet with the *Gods Penates*, a long time before *Mofes*, and confequently before the *Grecians*, for thefe were the *Gods* of *Laban*, which *Rachel* his Daughter, the Wife of *Jacob*, carried away, and hid under the Harnefs of a Camel, when fome came into her Tent to fearch for them, from whence we may conclude, that they were not very large Images. Neither did *Laban* in this do any thing, but follow the Cuftom that had been in ufe a long time before him; for *Thares*, the Father of *Abraham*, made alfo Images among the *Chaldeans*, and thefe Images could be nothing elfe but Publick *Idols*, or the Tutelar *Gods*.

The Original of thefe *Idols*, had nothing that was Evil in it, and they were at firft only Figures, by which Men endeavour'd to Reprefent their Dead Fathers, or their Sovereigns from whom they were far diftant, and to whom they could not pay Perfonal Honours; for thus they Labour'd to fupply by their Art, what Nature had taken away from

them, or what the great distance of Places hinders
them from seeing: Which was only a sign of the
Love and Reverence which Children well-born
ow'd to those from whom they receiv'd their Being,
or of that Submission and Homage which faithful
Subjects owe to those whom Heaven has appointed
their *Gods*.

We find in the 14th. Chapter of the Book of *Wisdom*, one of the occasions which might give a rise to
Superstition, with respect to the Images set up in
Honour of Dead Parents, which the wise Man attributes to the love of a Father for his Son, and
which would have been no less innocent than the
former, if the Father had confin'd his grief within
just bounds, and had not carried the Matter so high,
as to Reverence for a *God* in the midst of his Family, him whom he lamented as a Man that was
Mortal.

Plato gives to these *Gods*, *Penates*, the Name of
ὁμογένεοι θεοι, which properly signifie the *Gods* born
of the same Family, for ὁμογέ'νεια signifies Kindred:
Now 'tis certain, that by these *Gods* whom the Ancients look'd upon as their Kindred, and whom they
call'd by that Name, they could not understand any
other than their Ancestors, who were Dead, and
for whom Men had a very singular Veneration in
the first Ages of the World; or in general all those
of their Families, who had been very dear to them
in their Life-time.

There is very great reason to believe, that for the
most part, they had at first only a Reverence and
Veneration for these Images, and that they look'd
upon them only as we do now on the Picture of a
Dead Father, whom we tenderly lov'd, but that
insensibly, by little and little, they carried the Matter higher.

For instance, perhaps when they found themselves in Adversity, and cast their Eyes upon these
Images

Images, which call'd to mind their Grandfathers, who had such a tender love for them, that they would have reliev'd them, if they had been now Alive, or at least would have shar'd with them in their Misfortune; they began at first with Mourning for the loss of them, which was very Natural; but not being satisfi'd with this Sorrow, which gave them no ground to hope in them, and nothing being more grateful to the Mind of Man, in his Misery, than a glimmering of Hope, tho' it be as ill founded as is possible; after they had wish'd they were now alive, to afford them that Protection they now stood in need of, they began to doubt, whether they might not still grant it to them, tho' they were Dead, (which they grounded upon the belief of the Immortality of the Soul) and at last they ventur'd so far, as to desire it of them.

It was therefore necessary, to this end, that they should proceed to Invocation, and to confirm them in this Advance which they made with a doubting Mind, it was sufficient, that upon Tryal they were for the future deliver'd from their Misery, and found themselves in a better Condition; for in all probability they would not fail to attribute the Success to the Remembrance and Power of those, whose Assistance they implor'd.

Thus then, after some Generations we past, when their Posterity understood, that their Ancestors had invok'd the chief Heads of their Family, and that their Prayers were heard; when from Father to the Son, they heard their Virtues mention'd, and Celebrated with a great *Elogium*; when they saw still before their Eyes, the Images of them which had been carefully preserv'd; upon these Accounts, they proceeded openly to Adoration, which always continued; and the Minds of their Posterity were so much the more confirm'd by the Idea which Men have always had of the times preceeding their own;

viz.

viz. That every thing in them was Great and Virtuous, that their Predecessors were free from those Faults that were observ'd in the Men of their own time. And this is what *Solomon* expresly condemns treating of the same Folly. *Say not thou, what is the cause that the former Days were better than these? For thou dost not enquire wisely concerning this,* Eccles. 7. 10.

Thus by degrees, *Idolatry* crept into the World, which in its Name, still preserves something of its Original, for the word *Eidolon* (which comes from ἴδω, *video*) signifies no more than an Image, a Representation, or a Picture, which renders things distant actually visible to us, or even those things which are not in being.

Some have made *Nimrod* the Author of the first Statue that was cut in Honour of Dead Kinsfolk, which Opinion seems to me not to be well-grounded: For first, we cannot make use of the Authority of the Wise-Man, in his 14th. Chapter, to Support this Opinion, because *Nimrod* had a Son, *viz.* *Jupiter Belus* who Succeeded him, and therefore he could not make an Image for this Son when he Dy'd, since he himself Dy'd a long time before him. Secondly, Neither can we say, that it was done in Honour of some other of his Sons, since we know of no other but this: Yet I do not pretend to say, that he had no other than *Belus*; but since History says nothing of them, I cannot see what right any Man has to suppose them, unless he will have recourse to Tradition, which in this case, I think, would be a very weak Argument.

Yet it seems to be very probable, that the Statue of *Jupiter Belus* was the first that was erected to any Mortal; for besides that there we find the beginning of all the *Grecian* and *Roman Idolatry*, we see in *Daniel*, Chap. 3. that the Famous *Idol* of *Belus* was still Ador'd in his time at *Babylon*; and therefore we may more probably attribute the erecting of

the

the firft Statue to *Ninus* the Son of this fame *Belus*, and Grandfon of *Nimrod*, who in Reverence to the Memory of his Father, caus'd it to be erected to him.

As to the beginning of the *Grecian* and *Roman Idolatry*, which I faid might be found at *Babylon*, by fuppofing that the Statue of *Jupiter Belus* was the firft that was erected to any Mortal; It may perhaps be objected, that the *Jupiter*, who was the Foundation of fabulous Hiftory, did not Reign at *Babylon*, but was King of *Crete*, which is now *Candia*.

To this I might anfwer, that there have been many Princes that had the Name of *Jupiter*, and whofe Actions were attributed to one only. This is the Opinion of *Varro*.

Cicero relates the fame thing in his *Third Book of the Nature of the Gods*, where he fays, That the *Romans* acknowledg'd three *Jupiters*, the firft of whom was born in *Arcadia*, was the Son of the *Air*, and begat *Proferpina* and *Bacchus*; the fecond alfo was born in *Arcadia*, who had the *Heaven* for his Father, and begat *Minerva*; and laftly, the third was he of the Ifle of *Crete*, who was the Son of *Saturn*, whofe Sepulchre is to be feen ftill in that Ifle. The manner in which the Antients give an account of *Jupiter*, confirms alfo this Opinion, fince they tell us many things of him, which at that time could fcarce agree to any one Man; for who could, for inftance, affirm, that the *Jupiter* who Reign'd in the Ifle of *Crete*, was the fame, who upon Mount *Olympus*, which is between *Theffaly* and *Macedonia*, Sacrific'd firft to the *Heaven*, which he call'd his Grandfather, by the Name of *Uranus*, as *Lactantius Firmianus* relates, *lib.* 1. *cap.* 12. Wherefore I think, that tho' one was King of *Crete*, this does not hinder, but another might Reign at *Babylon*, and lay the Foundation of Fabulous Hiftory.

To

To return to the Tutelar *Gods* ; they were plac'd in several parts of the House, but most commonly in a sort of little Niches that stood near the Fire, as being the place where those of the Family did most commonly meet together ; and hence they sometimes made use of the word *Estia, Focus,* to signify the *Gods Penates* ; and by turns the word *Penates* was sometimes us'd to signify the Fire, or even the whole House ; but since the *Indians* had no Chimneys in their Houses, they plac'd their *Penates* indifferently in any place of their Habitation.

ARTICLE. VIII.

Of their *Lustral* Waters.

THE *Jews* also had their *Waters* of Lustration and Purification, of which they threw a little on a Man that was Unclean, the third day after he was declar'd to be so, and the seventh on which he was Purified.

It was nothing but clean *Water*, in which was put the Ashes of a red Heifer ; which was burnt without the Camp, with his Entrails ; the Priest threw into the Fire that consum'd it, some *Cedar-wood*, *Hyssop*, with a little *Scarlet*.

The *Pagan Indians*, have also these *Waters* of Lustration, which they take from a Cow ; but because they believe it a capital Crime to burn it, they use only its Urine, wherewith the devout People do carefully *Water* every Morning, the place before the Door ; for by this means they fancy, that they keep off all kind of Misfortune from their Houses, and bring down upon them the peculiar Protection of the *Gods* ; and indeed they look upon every thing as Sanctified, nay, as Divine, which comes from this Animal.

The

The Reverence which they have from Cows, appears to me to be deriv'd much higher than from the pretended *Metempſychoſis* of *Phoe*, or that which they tell us of *Parmeſer, viz.* that when he liv'd upon Earth, he was very willing to keep them; for if, according to them, they had an affection for theſe Animals, it is, as they pretend, becauſe they are the beſt and moſt perfect of all others; and ſo without any reſpect to the Honour which was done them, either in receiving the Soul of *Phoe*, or in being kept by one of their *Gods*, they were always held in great Veneration by them.

The *Indians* are not the only Perſons that have great reſpect for a Bull, a Calf, and a Cow, as *Deities*; for theſe are the Animals which have been moſt generally Worſhipt by *Idolaters*.

The *Egyptians* Worſhipt an Ox, under the Name of *Apis* and *Serapis*, which ſignify the ſame thing. Some would have *Apis* to be nothing but a *Hieroglyphic* of *Joſeph*, who invented the way, how the *Egyptians* might enjoy a happy Plenty, during the time of a great Barenneſs, becauſe in effect among them and all other *Pagans*, the Ox Repreſents Fruitfulneſs and Abundance; Others think that *Apis* was a Prince, who firſt Reign'd among the *Argives*, and afterwards among the *Egyptians*, and who taught the latter the way of Planting and Dreſſing the Vine, and that *Egypt*, in acknowledgment for this Benefit, Worſhipt him after his Death, under the ſhape of an Ox. 'Tis ſaid that this Prince aſſum'd there the Name of *Oſiris*, ſo that *Apis, Serapis* and *Oſiris*, were the ſame thing.

Mr. *Voſſius* pretends that there were three *Oſiriſes* in *Egypt*. He ſays, that *Cham*, or his Son *Miſraim*, was the firſt; and indeed the Name of *Miſraim* continu'd to be given to *Egypt*, and ſo it is call'd in the *Hebrew* Text. The ſecond, according to him, was *Joſeph*, and the third, *Moſes*. But as to the laſt it

is

is no ways probable. However, this is certain, that under the Name of *Apis*, *Serapis* and *Ofiris*, the *Egyptians* Ador'd the Ox, and they look'd upon it, perhaps as the *Hieroglyphic* of one of these three Princes we have just now nam'd.

The *Jews*, after their Example, made a Golden Calf in the Wildernefs, and bowed the Knees before it. When the Kingdoms of *Judah* and *Ifr..el* were divided, *Jeroboam* caus'd two Calves to be set up, one at *Dan*, the other at *Bethel*, whom the *Ifraelites* Worfhipt as *Gods*, who had deliver'd them out of *Egypt*: And *Jupiter* was Worfhip'd under the fhape of a Bull, which they say he affum'd, that he might carry away *Europa*; which Fable is very Ancient, and is mention'd by *Anacreon* in *Ode* 95. In fine, there is fcarce any Country in the Fabulous times, where the Ox was not either Ador'd as a *God*, or Reverenc'd as the Symbol of Fruitfulnefs and Plenty.

Diodorus Siculus relates, that the *Troglodites*, whom we have already mention'd in the Article of *Circumcifion*, Strangled with the Tail of an Ox, the old Men, that were not capable of Labouring and Keeping the Flocks, and generally all thofe that were in a languifhing Condition, and were feiz'd with any incurable Difeafe, believing that they did them a great piece of Service, to prevent them from languifhing a long time, and to fend them quickly into the other World: And befides, they imagin'd, that they did them a great Honour, in Strangling them with the Tail of fuch an Animal, as an Ox or a Cow.

The *Indians* indeed do not pufh their Charity fo far; but always look upon it as an Honour, and an enfurance of Eternal Happinefs, if they can Die, ʒolding the Tail of a Cow in their Hands.

The *Egyptians* Worfhipt an Ox, under the Name of *Apis* and *Serapis*, as we have already obferv'd; from whence it may be inferr'd, that they did not kill it at all: And therefore when *Pharaoh* commanded

ed

ded the Children of *Ifrael* to offer Sacrifices to their own *God*, without departing out of *Egypt*, *Mofes* told him that this could not be done, and that the *Egyptians* would Stone them, if they fhould fee them offer thofe Animals which they ador'd. *And* Mofes *faid*, *It is not meet fo to do, for we fhall Sacrifice the abomination of the* Egyptians, *to the Lord our God. Shall we Sacrifice the abomination of the* Egyptians *before their Eyes, and will they not Stone us?* Exod. 8. 26. If therefore the *Egyptians* could not without Horror, fee the *Jews* Sacrifice thofe Animals which they ador'd, 'tis very probable, that themfelves did not kill them. Befides, *Juvenal* informs us, that in *Egypt* they did never Eat of any Animals that bore Wool, and that it was a Crime to cut the Throat of a Goat,

———*Lanatis animalibus abftinet omnis Menfa, nefas illic fœtum jugulare capellæ.* Juv. Sat. 15.

If the *Egyptians* therefore, durft not kill either Sheep or Goats, 'tis very probable, that neither did they kill Oxen, for whom they had fo great a Veneration ; yet they permitted the *Jews* to Kill and Eat them, and *Plutarch* relates, that themfelves Sacrific'd Red Oxen to *Typhon*. While the *Ifraelites* were there, they did Eat of Lambs, contrary to the Cuftom of the *Egyptians*, related by *Juvenal*, who fays, that they never Eat of any Animals that bear Wool; from whence we may conclude, that they did not oblige the *Jews*, to follow their particular Cuftoms, and that they gave them leave, provided they did nothing publickly that was contrary to their Religion and Ceremonies.

We ought not, I think, to attribute that Veneration which the generality of *Idolaters* paid to the Ox, to any thing elfe, but the good Services which Men receive from it. Many Perfons, for inftance,

even

even after the Deluge it self, fed only upon the Fruits of the Ground, and upon Milk ; and so the Cow furnish'd them with that which they most commonly us'd for Food, the Ox Till'd the Ground, carried the Baggage of Travellers, and drew their Carts, and in the Desarts, where they have no Wood, they made use of their Dung to make Fire ; having mingled it with a little Straw, and dry'd it at the *Sun*, which the *Indians* still do in those Places where Wood is scarce. Thus these Animals were very beneficial to them.

Hence it came to pass, that Men insensibly accustom'd themselves to take care of the Preservation of an Animal, which did them so much good, and was in a manner necessary to them, and that they did not take the same care of other Animals, which was very reasonable ; but at last they carried this Care and Acknowledgment so far as Reverence, which quickly degenerated into Adoration : So true it is, that Men seldom stop at a just Mediocrity, but for the most part, generally push things on to extreams.

The *Indians* still continue in many Places, to set under a kind of a Pillar, a little Cow, made either of Wood or Stone ; but I am not fully inform'd, whether they look upon these Representations as *Idols*, or as *Talismans*.

I have observ'd something very like this before I entred into the *Indies*, and I saw in the Isle of *Moeli*, which is inhabited by *Mahumetans*, the Bone of the Head of an Ox, full of *Arabic* Characters, but which were almost all defac'd : Whereby I am persuaded that they look'd upon it as a *Talisman*, which conduc'd to the Preservation and Prosperity of the Flocks in the Isle ; for the *Arabians* attribute very much to this kind of Mysteries.

The *Jews* themselves, were not altogether free from this Superstition, and it would be a favourable Opinion of them, to say, that they did only Reverence ᵭence as a *Taliſman*, the Brazen Serpent which *Moſes* caus'd to be erected in the *Wilderneſs* ; for it is very rare, that Incenſe is offer'd to *Taliſmans*, which were often hid under the Foundations of Buildings, or Cities, that were put under their Protection ; or plac'd on the top of Towers and Pyramids : Yet ſome were plac'd in certain little private Temples, but they were not expos'd to publick View ; and the Scripture informs us, that they offer'd Incenſe to it until the time of *Ezechias*, who caus'd it to be broken in pieces. *And he brake in pieces the brazen Serpent which* Moſes *had made, for unto thoſe days, the Children of* Iſrael *did burn Incenſe unto it*, 2 Kings 18. 4. The *Palladium* of *Troy*, for inſtance, was alſo a *Taliſman*, and there was ſcarce any City, which had not alſo ſomething peculiar to it, upon which, in the People's opinion, its deſtiny depended.

ARTICLE IX.

Of the River Ganges, *and the Lands which it Waters.*

SOme of the Ancients, and chiefly St. *Jerom*, have deſcrib'd to us the River *Ganges*, in very Pompous terms, and as a thing too extraordinary for us to paſs it over in ſilence.

This Holy Father writing to the Monk *Ruſticus*, tells him from the Scripture, that *Ganges* which is call'd *Phiſon* in *Geneſis*, runs thro' all the Land of *Havilah* : There, as he obſerves, are bred the *Emerald* and *Carbuncle*, and there are Mountains of Gold, which 'tis impoſſible for any Man to approach, becauſe of the *Gryphons, Dragons*, and many other Monſters that dwell there. *Ad* Indiam *pervenitur & ad* Gangem *fluvium, quem Phiſon ſacra Scriptura commemorat, qui circumit totam terram Evilath*———— *ubi naſcitur Smaragdus & Carbunculus* ———— *monteſque auri,*

quos

E

quos adire propter Gryphos & Dracones, & *immenso-*
rum corporum monstra, hominibus impossibile est. Hieron.
Ruftico Epift. 13.

When the Scripture deſcribes to us *Ganges* (ſuppoſing it were the ſame with *Phiſo*) I think that
it deſcribes it ſuch as it was before the Flood, and
immediately after the Creation of the World, making it, with three other Rivers, iſſue from the ſame
Spring-head ; but 'tis very probable, that the Waters which cover'd the whole Earth, did perfectly
change the Courſe and Situation of theſe Rivets, ſo
that what we call now *Tigris, Ganges* and *Euphrates* ;
are not the Ancient Rivers which iſſued out of the
Terreſtrial Paradiſe, and have nothing in common
with them, but the Name.

Hence it appears, that we may, without fear of
contradicting the Scripture, be ſo bold as to lop off
from the Deſcription which St. *Jerom* has given us
of *Ganges*; the *Emeralds, Carbuncles,* and *Mountains*
of *Gold* ; the Country which this River waters, being Rich only by the Fruitfulneſs of its Soil, by
its Silks and Muſlins, which invite thither Foreigners,
for almoſt all the Gold of the *Indies* comes from *Achim,*
which is in the Iſle of *Sumatra,* and is diſtant from
Ganges more than 300 Leagues.

Some think that this City of *Achim,* was the *Ophir*
mention'd in the Scripture, whither it ſays that
Solomon ſent to fetch Gold ; neither is this a ground-
leſs aſſertion, for the Fleet of this Puiſſant King, was
Built at *Ezion-geber,* which was a City of *Idumea,* ſitu-
ate upon the Banks of the *Red-Sea,* which in all probability was not far diſtant from the Place which is
now called *Moca* ; neither does it appear, that theſe
Veſſels going out of the *Red-Sea,* had any other
place to Sail to, where they could find ſo great a
quantity of Gold, but only the Iſle of *Sumatra* ; and
yet this is ſo far diſtant from it, that they could not
at that time go thither, but with much difficulty,
and

and great length of time; for fince they knew not the ufe of the Compafs, they durft not venture far into the *Ocean*, but were forc'd to Sail always near the Land. It was perhaps, upon the occafion of this long Voyage, that *Ecclefiafticus* fpeaking of *Solomon*, fays, *that his Reputation was fpread unto the moft diftant Ifles*, Eccl. 47. ver. 17.

The Famous Mr. *Huetus*, fpeaking of the *Canal* that join'd the *Mediterranean* to the *Red-Sea*, and thro' which the Veffels of *Solomon*, or *Hiram* might return with their Lading into *India*, or *Phenicia*, thought neverthelefs, that *Ophir* was the *Eaftern* Coaft of *Africa*, call'd *Zanguebar*; but this Coaft falls far fhort of *Achim*, for abundance of Gold; and befides, it would be to no purpofe, for him to object, that *Achim* is too far diftant for People that were not very skilful in Navigation, for this Learned Prelate affirms, that they made a Voyage much longer, and more dangerous, and makes them to return from *Spain* into the *Red-Sea*, by fetching a compafs round about *Africa*; This he affirms of thofe who return'd from *Tarfus*.

As to the Savage Beafts which live about *Ganges*, *Dragons* and *Gryphons* are not commonly to be feen there, but *Crocodiles*, *Rhinoceros's* and *Tygers*, are very common and numerous there. The laft efpecially make a ftrange havock there, for they come even into the Houfes, and carry away Children, and when a Man is gone a little way into the Woods, he runs the hazard of being devour'd by them. I once faw when I was a Hunting below this River, the frefh Footfteps of one of thefe Animals, which without ftraining the Matter, were feven Inches in Diameter.

Crocodiles are alfo there in very great numbers: They commonly keep in the Water, and delight in the little Brooks that run into the *Ganges*, becaufe, there they find greater plenty of Food than in the great Water, and when they go on Land, they seldom remove far from the River-side. I have heard very strange things of the Prodigious Strength of these Animals, and the People of the Country have assur'd me, that many of them taking the Oxen by the Snout, when they went to Drink, have drag'd them with ease down to the bottom of the Water; so dangerous it is to Bathe there.

The *Indians* have a very singular Veneration for the *Ganges*, which they look upon as a *God*, and to which they offer Sacrifices every Day, setting upon its Banks, little Lamps, which the Current carries away; and this make a very pleasant Prospect in the Night-time.

Many of those who dwell on the Grounds which it waters, desire it as a particular Favour, when they see themselves at the point of Death, to go and Expire there, thinking those happy who give up the Ghost in its Waters, and believing, that by this means all their Pollutions and Crimes are wash'd away.

> *O faciles nimium qui tristia crimina cædis,*
> *Flumineâ tolli posse putatis aquâ.*

When once a Man has desir'd to be Conducted thither, he cannot retract his word, and therefore he is carried to it; where first they put his feet in, and then make him Drink a great deal of Water, exhorting him to drink it with Devotion and Confidence, and to look upon it as a certain means of washing his Soul, and blotting out all his Sins; and at last they push him into it over Head and Ears, even tho' he should desire to return Home: For many are thrown in after this manner, whom an indiscreet Devotion, or some Discontent in their Family had brought thither, who were not Sick enough to think of Dying so soon, and Repented
very

very much of the Fault they had committed; but
it was too late.

Thofe who are far diftant from it, fatisfy themfelves with Drinking a little of the Water, before
they Die, when they can get it ; and believe that
they are fully Purg'd from all their Crimes by fo
doing. There come People often from remote
Places to carry it into their own Country, and furnifh their principal *Pagods* with it, of which they
are feldom deftitute ; and I faw once pafs thro'
Pondichery (which is diftant at leaft 300 Leagues
from it) a httle *Caravan* of thefe *Devoto's*, who had
many great Pots garnifh'd with *Rattain*, and fill'd with
the Water of the *Ganges*. Thefe poor Wretches
guarded them with great Care and extraordinary
Refpect, and they had ftill a great part of their way
to go before they got Home.

And here a fair occafion is offer'd me, to make a
little reflexion upon the Darknefs into which thefe
Idolaters are plung'd, and to obferve, *en paffant*, what
a grievous thing it is, that Falfhood and Truth fhould,
if I may fay fo, make the fame Impreffion upon the
Minds and Hearts of Men, who are no lefs conftant
and exact in their grofs Superftitions, and palpable
Deceits, than others are in a Religion that's wholly
True, and perfectly Pure ; and how aftonifhing it
is, that what we call the force of Truth, does not
exert itfelf, and make thefe poor Blind Creatures
fenfible of it, and open their Eyes to perceive their
Errors. In truth we have great need upon this occafion, to have recourfe to the depth of *God's* Judg-
ments, and to that Abyfs of Wifdom which the
the Eyes of no Creature can penetrate into, and
which *God* alone can comprehend. But enough of
this Matter, I return now to *Ganges*.

Perhaps the Reverence which the *Indians* have for
this River, is with them the Remnant of a Tradition
which they learn'd from their Fathers, That *Ganges*

was the fame with *Phifon* mention'd in the Scripture, which fays, that it came out of the *Terreftrial Paradife* (fuppofing that Tradition to be true, which many have doubted of upon good grounds) and that they mingled with it what they had heard of the firft Men, with the Fabulous Hiftory of their *Gods.*

But they have not only a Veneration for *Ganges,* which they always look upon as moft Holy, and which they pretend to be no lefs than a *Deity*; but they Reverence in general all Rivers, and the *Devoto's* among them take Care, before they put their Foot in water, to take fome of it and wafh their Hands with it, making at the fame time a fhort Prayer to the *Gods.*

This Cuftom of fhewing a refpect to Rivers, and wafhing their Hands in the water before they go into them, is very Ancient; and *Hefiod* recommends it in thefe words: *Neque unquam perennium fluviorum limpidam aquam pedibus tranfito, priufquam oraveris afpiciens Pulchra fluenta, manibus lotis amœnâ aqua limpida.* *Hefiod oper. & dier. lib.* 2.

This Reverence was founded upon a Fancy of the Ancients, that each River had a particular *Deity* that delighted in it, and prefided over its Waters.

ARTICLE X.

Of the Tranfmigration of Souls.

THE *Indians* believe the *Tranfmigration of Souls,* and their Hofpitals at *Suratt*, into which they receive, and where they give Food or Medicines to all Sick or Maimed Beafts, are a convincing Proof of it; but I could never difcover upon what grounds this Doctrine was eftablifhed among them, and I believe 'tis difficult to do it; for I have known
People

People of the same Religion, who go to Worship their *Gods* in the same Temples, who use the same Ceremonies, and besides are of the same Tribe, yet have different Opinions about this Article.

There are, for instance, certain *Brahmans*, who live only upon Herbs, Milk, Butter, and Fruit; some that Eat only Hens, and some that Eat Kid. There are other Tribes that Eat Pork, but generally they all abstain from the Flesh of an Ox and a Cow, for whom, as I have already said, they have a great Veneration.

The *Banians*, who are a particular Tribe of Merchants, of whom I shall speak hereafter, are those, of all the *Indians*, who follow most exactly the Doctrine of *Transmigration* of *Souls*, and who practise most Religiously even the smallest things, to which this Opinion obliges its Followers. They kill no sort of living Creatures, and they Eat of nothing that has Life : Many also among them, carry this Matter to that degree of Exactness and Scruple, that they keep Servants to blow the *Air* with a Fan, while they are Eating, that they may drive away from them all the little Flies, which in this Country are very numerous, for fear lest any of them should mingle with their Meat, and so Choak them when they are Eating.

I think we may conclude, from this diversity of Opinions, concerning *Transmigration* of *Souls*, That when it was first propos'd to them, they had a determinate Worship and Religion independent upon this Doctrine ; and so it was only receiv'd at first as an Opinion, which having nothing that's ill in it, might be either embrac'd or rejected, by each private Person, as he should think fit ; That some Fathers of Families, espous'd this new Philosophy, and follow'd it in its utmost Rigour ; and others, thinking that the *Souls* of Men could not pass into the Bodies of certain Animals, did not believe that they

ought

ought to abstain from them. Every one communicated his Opinion to those of his Family, who insensibly transmitted it to their Posterity, who always Preserv'd it, and look upon it at present as a Rule, which they are indispensably oblig'd to follow, by the Veneration and Reverence, that they have for all the Customs that are deriv'd from their Predecessors.

For if the *Metempsychosis* had been establish'd at first among the *Indians*, as a point of Religion, there would not be so much Division about this Opinion, their Sentiments would be more uniform ; or at least those that differ'd from the publick Opinion, and did not follow this Doctrine in all its Purity, would have been the Authors of what we call a *Schism* ; and so being separate from the rest, would not have had in common with them, the same Temples, the same Priests, and the same Sacrifices.

Besides, it may be ask'd, whether the *Indians* receiv'd the Doctrine of *Transmigration* of *Souls*, from *Pythagoras* or some of his Followers ? For this Philosopher is commonly look'd upon as the Author of this Opinion, or at least, as he who first taught it.

If any give an Answer to this Question, agreeable to the new Discoveries that have been made in our Days, in the *Empire* of *China*, it must be granted that the *Indians* knew the *Metempsychosis* at least 500 Years before this Philosopher, who did not flourish till the time when the *Romans*, being weary of the Tyranny of *Tarquinius Superbus*, drove him away from *Rome*, and erected a *Commonwealth* : For, from the time of *Solomon*, an *Indian* Philosopher called *Phoe*, Born in the Isle of *Ceilon*, as many think, or in the Neighbouring Continent, according to some others, Publish'd this Doctrine in the *Indies*.

To add greater Weight and Authority to this new Philosophy, 'and make it to be receiv'd with the greater Respect, he asserts, that he receiv'd it from
Heaven ;

Heaven; he procur'd himself to be lookt upon as a Prophet, and magnified himself so far as to say, that upon Earth there was not his Equal.

He had two sorts of Doctrines, one Internal, or Secret, and another External, or Publick.

His Internal Doctrine which he Communicated only to his most beloved Disciples, (whom he knew to be entirely addicted to him, and of whose Fidelity he was certain) asserted as I may say, the Annihilation of the *Soul* after Death; for he said, that after it was separated from the Body, it was scatter'd in the *Air,* and resolv'd into an Ethereal Matter; which in effect, is nothing else but *Atheism,* such, as some pretend, is still follow'd by the generality of the Learned *Chinese.*

His External Doctrine which he commonly taught the People, consisted in the *Transmigration* of *Souls,* which he said he had Experienc'd in himself an infinite number of times, having liv'd upon Earth in the shape of an Ape, a Calf, an Elephant, and many other Animals; and upon these different sorts of Beasts, into whose Bodies, he says, his *Soul* had pass'd, almost all the Religions of the *Indies* are Founded; who before this time, probably had no other, but the Acknowledgment of some Sovereign Being, or in general of some *Deity,* to which they might offer Sacrifices.

Nevertheless, I do not intend by this to affirm, that this Acknowledgment of a Sovereign Being among the *Indians,* was such as it should be, *i. e.* That they own'd only the true *God,* that the Sacrifices they offer'd, were only Address'd to him, and that, till the time of this false Prophet, they had a Religion free from *Superstition* and *Idolatry* : For this would be to advance a strange Paradox, *viz.* That (while all *Palestine* was in Error, insomuch that *God* was oblig'd, if I may so say, to separate *Abraham* from all other Men, to make him the Head of a People

ple, who fhould Adore and Serve him, without Superftition, and without dividing their Adoration between him and falfe *Gods*) the Truth fhould find a
place of Refuge among the *Indians,* that it remain'd
there whole and entire till *Solomon*'s time ; and that
while the *Jews* were continually falling into *Idolatry,*
the Idea of one only *God,* fhould be preferv'd there
without Mixture, and that the Worfhip which is
due; fhould be paid him in all its Purity.

Phoe therefore propos'd his new Doctrine to the
Indians, and without much trouble perfuaded them
to receive it, and to add his Follies to what hey
had believ'd until his time, as to the *Deity* ar the
Soul ; for Novelty does powerfully Charm Men, but
more efpecially the Common People, and chiefly
when it is defign'd, to improve and perfect their
Religion.

Befides, the eafy Reception which the Doctrine
of the *Tranfmigration* of *Souls* met with in the Minds
of Men, proceeded from the Idea which all the
World had of the Soul, *viz.* that it does not Die
with the Body ; and that after it is feparated from
the Body, it goes to fome place, which at different
times has produc'd very different Opinions : For fome
imagin'd that the *Souls* of Wicked Men, immediately after Death, defcended into a place of Punifh-
ment, where they were tormented proportionably
to their Crimes ; and this Opinion was moft generally receiv'd by all the *Pagans.* Some again faid,
that the *Gods* made them pafs into the Bodies of the
more falacious and viler Animals; and others thought
that they wandred round about the World, and did
not reafcend into Heaven from whence they came,
until they had remain'd many Ages in this continual
agitation. *Cicero,* in all probability, was of this laft
Opinion, as may be feen in his *Somnium Scipionis,*
where he fays, *Qui & Deorum & hominum jura viola-
runt, corporibus elapfi, circa terram ipfam volutantur,*

nec

*nec in hunc locum niſi multis exagitati ſeculis rever-
tuntur.*

Phœ wrote Forty Volumes, which remain'd in the *Indies* until the 65th. Year of *Jeſus Chriſt,* that the Diſciples of this Philoſopher carried them into *China,* under the Reign of *Hiaomim-Hoamti.* The *Chineſe* immediately tranſlated them into their Language ; they juſtify the time in which his Followers ſay he liv'd, by the different circumſtances they find in his Works, and which have ſome relation to what they know of the *Indians:* And this Doctrine had no ſooner appear'd among them, but it found an infinite number of Followers.

ARTICLE XI.

Of the Charitable manner, in which the Indians *give Drink to Paſſengers:*

JEſus Chriſt intending to inſtruct us in his Goſpel, that every thing we do for Him, ſhall have its Reward, Promiſes one to thoſe that in his Name, and from a deſire to pleaſe Him, ſhall give ſo much as a cup of cold water.

A Cup of cold Water will ſome ſay, is a very ſmall thing ; yet it is a worthy good action to give it as many *Indians* do, who go ſometimes a great way to fetch it, cauſe it to be boil'd, that it may do the leſs hurt to Travellers that are Hot ; and after that, ſtand from Morning till Night, in ſome great Road, where there is neither Pit, nor Rivulet, and offer it, in Honour to their *Gods,* to be drank by all Paſſengers.

This perhaps is a Work of Charity, which was equally Practis'd, both among the *Jews,* and the People that liv'd near them, who knew the *Jewiſh* Cuſtoms, and to which *Chriſt* aſſures us, that there is a Reward annex'd.

'Tis

'Tis very certain, that as to what concerns the Neceſſaries of this Life, the *Eaſtern* People have much more Charity than the *Europeans* ; unleſs the Country be afflicted with Famine, they ſcarce know what it is to refuſe Meat to a Paſſenger ; wherein they have preſerv'd the Cuſtom of the Primitive Times, when no Paſſenger was ſuffer'd to paſs by, but they offer'd him ſomething, and refreſh'd him for a ſmall time. Thus *Abraham* perſuaded three Angels to reſt themſelves, and gave them ſomething to Eat, who appear'd to him in the ſhape of three Men, that were paſſing thro' the Valley of *Mamre*, whither he was then come to fetch *Lot* out of *Sodom*, *Gen.* 18. And when they were come to that City, *Lot* would not ſuffer them to continue in the Place, but carried them away to his own Houſe, tho' he knew them not, *Gen.* 19. The Stranger who dwelt at *Gibea*, offer'd likewiſe his Houſe to a *Levite*, who was very much ſurpriz'd that no Body would receive him, *Judg. chap.* 19. *ver.* 20. For at that time, a Place for ſhelter was not deny'd to any Perſon whatſoever ; but on the contrary, they took Pleaſure in giving Meat to Travellers, without requiring any thing of them.

ARTICLE XII.

Of their way of Eating Locuſts.

THE Goſpel relates, that St. *John Baptiſt* liv'd upon *Locuſts* and wild *Honey*, and ſome Interpreters, who could not imagine that he ſhould Eat this kind of Inſects, have ſaid, that by *Locuſts*, are meant the tops of the Branches of Trees, and pretend that this *Hermite* fed upon them ; but they were not at all acquainted with the Cuſtoms of the *Indians*, who Eat *Locuſts* with pleaſure, after they

are

T Slater Sculp

are Drefs'd ; and tho' thefe People are fhap'd like thofe we fee in *Europe,* yet none of them finds the leaft Inconvenience by Eating of them.

Neither was this any extraordinary thing among the *Jews,* whom *God* had permitted to Eat of thefe Infects, as he prefcribes to them in *Leviticus,* Chap. 11. Ver. 21, 22. *Of every flying creeping thing that goeth upon all four, which have Legs above their Feet to leap withal upon the Earth: Even thefe of them ye may Eat, the* Locuft *after his kind, and the* Bald-Locuft *after his kind, and the* Beetle *after his kind, and the* Grafhopper *after his kind.*

ARTICLE XIII.

Of the Fortified Places, to which the Shepherds *retire with their* Flocks.

THE Scripture informs us, that *Uzziah* caus'd Towers to be built in the *Wildernefs,* and digged Gifterns upon the account of the great multitude of *Flocks* that he had : *Alfo he built Towers in the Wildernefs, and digged many Wells, for he had much Cattel,* 2 Chron. 26. 10.

By thefe Towers, I believe we muft underftand what the *Indians* call *Pagods,* not fuch as ferv'd for Temples, but certain other Great Buildings which are in the Fields, which they call by the Name of *Pagods ;* either becaufe above their Gates, they rais'd high *Pyramids,* full of Pictures of their *Gods,* as are thofe at *Villenoura,* and many others ; or becaufe, within their Circuit, there was always a multitude of little Chapels, every one of which contain'd an *Idol.*

Thefe Buildings are commonly encompafs'd with good Walls, and there the *Flocks* are gather'd together, in cafe of any alarm ; for tho' the Prince is not at War with any Body, yet the People have al-
ways

ways reason to be upon their Guard, because in these Countries, the Soldiers are very ill Paid, and the Commanders who detain their Pay, permit them to take what they can get ; whereupon they fall upon the Beasts, when the *Shepherds* think least of it. These *Maraduers* have often made us take Arms at *Pondichery*, and we had the Misfortune in one of these Sallies, to lose a brave Officer, and to have one Wounded, and some of the Country People, who took our Pay, Maim'd. After this, 'tis in vain to demand Justice of the Commanders, and to represent to them, that since they are at Peace with the *Great Mogol*, their Troops do very ill, to make Incursions upon your Lands ; for they will always Promise you very much, but Perform nothing, because they must either Pay their Soldiers, or permit them to Pillage. Travellers also retire into these *Pagods*, as they do in *Persia* into the *Seralio-Caravans*, and in *Arabia* into the *Caravan-Beites*, i. e. the Houses of the *Caravans*.

In the Places where there are none of the *Pagods* of this kind, there are commonly other Buildings, which are call'd *Chaudries*, where Travellers may as well shelter themselves, but not with the same Conveniencies.

We find in the *Indies*, that which is very near the same thing with the Cisterns which the King of *Judah* caus'd to be Built in the *Wilderneß* ; for the *Pagans* look upon it as a work of Charity, to dig Pits and Lakes in By-places, for the convenience of Travellers and Flocks ; and this is often done, as the Performance of a Vow which they made to their *Gods*, in hopes of obtaining from them, either Children, or good Success in their Undertakings, or in general, some Favour.

ARTI-

ARTICLE XIV.

Of their Publick Buildings.

THE *Pagods* and other publick Edifices of the *Gentiles*, are commonly built of great Black-ftones of an extraordinary length : The Pillars which are always very numerous in them, are al-moft all of one piece, and fupport the Rafters of the fame Matter which Form the Roof; and thefe Rafters of Stone, are commonly between 17 and 18 Foot long, and 3 and a half, or 4 broad. They join them all together, and put a little Lime between them, to hinder the Water from paffing thro'; and fo in thefe great Buildings, there is not one bit of Wood.

The difficulty they meet with, to find out thefe Stones, to Tranfport them, and put them in their Places, makes them to be of great Price, and of the fame precious Maffes for length and thicknefs; the Walls of *Jerufalem* were built, *Lapides pretiofi muri tui* Jerufalem.

Solomon made ufe of them alfo, to lay the Foun-dations of his Houfe, and of that which he built for the Daughter of *Pharaoh*, according to that Paffage : *And the Foundation was of coftly ftones, even great ftones, ftones of ten Cubits, and ftones of eight Cubits*, 1 King. 7. 10. Which contributed very much to the duration of thefe famous Building, which held out againft the Injury of times, and the Revolutions of Ages. — The Mode at prefent, is very much chang'd, for without troubling our felves much, whether any hing we do will be grateful to our Pofterity, we confult only our own Eafe, and take care to pleafe our felves.

The *Indians* that are Rich, do ftill agree very well with the *Jews*, as to their manner of Building; for almoft all their Roofs are made in the Form of a
Terras,

Terras, as those in *Palestine* were, and as they are still in almost all the Hot Countries : And besides, they have for an entrance into the House, what the Scripture calls *Atria*, which is a kind of a Gallery that makes up the Frontispiece of it. This is the place where they receive their Visits, and where they also make their Feasts in a Rainy Season ; for in Fair Weather, they commonly make them in their Courts, their Tents, and under their shady Trees, where they regale themselves.

They never admit any Body into their House, who is not design'd for them or their Women, and they take great care that no Window be open to the Street, to prevent by this means all occasion of Courtship ; for they are jealous in this Country to the last degree. They do not only refrain from paying Visits to Women, but even from asking any Questions about them, and the worst Complement that one could make to a Man, would be to ask how his Wife does, so that you must live with them, and talk with them no more about their Wives, than if they never had any.   They would answer any that should ask about them, That it was their proper concern to take care of them, whether they were Well or Sick ; and since they were design'd for them only, none but they had a right to concern themselves about their Health, or meddle with any thing that belong'd to them : And, besides this, perhaps, one such-like Question, might be fatal to the Person of whose Health they enquir'd. From whence, any one may understand, how idle many Persons would be in this Country, which are not so in *Europe* : 'Tis true, the Bondage in which the Women are kept, makes them omit no opportunity they can find, and the Men can only keep themselves upon the Defensive, by taking care to prevent all opportunities.

ARTI.

ARTICLE XV.

Of the Black, *which the* Indian *Women use to improve the* Whiteness *of their* Complexion, *and of the* Mirrors *that are in use among them.*

Ezechiel defcribing the *Idolatry* of *Jerufalem*, under the Figure of a *Lewd Woman*, accufes her of rubbing her Eye-lids with *Black-Lead*, when her Lovers came to wait upon her, *Et circumlinifti ftibio oculos tuos*, Ezech. 25. 40. This is what we find alfo in the Book of *Kings*, that *Jezebel* did, on purpofe to pleafe *Jehu*, and to fhun by this means that Death, which fhe knew her Crimes had very well deferv'd: *Porro* Jezebel, *introitu ejus audito, depinxit oculos fuos ftibio, & ornavit caput fuum*, 2 Kings 9. 30. And *Jezebel*, hearing of his coming, Painted her Eye-lids with *Black-Lead*, and put Ornaments upon her Head. This *Black-Lead* therefore blacken'd their Eye-lids, which, if we may judge, according to our Fafhions, was not very fit to render Women more enticing? Yet this Cuftom is ftill in ufe among the *Indians* that are *White*, who to heighten the luftre of their Complexion, and render their Eyes more languifhing, put a little Black about them, and this ferves to almoft the fame purpofe with the Patches, that are us'd by our *European* Dames.

With refpect to the Ornaments of Women, I will add fomething, *en paffant*, of their *Mirrors*, and the manner in which they are made. They are commonly very little, made of Brafs, well-polifh'd, and exactly reprefent the Complexion. Many People of *Europe* do now make ufe of them, and the *Jews* did fo formerly; for the Scripture informs us, that *Bezaleel* made a great Brafen Veffel with its Bafis, of the *Mirrors* of the Women that came to Watch and Pray at the Door of the Tabernacle: *And he made*

F

the

the *Laver of Brass*, with the Foot of it of *Brass*, of the *Looking-Glasses of the Women Assembling*, which *Assembled at the Door of the Tabernacle of the Congregation*, Exod. 38. ver. 8. And here give me leave to say something of the Women that came to Watch at the Door of the Tabernacle, with respect to the consequences, which some Authors would draw from that Passage I have related. For, by this they pretend to prove, that under the Written Law, there were *Nuns*, *i. e.* Virgins Consecrated to *God*, and who had their Cells in the outer-parts of the Tabernacle; but in truth, This is to carry their Love to a *Monastic Life* too far, and to Assign it an Original more Ancient than ever it had. It may suffice therefore to say, that this State is Good and Holy, that it is approv'd by the Church, without searching for such Ancient titles, as were more than 1500 Years before *Christ*. Besides, the *Nuns* must have been very numerous, and their *Looking-Glasses* very great, or they must have had great plenty of them, since of these *Mirrors* was made so great a Brasen Laver : And it seems these two last Conditions do not well agree with *Nuns*, who should forget their Beauty, if they have any, and consequently have no need of so great a number of *Mirrors*. But if it were true, that there was a *Monastick State* in the days of *Moses*, what will become of the pretensions of the famous Successors of *Elias*, who maintain stoutly, that it was begun by them ?

These Women therefore, that came to Watch at the Door of the Tabernacle, were not *Nuns*, but Secular Women, who out of Devotion, went to spend the Night in Prayer, near the House of the Lord. This Devotion was also in use in the days of *Eli* the *High-Priest*, and one of the Crimes of his Children was, that they Debauch'd these Women: The Scripture does not use in this place the word *excubabant*, as in the Passage of *Exodus*, but the word *observabant*,

obfervabant, whereby it appears, that it ought to be expounded by *Meditating*, and not by *Guarding* or being *Centinels*; for the *Levites* were numerous enough, to make a good Guard about the Tabernacle, without making ufe of Women to that purpofe.

ARTICLE XVI.

Of their Cuftom of fuffering their Nails *to grow.*

AMong the *Indians*, both Men and Women fuffer their *Nails* to grow to an extraordinary length, and all the *Pagans* anciently us'd to do fo : But the *Jews* fearing, left fomething that is unclean fhould lurk under their *Nails*, and mingle with their Meat, par'd them off very carefully, and made all thofe that kept them long, to cut them off; wherefore the Scripture permitting them to Marry a Woman whom they took from their Enemies, commanded them to caufe her Head to be Shav'd, and her *Nails* cut, *Quæ radet Cæfariem & circumcidet ungues*, Deut. 21. ver. 12.

ARTICLE XVII.

Of their Nuptial *Ceremonies.*

ST. *Matthew* relates a Parable, which I think may be Explain'd by a Ceremony of the *Indians*. This *Evangelift*, fpeaking of the five foolifh *Virgins*, who never thought of getting Oyl, till the Bridegroom was ready to come in; tells us, that at Midnight they heard a great cry which awak'd them, and gave notice of his Coming, *Matth.* 25. 6. *At midnight there was a great cry made, Behold, the Bridegroom cometh, go ye out to meet him.*

It

It appears to be ſcarce agreeable to our Cuſtoms, that a Man ſhould go out on his Marriage-Night, and not return to his Houſe till Midnight, and therefore it may be ask'd, whether there was any Law that oblig'd him to do after this manner, ſince he arriv'd in great Ceremony, at his Houſe, where the Women were ready with Lamps to go out and meet him, and a Feaſt was prepared for him.

'Tis not difficult to anſwer this Queſtion, if we do it agreeably to the Cuſtoms of the *Indians* ; for on the Day of their Marriage, the Husband and Wife being both in the ſame *Palki*, or *Palanquin*, (which is the ordinary way of Carriage in the Country, and is carried by four Men upon their Shoulders,) go out between ſeven and eight a Clock at Night, accompanied with all their Kindred and Friends : The Trumpets and Drums go before them, and they are lighted by a multitude of *Maſſals*, which are a kind of Flambeau's, the Make whereof, I ſhall quickly explain.

Immediately behind the *Palanquin* of the New-Married Couple, walk many Women, whoſe buſineſs is to Sing Verſe, wherein they wiſh them all kind of Proſperity, as the *Greeks* and *Romans* formerly us'd to do, in their *Epithalamiums*.

I believe it is of theſe Publick Singers that the Scripture ſpeaks, when it ſays in the laſt Chapter of *Eccleſiaſtes*, ver. 4. *And all the Daughters of Muſick ſhall be brought low*, intending by that, to give us one Sign of a publick Deſolation. The Royal Prophet alſo mentions this ſort of Women, and calls them, *Juvenculas tympaniſtrias*. Pſal. 67. 26.

The New-Married Couple go abroad in this Equipage, for the ſpace of ſome Hours, after which they return to their own Houſe, where the Women and Domeſticks wait for them. The whole Houſe is enlightned with little Lamps, and many of theſe *Maſſals* already mention'd, are kept ready for their arrival,

rival, befides thofe that accompany them, and go before their *Palanquin.*

This fort of Lights, are nothing elfe but many pieces of old Linen, fqueez'd hard againft one another, in a round Figure, and forcibly thruft down into a Mould of Copper. Thofe who hold them in one Hand, have in the other a Bottle of the fame Metal, with the Mould of Copper, which is full of Oyl, and they take care to pour out of it, from time to time, upon the Linen, which otherwife gives no light.

When the Bridegroom and the Bride are come into the Houfe, the Wife retires with the Women, and the Husband fits down with his Friends upon Tapiftry or Mattreffes, where their Meat is ferv'd up to them : The Company is always very numerous, and I doubt, if among the *Greeks,* there were fo many Bride-Maids as there are among the *Indians.*

The Parable in the Gofpel, appears plainly to have rela   to this Cuftom, and perhaps the *Jews,* at leaft in the Days of *Jefus Chrift,* us'd fome Ceremony that came near it, without which I cannot fee, that a clear Explication can be given of this return of the Spoufe at Midnight, and the Feaft that is followed immediately after his arrival : And yet thofe who have written of the *Jewifh* Traditions, have faid nothing of it.

It may very well be, that *Chrift* fetch'd this Example from other Nations, which were near to *Judea,* and whofe Cuftoms and Ceremonies the *Jews* might know.

It were in vain to allege, that this is only a Parable, for all thofe which our *Saviour* made ufe of, were founded either upon the Cuftoms of the *Jews,* or of the other Nations that lay near to *Paleftine.*

ARTICLE XVIII.

Of their different Tribes *or* Clans.

THE *Pagan-Indians* are divided into *Tribes*, as formerly the *Jews* were, but I could never exactly difcover how many there are of them; for befides the general Divifion, each *Tribe* is divided into an infinite number of others, which are quite different from one another, either in their Food, or in fomething elfe.

What the *Jew* call *Tribes*, that the *Indians* call *Caftes*, i. e. *Clans*; but there is a much greater Difproportion betwixt thefe *Caftes*, than there was between the *Tribes* of *Ifrael*, which were neverthelefs unequal: For not to mention the Preheminence which the Priefthood gave the *Tribe* of *Levi*; there were alfo different Degrees among the reft: That of *Benjamin*, for inftance, was the leaft, as *Saul* obferv'd to *Samuel*, when this Prophet told him, upon occafion of the *Affes* he fought after, that the defire of all *Ifrael* was towards him, *Am not I a* Benjamite *of the fmalleft Tribe of* Ifrael? 1 Sam. 9. 21.

Neverthelefs, this Superiority of the People in different *Tribes*, did not hinder them from Vifiting one another, and from Eating together: It was alfo permitted, that one fhould take a Wife in another *Tribe* than his own, provided fhe was not an Heirefs, becaufe it was forbidden to remove an Inheritance from one *Tribe* to another, *Neque commifceatur poffeffio filiorum* Ifrael *de Tribu in Tribum, omnes enim viri ducent uxores de Tribu & cognatione fua*, Num. 36. ver. 7. Thus *David*, who was of the *Tribe* of *Judah*, Married *Michal*, who was of the *Tribe* of *Benjamin*, becaufe fhe was not an Heirefs.

The *Indians* do not allow of this, and they have among them fome *Caftes* fo contemptible, fuch as

that

that of the *Parias*, that a House would be in a manner Defil'd, if any one of them should dare to enter into it. They are defign'd for the vileſt Works, and dare not ſo much as touch others, which would be entirely Baniſh'd from their *Caſte*, and look'd upon as Infamous, if they ſhould have the leaſt familiarity with them.

This Horror which the *Pagans* have for that unhappy *Caſte*, is one of the greateſt hindrances which the *Miſſionaries* meet with in the Converſion of theſe *Infidels*, who cannot be prevail'd upon to ſubmit to a Law, by which they ſee themſelves in a manner oblig'd to take the Communion from the ſame Hand, which Adminiſters this Sacrament to the *Parias*, and conſequently expos'd to the danger of touching with their Lips and Fingers, what a *Paria* may have touch'd with his; and therefore, they are forc'd upon this occaſion, to uſe extraordinary precautions.

They refuſe alſo, to be preſent in the ſame Church with theſe *Parias*; and in condeſcenſion to this weakneſs, the Reverend Fathers *Jeſuits*, have built at *Pondichery*, a little Chapel near their Church, to ſhelter theſe poor Wretches, who before were obblig'd to ſtand without, and aſſiſt at Divine Service, where the Rain falls upon them, and the Heat of the Suu burns them up.

Some People may perhaps condemn this Method, and ſay, that the firſt effect of *Chriſtianity* being *Charity*, we ought not to ſuffer this averſion and abhorrence which they have for the *Parias*, whom *Baptiſm* has made their Brethren in *Jeſus Chriſt*, and that they ſhould apply themſelves to overcome that Natural Antipathy which all the other *Caſté's* have for this of the *Parias*.

This is indeed what is done with a Zeal truly Apoſtolical, by the Reverend *Jeſuits* and *Capuchins*, where they have the direction of *Souls*; and what the Gentlemen of Foreign *Miſſions* do with the like

F 4　　　　　　　　　　Appli-

Application; but this fort of Weakness is not to be overcome all on a fudden. When a Chuch is newly Planted among Men, who, as I may fay, are wavering between *Christianity* and *Idolatry*, and have their Hands ftill Reeking with the Incenfe, which they have offer'd to falfe *Gods*, they ought to take fpecial heed, that no fuch fudden Changes be attempted in a Place where they would have the *Christian Religion* to flourifh, and to be fettled for a long time to come.

We fee, for inftance, in the *Acts* of the *Apostles*, that tho' thefe firft Preachers of the Gofpel, being Affembled at *Jerufalem*, thought fit, that the *Gentiles* that were Converted to *Christianity*, fhould not be oblig'd to *Circumcifion*; *It feem'd good to the Holy Ghost and to us, to lay upon you no greater burden than thefe neceffary things*, Acts 15. 28. Yet St. *Paul* Circumcis'd *Timothy*, becaufe of the abhorrence which the *Jews*, to whom he was going to Preach the Kingdom of God, had for every one that was not Circumcis'd. *And took and circumcis'd him, becaufe of the* Jews *that were in thofe Quarters, for they all knew that his Father was a* Greek, Acts 16. 3.

We have alfo in the *Old Teftament* an Example of a much greater Toleration than this, which I am perfuaded would not have been allow'd under *Christianity*. And that was when *Naaman* General of the King of *Syria's* Army, was cur'd of his *Leprofie* by *Elifha*: He promis'd this Prophet, that he would never adore any *Idol* for the future, and that he would Worfhip only the true *God*, to whom he ow'd his Cure. Yet, becaufe his Office oblig'd him to wait upon his Prince into the Temple of *Rimmon*, and to ferve him as an *Efquire*; upon this account he pray'd *Elifha* to entreat the Lord, if when the King lean'd on him, and Worfhip'd the *Idol*, he Worfhip'd it alfo, ʓ. e. bow'd himfelf before it. *In this thing Pardon thy fervant, that when my Mafter goeth into the Houfe of*
Rimmon

Rimmon *to worship there, and he leaneth on my Hand,* and *I bow my self in the House* Rimmon, *when I bow down my self in the House of Rimmon, the Lord pardon thy servant in this thing,* 2 Kings 5. 18. And the Prophet *Elisha* answer'd him in such a manner, as makes us believe that he consented to it, for after this request, he said, only, *Go in peace.* At least, it cannot be said that he condemn'd him.

I have related these Examples, only to show, that certain things may be sometimes allow'd for the hardness of Mens Hearts; especially, when they are not directly opposite to the fundamental points of Religion, and when we see great danger would ensue upon refusing of them : But this must be done so, that Men may not be able to draw consequences from it for the future, and look upon it as a formal Grant, and an absolute Consent, which was only a pure Sufferance for a time, and therefore great care should be taken, to inform them of this before-hand.

These Matters are indeed very nice, and require great Prudence and Discretion, which perhaps are the two things most necessary in the *Missionaries,* and which I am persuaded the Holy Labourers in the Lords Vineyard, are perfectly possess'd of; for there is Reason to believe, that Heaven which has inspir'd them with such a glorious design, as the Conversion of the *Gentiles,* would not refuse them those Vertues they stand in need of, to acquit themselves worthily ; at least, *Charity* obliges us to think so of them.

We ought therefore to hope, that in Process of time, some means may be found out, to destroy by degrees this strong Antipathy, which all the *Pagan-Indians* have for the *Parias* : Time alone, does often remedy some things, which it would be vain and dangerous to attempt at the beginning : And besides we ought not to doubt, but when the wise Di-

rectors

rectors of *Souls*, shall find the least prospect of settling *Christian Charity* in its Purity, in the Hearts of the *Indians*, they will employ all their Power to do it.

This distinction of *Tribes* and *Families*, and the care that was taken to prevent as much as is possible, the Marrying into other *Tribes*, did in Ancient times, Authorize these Marriages between those that were near a-kin. *Jacob*, for instance, rather than take a *Canaanitish* Woman to Wife, Married his two Cousin-germans, *Leah* and *Rachel*, who besides were Sisters ; and before the written Law, this kind of Marriages was frequent. In Process of time, these things were carried much higher, for *Solon* permitted to the *Athenians*, the Marriages between Brethren and Sisters, provided they had the same Father, but not the same Mother : *Lyeurgus*, on the contrary, allow'd of Marriage between Brethren and Sisters, who had the same Mother, but not the same Father ; and the *Egyptians* permitted Marriage indifferently, between the one and the other. We see at this day among the *Persians*, Marriages much more Monstrous ; the Son, for instance, may Marry his Mother : All Persons of Quality, Marry thus among them, as *Philo* relates, *de special. Leg.* and those who were Born of these Marriages, were the more Honour'd, and counted worthy, as they say, of a Throne, upon this account, that a Man ought to be esteem'd so much the more perfect, the less his Blood is mix'd.

ARTICLE. XIX.

Of the Head of each Tribe *or* Caste.

EVery *Caste* has its Head, who is appointed to maintain its Privileges, and to promote the Observation of the Laws, and in general to take care, that all
Business

Bufinefs be orderly manag'd: And when they treat of any Article that concerns the whole Nation, chiefly when it relates to their Cuftoms, Rights, and Juftice, or generally to all Affairs of Policy, thefe Heads affemble to Examine and Determine what is fit to be done.

Thefe are what the *Jews* call the Princes of their *Tribes*, of whom 'tis faid, That they fate upon twelve Thrones, judging the twelve *Tribes* of *Ifrael*, and who are alfo mention'd in *Deuteronomy*, Chap. 5. 23. and Chap. 29. 10. They did nothing confiderable without their confent: And becaufe every one of them in his *Tribe*, had Authority to oblige the People to obferve the Rules which the Lord had prefcrib'd, and to reform the Abufes which were committed againft them, *God* begun always with Punifhing thofe Sins, which they did not oppofe, as may be feen in *Numbers* ; where we read, that when the *Ifraelites*, being entic'd by the *Moabitifh* Women, had Worfhip'd their *God, Beelphegor*, he order'd *Mofes* in the firft place, to caufe all the Princes of *Ifrael* to be Hang'd up, *i. e.* the Heads of the *Tribes, Take all the Heads of the People, and hang them up before the Lord, againft the Sun, that the fierce anger of the Lord may be turn'd away from* Ifrael, Numb. 25. ver. 4.

The *Grecians* had alfo fuch as prefided over each of the Ten parts which made up the City of *Athens*, which the *Athenians* call'd *Phule*, which was the fame thing with the *Tribes* among the *Jews*, and to every one of thefe Heads, they gave the Names of *Archiphulos, Phylarchos, Archos* or *Archegos*.

This diftinction of the principal Families which made up the *Tribes*, was alfo us'd among the *Ifraelites* ; They had twelve *Tribes*, and each of them had its Head or Prince, as the Scripture informs us. *Thefe are the Sons of* Ifhmael, *and thefe are their Names by their Towns, and by their Caftles ; twelve Princes according to their Nations*, Gen. 25. 16.

Thofe, who in Ancient times firft founded thefe
Mo-

Monarchies, which in Procefs of time became fo famous, were nothing elfe but the Heads of *Tribes*, and affum'd no other Title but that, at firft among their Equals : but by degrees, abufing that Dignity, they forfook at laft the Title of Father, to affume that of Emperor and King, and often chang'd, even the Name of *Protector* into that of *Tyrannus*.

ARTICLE XX.

Of their Excommunicate *Perfons*.

THE *Indians* have among them fuch Perfons as are *Excommunicate*, as formerly the *Jews* had. He that is *Excommunicate* is faid to lofe his *Cafte, i. e.* he is no more to be reckon'd as one of the Members of his *Tribe*. Thofe who are in this condition, are lookt upon as infamous, and every Body fhuns them; and if any one does fo much as frequent their Company, he partakes of their Infamy, and is judg'd no lefs to have loft his *Cafte*; and the others have fo great an abhorrence of them, that they break in pieces all the Earthen Pots, they have made ufe of : And this they do likewife, whenever a *Foreigner* or a *Paria*, does fo much as touch the Pots which are defign'd for their own ufe, looking upon every thing as Profane which has pafs'd thro' their Hands.

The moft common Caufes of *Excommunication* are, for inftance, To Drink Wine, to Eat of a Cow, to Eat with Foreigners, or with *Parias*, or even to Eat of that which they have made ready.

When a Man is once declar'd to have faln from his *Tribe*, it cofts him much Mony to reftore himfelf, befides many Wafhings he is oblig'd to ufe, that he may wipe off the Defilement they pretend he has contracted.

All the Ancient *Pagans* had likewife *Excommuni-cates,*

cates, who were forbidden to approach their Temples, or the ſacred Groves in which they offer'd Sacrifices, and where Prayers were made to the *Gods.*
Before they begun their Ceremonies, the Prieſts
took care to advertiſe thoſe, who by ſome ill actions,
were become unworthy of partaking in them, to
withdraw, and not to defile by their preſence the
Holy Places, which were Conſecrated to the *Deity,*
as *Virgil* relates in the ſixth Book of his *Æneids.*

—— *Procul, O procul eſte Profani,*
Conclamat vates, totoque abſiſtite luco.

The word *Excommunicate,* ſignifies among us, one
excluded from the Communion, as the word *Profa-*
nus, ſignified among the Ancients, one excluded
from the Temples, and Sacrifices, for *Profanus* is as if
one would ſay, *procul à fano.*

ARTICLE XXI.

Of their manner of Building and watering Gardens.

SOlomon relating in his *Eccleſiaſtes,* all the Works he
had made for his own ſatisfaction, that he might
ſpend his Days in great Eaſe and Pleaſure, and make
himſelf in appearance a happy Man, tells us, that
he made Pools of water, to water therewith the
Plantation of young Trees ; *Et extruxi mihi piſcinas,*
ut irrigarent ſylvam lignorum germinantium, Ecclef. 2. 6.
I think that the moſt Natural way of underſtanding this Paſſage, agreeably to our Cuſtoms, were to
ſay, that the Scripture underſtands by this Wood of
young Trees, a *Seminary,* where the young Trees
are Planted as thick by one another as in a Wood ;
yet it ſeems, that by this we are to underſtand in
general, the *Gardens* which *Solomon* Planted, after
he

he was advanc'd to the Throne; for among the *Jews, Gardens* were nothing elfe but real Woods of Fruit-trees, upon which account they are often in Scripture call'd *Pomaria*.

The Gardens of the *Indians* are built very near after the fame manner, and are nothing elfe but a confus'd heap of all forts of Trees, Planted for the moft part without any Order or Symmetry, which neverthelefs have a peculiar agreeablenefs, and which I would prefer in the Hot Countries, to the great open Walks, accompanied with fine Plats, which may indeed pleafe the Sight, but afford no fhelter againft the Rays of the fcorching *Sun*, to which 'tis very troublefome to be expos'd.

Thefe Pools of water, which *Solomon* fpeaks of, and which he fays he made, for watering this Foreft of young Trees, are us'd alfo among the *Indians*, and perhaps it will not be difficult to apprehend the manner in which they ufe them.

There is commonly in thefe Gardens, a great Pit, or kind of Fifh-pool, which is full of Rain-water; and juft by it there is a Bafon of Brick, rais'd about two Foot higher then the Ground: When therefore they have a mind to water the Garden, it is fill'd with water from the Fifh-pool or Pit, which, thro' a Hole that is at the bottom, falls into a *Canal*, that is divided into many Branches, proportionable in bignefs to their diftance from the Bafon, and carries the water to the Foot of each Tree, and to each Plat of Herbs; and when the Gardiners think they are watred enough, they ftop up, or turn afide, the *Canals* with clods of Earth.

After this manner, the *Romans* water'd their Gardens, and even their Meadows; and of thefe *Brooks* or *Canals*, *Virgil* fpeaks, when he fays, *Claudite jam rivos pueri, fat prata biberunt*.

The *Italians* have preferv'd the fame Cuftom, which is alfo follow'd by almoft all the People of the
Levant,

Levant, and which is more Commodious than the way we make ufe of, for by the means of thefe *Canals*, a great Garden may be fooner water'd, than one fingle Square-plat by our Water-pots.

ARTICLE XXII.

Of the Abhorrence they have for every thing that is contrary to Decency.

THeophraftus obferves in his Characters, that at *Athens* (which in his time was the Seat of *Civility*) there were fome Men fo very fcrupulous and nice, that they would not go into any place where they fhould fee a Bird of a bad *Omen*, without throwing before them in their way, three little Stones, or fpitting in their Bofom to remove as it were far from them, the confequences of this bad Prefage.

There are many among the *Indians*, who follow this Cuftom : And one day when I was at *Balaffor*, a *Pagan Indian* ftopt fhort, and fought out three Stones, which he threw into a place thro' which he was to pafs, and where he had feen a *French* Seaman, in fuch a Pofture, which tho' neceffary, was not very decent, and which they abhor above all things ; and therefore when Nature obliges them to any fuch thing, they ufe all the precautions imaginable to hide themfelves.

Upon occafion of this abhorrence, which the *Indians* have for every thing that in the leaft is contrary to Decency, I will relate one of their Cuftoms, which is mention'd by an Ancient Author in his Works, and is by him recommended to his *Contemporaries* : But fince I cannot make ufe of fuch terms in our Language, as are employ'd by others, without offending againft Decency, I fhall ufe only the *Latin* for a few Lines.

Inter prudentes tum Religionis, tum Urbanitatis regulas, quas temporis sui homines Docere conabatur Hesiodus, *hæc invenitur.* Neque in via, neque extra viam progrediendo meias, neque denudatus —— Sedens vero divinus vir & prudens mingit, aut idem accedens ad parietem bene septi atrii. *Hanc ultimam consuetudinem scrupulosè tenebant* Judæi, *ut videre est in Scriptura Sacra; ubi cum Deus alicui familiæ destructionem minatur, semper fere dicit,* Delebo de familia ejus omnem mingentem ad parietem: *His verbis indicans mares, quibus sublatis & familia tollitur. Primam vero non minus exacte tenent* Gentiles Indi; *quippe semper ad terram usque inclinati, & quodammodo sedentes mingunt, stantemque, vel ad solem conversum, vesicam exonerare, apud ipsos abominabile est.*

ARTICLE XXIII.

Of the bad Presages they make from the Situation or Croaking of Crows.

Altho' *Crows* are very common among the *Indians*, yet the *Pagans* look upon them as Birds of a bad *Omen*, and particularly the *Banians*, who are a peculiar *Caste*, that applies it self only to Merchandize. They would not for all the World undertake any Business if going out of their Houses, in a Morning, they found a *Crow* sitting before their Door.

The Ancients did likewise look upon that Place as unhappy, where a *Crow* had Croak'd in the Morning; and *Hesiod* forbids to leave a House imperfect, for fear lest a *Crow* should come and Croak when sitting upon it. *Neque domum faciens imperfectam relinquito, ne forte insidens crocitet stridula cornix.*

Neither

Neither is *Europe* itself perfectly free from this Superstition, and I remember that I have heard some People of good Quality in *France* say, that when the *Crow* or *Owl* make a Noise before Day on the top of a House, it was an infallible Sign, that somebody was to *die* there; and I believe, that the Natural Inclination which some People observe these *Birds* to have for *dead Bodies*, and in general for all kind of *Corruption*, is the Cause of that *doleful Omen* they make from their Voice, and every thing that belongs to them. Yet some pretend, that these Animals are in effect sensible of the *Bodies* which begin to be *disorder'd*, and because they love *Corruption*, they come always as near them as they can.

ARTICLE XXIV.

Of the Aversion some of them have for a Mouse, *which yet some among them do eat.*

IF the *Indians* abstain from eating certain Animals, out of the Respect and Veneration they have for them, there are also others from which they abstain out of an Aversion; because they look upon them as unclean, and which they dare not eat of, under Pain of being cast out of their *Tribe*, and being reputed Infamous.

The *Mouse*, for Instance, is one of these Animals to which they have a great Aversion; and yet there are some among them who publickly eat it, because they run no Hazard from their *Caste*, neither can they be thrust down lower than they are: Such are the Carriers of *Palanquins*, who are commonly call'd *Boes*.

Altho' this Animal was likewise abhorr'd among the *Jews*, and in *Levit.* 11. 29. they were forbidden to eat it, yet there were many of them who

G   trans-

transgress'd this Prohibition; as may be seen in the last Chapter of *Isaiah*, where the Prophet threatens them with the Wrath of GOD: *They that eat Swine's Flesh, and the Abomination, and the Mouse, shall be consumed together, saith the LORD,* Isa. 66. 17.

ARTICLE XXV.

Of their Funerals.

THE *Indians* have no general Rules for their *Funerals*: Some throw the Dead into the *Ganges,* many Bury them under Ground, and others Burn them. Those who Interr them, take care to carry, for a certain Number of Days, Rice, Fruit, and Flowers, and lay them on their Graves: And all the Ancient *Pagans* us'd to do this; so that the Custom which crept into the *Church* in the Primitive Times, was a Relique of *Paganism*, which S. *Austin* rebukes in the *Christians* of his Time.

Whether they interr the Bodies or burn them, they never fail to wash them well before-hand, and afterwards to rub them with Oil. All Antiquity religiously observ'd this Custom of washing their Dead before they buried them, and thought that this was the true way of knowing whether they were really dead, or only in a Lethargy; because if they had but a little sense left in them, this Water would rouze them out of their dead Sleep; and so much the rather, because many of them wash'd with Water boiling-hot. This Custom is still continu'd in *Europe* of Washing dead Bodies; but they use for that purpose only lukewarm Water, because they wash them only to make them clean, and have no thought of discovering by this means, whether they be truly dead or no.

The

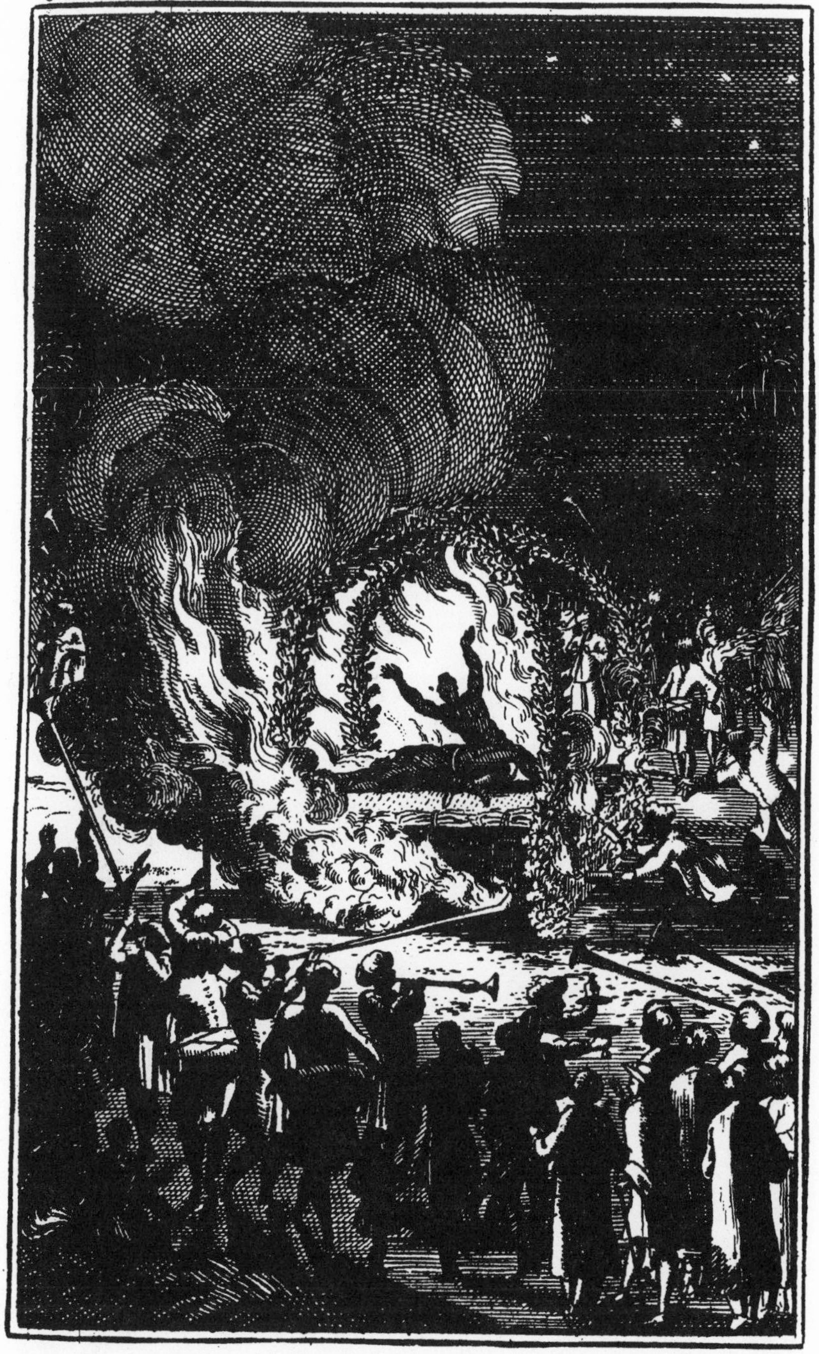

The *Jews* commonly wa.h'd the Dead, and we find that thus they us'd *Tabitha. And it came to paſs in theſe days, that ſhe fell ſick and died, whom when they had waſh'd, they laid her in an upper-chamber,* Act. 9. 37. This Cuſtom was alſo retain'd under *Chriſtianity;* and St. *Gregory* of *Tours* ſpeaking of St. *Pelagia,* ſays, that after ſhe was waſh'd according to cuſtom; ſhe was put into a Bier, and carried to Church. *Abluta juxta morem, collocatur in feretro, atque in Eccleſiam deportatur.* Greg. Turon. de Glo. Conf. c. 104.

The *Jews* did not only *waſh* their dead Bodies, but alſo *embalm'd* them, and *rubb'd* them with *Spices* to preſerve them, as much as poſſible, from Corruption; eſpecially the Bodies of *Princes.* Thus *Joſeph* caus'd his Father *Jacob* to be *embalm'd,* and in proceſs of time they did the ſame thing to the Kings of *Iſrael* and *Judah:* Yet ſome of them, upon the account of their Wickedneſs, were depriv'd of this Honour; as for inſtance, *Joram* King of *Judah,* who was indeed laid in the *Sepulchre* of his *Anceſtors,* but without *Embalming,* and all the other Ceremonies, which are uſually obſerv'd upon ſuch-like Occaſions: At leaſt, it ſeems that this is the only Senſe that can be put upon that Place of the *Chronicles: And it came to paſs in proceſs of time,*—— *his Bowels fell out by reaſon of his Sickneſs; ſo he died of ſore diſeaſes, and his People made no Burning for him, like the Burning of his Fathers,* 2 Chron. 21. 19. For indeed they muſt paſs thro' the *Fire,* in order to *Embalming;* and it was neceſſary that the *Spices* they made uſe of, ſuch as *Myrrhe, Incenſe, Gum-Arabic, Cedar-Water,* and all the other things they employ'd to this purpoſe, ſhould be boiling-hot, to make them penetrate into the *Fleſh;* ſo that it was indeed *burning* of them, to *rub* them ſo very *hot into* the *Body,* as the Cuſtom was.

　　　　　They

They had learn'd from the *Egyptians* this Way of *Embalming* Bodies, and the Bodies thus *embalm'd*, are what we call *Mummies*. Among the rest, I saw one at *Leyden*, which was very fair; it has all its Teeth still, the Skin is black and shrivel'd, the Body is all wrapt up in gummy Bandages; and the Arms do no-where appear, being plac'd like those of an *Infant* in *Swadling-Cloaths*: It is indeed wonderful to see, that *Spices* should be able to preserve *Bodies* in their full Proportion, for the space of perhaps 3000 Years.

Sometimes *Honey* has been employ'd to preserve Bodies, and to keep them from Corruption; and *Nicephorus* informs us, that those who accompanied the Body of *Epiphanius*, made use of this Preservative to carry it as far as the Isle of *Cyprus*. *Epiphanium verò in mari mortuum esse intellexi, quem comites ejus melle oblitum, ne quid fortè ingratum corpori accideret, in Cyprum detulerunt.* Nicephor. *Hist. lib.* 12. *cap.* 46.

To return to the *Indians*, we see still at their Interments, what the *Scripture* calls the *Trumpeters for the Dead;* who are a sort of Men, that go a little way before the dead Corps, and play upon a long Trumpet, whose doleful Sound is very agreeable to the sad Occasion.

Before the *Mogol* became Master of the *Indies*, and while the *Pagans* had yet their particular Princes, the Wife of him that died, who was to be burnt, was oblig'd to sit upon a Load of *Wood*, holding the Body of her *Husband* upon her Knees, and so the Fire consum'd them both together.

I say she was oblig'd, for tho' the Relations of the Deceas'd could not absolutely compel her, yet she was so far under a Force, by the Manner in which she must pass the rest of her Life, in case she refus'd to follow her Husband, that she became in a manner a Slave to his Relations, and by them was

treated

treated with that Difgrace and Cruelty, which was a thoufand times worfe than Death.

Yet there remain'd one way to avoid at once Death and the bad Treatment of his Family, which was to make herfelf a *Publick Woman*; for then the Relations of her *Husband* had no Power over her; it being exprefly forbidden by the Law to abufe this fort of *Women*.

Thefe are they that commonly go in Crowds to Sing and Dance at *Marriages*, and other Publick Occafions of *Rejoicing*, and in general to any Place whither they are call'd. While their *Good Days* lafte, they are well-receiv'd wherefoever they go, altho' they are publickly known to be what they are; but they are miferable when they begin to decline; and and it is happy for them in this Condition, if the Younger Sort will make ufe of them as Servants, and give them their Food.

But to return to my Subject. Becaufe it was a Difgrace to his *Family*, whofe *Wife* was not burnt, they us'd their utmoft Endeavours to perfuade her to refolve upon it. And for this end they attack'd her in the time of her greateft Grief, when fhe feem'd to be moft affected with the Death of her *Husband*; and fet before her Eyes all his Good Qualities, and heightned the Love he had for her: In fine, they made ufe of every thing which might beget a Tendernefs for him, and make her willing to fay, fhe would not furvive him: For when fhe had once pronounc'd this Fatal Affent before three or four Perfons, it was like the Interment in the River *Ganges*, and there was no way of Retracting it; befides, that they loaded her with Praifes, accompanied her with Drums and Trumpets, encircled her with Garlands of Flowers, and the *Brahmans* promis'd her Eternal Happinefs, when fhe had taken this Refolution · whence it came to pafs that few Women efcap'd.

She

She was therefore conducted in Pomp sitting upon the Load of Wood, and at such time as the Fire was put to it, the Drums and Trumpets made a terrible Noise, for fear her Cries should be heard.

After the same manner in ancient times did the *Ammonites*, when standing round about the Idol *Moloch*, they set Fire to it, and put a Child between its Arms to be consum'd : And the Noise of the Drums upon this Occasion, was the Cause why the Valley in which these abominable Sacrifices were offer'd, was call'd *Tophet*, which in *Hebrew* signifieth a *Drum*.

Since the *Moors* became Masters of this Country, they have, as much as they could, oppos'd this detestable Custom, and they have also laid a heavy Tax upon the Kindred of those, whose Wife shall be expos'd upon a Load of Wood; so that now they do not Burn so many.

I have endeavour'd to discover the Original of this Cruel Custom, but could never find any thing certain about it : Only they say, that formerly the Wives Poison'd their Husbands upon the least Discontent; and therefore to oblige them not to shorten their Days, but to endeavour by all means to prolong them, this great Disgrace was fix'd upon such a Wife, as durst survive her Husband ; that so they seeing themselves oblig'd in Honour to Die with them, or forc'd to pass the rest of their Days in a Miserable Condition, might account it their Interest to preserve them. And thus a Wife appear'd to take great Care of her Husband, when she did only take Care of Herself; and to shed abundance of Tears upon the Account of his Death, when at the bottom she only bewail'd her own.

They have something like the same Custom in *Guinea*; for there, when a great Lord dies, not only all his Wives whom he lov'd best are put to Death, but also the Servants that were most dear to him;

to the end, say they, that they may go to bear him company and serve him in the other World. Upon this account, it is no pleasure to be Mistress to a *Negro* of Quality; and I am persuaded if we should be so unhappy, as to have such a Wicked Custom here in *Europe*, the great Lords would be found more cruel than now they are, and that Celibacy would be more in vogue.

ARTICLE XXVI.

Of their Monks, *call'd* Fakirs.

IT has always been said, that the Devil has his *Martyrs;* but if there be any Place in the Universe, where it is so, 'tis certainly in the *Indies,* where there are *Fakirs,* who properly are the *Monks* of the Country; who do such things, as exceed a thousand times, what we read of the Mortification and Penance that was endur'd by the *Fathers* in the *Desarts.*

Many make a Vow to continue all their Life-time in the same Posture, and in that Posture they remain : So some of them never lie down, but are continually supported by a Cord, or Stick, upon which they lean with their Armpits; others have their Hands always lifted up to Heaven : And many other Mortifications they use, the least of which is to cut their Flesh in pieces with a Whip, or a Knife. They look upon themselves, as Men that are not of this World; and because they fancy, that they are above all the Passions of Humane Nature, and in a State of Innocence; many of them walk forth, or show themselves publickly quite naked, and never cover, what Decency forbids to be un-cover'd.

G 4 Those

These are not the only Persons, who have pretended to be free from *Passions*, and from all the
Inclinations that *Nakedness* can inspire; whom the
Adamites have imitated in this particular Custom:
For the Hereticks who came out from the Sect of
the *Carpocratians* and *Gnosticks*, assembled quite
naked, as St. *Austin* relates; and in this condition
they heard the Lectures that were made, they pray'd,
and even celebrated the Sacrament. *Nudi itaque
mares fœminæque conveniunt, nudi lectiones audiunt,
nudi orant, nudi celebrant Sacramenta. S.* Augustin. *de*
Hæres. *c.* 31. St. *Epiphanius* is cited as speaking too
severely of these Hereticks; and his Authority is
made use of, to prove that they committed all sorts
of *vile Actions* in their Assemblies, and that they
wholly rejected *Prayer. Diction. Crit.* of *Bayle.* Yet, as
we have just now shown, St. *Austin* says positively,
that they *pray'd*; and even St. *Epiphanius* says in one
place, that they follow'd the Rules of *Monks*; i. e.
they observ'd *Continence*, and even condemn'd *Marriage. Monachorum & continentium instituta sectantur,
nuptiasque condemnant.* St. Epiphan. *T.* 1. *l.* 2. And
therefore 'tis no wise probable, that they should at
first commit publickly all the *Crimes* that are im-
puted to them: But some pretend, that in process
of time they abandon'd themselves to their Lusts,
and that their *Nakedness*, which they look'd upon at
the beginning as a certain Means of restoring themselves to the State of *Innocence*, and being made
conformable to *Adam* before the Fall, plung'd them
afterwards into the highest degrees of *Lewdness*;
which appears to be probable enough.

The Common People are fully persuaded of the
Vertue and Innocence of the *Fakirs*, but then they
must appear to be abstracted from every thing that
can gratify the Senses, and to meddle in no Affairs
of this World: The greatest part of them maintain this Character well enough, and act their part

in

in publick tolerably well ; but in private they are accus'd of committing among themselves enormous Crimes ; and perhaps some talk too much against them.

We see in the Book of *Kings,* what strange Ways the Priests of *Baal* made use of to honour their *God,* to invoke him, and obtain some Favour from him ; and as the *Scripture* observes , to make Fire come down from Heaven upon their Sacrifice ; how they cut themselves with Knives and Lancets till the Blood gush'd out. *Clamabant ergo voce magna, & incidebant se juxta ritum suum cultris & lanceolis , donec perfunderentur sanguine,* 1 King. 18. 28. Which the *Fakirs* do still to this day, as we have already observ'd. Some of them make a Vow, to rowl themselves, for a certain number of Leagues , over every thing that comes in their Way , whether it be Stones or Thorns, whereby they tear all their Body in pieces : And this kind of Mortification is also very common among them.

The *Indians* have also another sort of *Fakirs,* who are less austere , or to speak properly , less foolish ; who assemble in Troops , and go from Village to Village, to foretel *Plenty,* or threaten *Barrenneß,* according as they are well or ill treated in any place ; to prophesie *good Succeß,* to promise *Children* to those that have none, and *Husbands* to those that are weary of the State of *Virginity :* But they are great *Rogues,* and 'tis dangerous to meet them in a solitary place, unless you be well provided to defend your self : Yet they are held in great Veneration among the *Pagans,* and also among the *Moors* , who have some of that Sort among themselves ; and it would be a capital Crime to beat any one of them.

These Assemblies of the *Fakirs* (setting aside their *Religion* and *Bad Conduct*) are among the *Indians,* what the *Schools* of the *Prophets* were formerly among the *Jews,* whose *Scholars* were call'd
Filii

Filii Prophetarum, Grex vel Chorus Prophetarum. Such were thofe whom *Saul* found, when he *Prophefied* in the midft of them. The *Scripture* faith, that they had *Drums* and *Trumpets*, and that it was at the Sound of thefe *Inftruments* they utter'd their *Prophefies. Et ante eos Pfalterium, & Tympanum, & Tibiam, & Citharam,* 1 Sam. 10. 5.

The fame *Scripture* informs us, That, when *Jehofaphat, Joram,* and the King of *Edom* were affembled againft *Mefha* King of *Moab,* and the want of *Water* reduc'd their *Army* to the greateft Extremity, *Jehofaphat* fent for *Elifha*, to obtain by his *Prayers* the Affiftance of Heaven; and that this *Prophet,* before he confulted GOD, demanded a Song : *Nunc autem adducite mihi Pfaltem, cumque caneret Pfaltes, facta eft fuper eum manus Domini, & dixit,* &c. 2 Kings, 3. 15.

To juftify this extraordinary Way of confulting GOD, and to give fome *Phyfical Account* of it, I think we may fay, That our Minds being fo much the fitter to receive the Commands of Heaven, and to be the more attentive to its Voice, the lefs Correfpondence it has with the Body; or the lefs the Body is capable to reprefent to it fuch things as may diftract it; every thing that contributes to lull the Senfes afleep, and hinder them from being affected with the Objects round about them, renders the *Prophet* fo much the more capable of receiving *Divine Infpiration* : But nothing is more fit to produce this Effect, than *Voices, Inftruments,* and all forts of *Mufick;* which do in a manner lull all the Senfes afleep by a languifhing Sound; or ftriking them all together by a confus'd and fudden Noife, keep them all in fufpence, and fix none of them : For altho' *Mufick* acts not immediately upon any Senfe but that of *Hearing*, yet this Senfe has an Influence upon the reft, as all the Senfes have upon one another. And this we find by daily Experience, that when one

Senfe

Senſe is ſtrongly affected , all the reſt ſeem to be hindred from doing their Office ; as when we *feel* an acute Pain , our *Eyes* do not diſtinctly perceive any Object, and our *Ears* perceive nothing but con-fus'd Sounds ; and after the ſame manner are our other Senſes affected.

The *Indian-Fakirs*, whom I lately mention'd, do likewiſe make uſe of *Drums* and *Trumpets* for venting their pretended *Prophecies*; and in their Crowds of *People* there are alwaysſome,who endeavour to poſſeſs themſelves with a furious Rage, by making the vio-lent Motions of their *Body* correſpond with the ſudden and confus'd Noiſe of their *Instruments* when they are falling ; and when by this means they have put themſelves out of Breath, then they pronounce certain Sentences, which the *Pagans* take for *Oracles* and *Predictions*.

It was ſo uſual among the *Jews*, to ſee the greateſt part of the *Prophets* become furious and be-ſide themſelves , when they had a mind to utter their *Prophecies* , that the Name of *Furious* was com-monly given to the *Prophets* ; and when they were poſſeſs'd with a *Rage* , then it was ſaid, that they *Propheſied*. This is the Expreſſion, which the *Scripture* makes uſe of with reſpect to *Saul*, both to denote that he became furious, and that he tor-mented his *Body* by violent Poſtures. *And it came to paſs on the morrow , that the evil ſpirit from God came upon Saul, and he propheſied in the midst of the houſe, and David played with his hand as at other times ,* I Sam. 18. 10.

Whether what we read in ſome *Poets* , and more particularly in *Lactantius* , about the *Sibyls* may be taken for a true *Hiſtory* , or only for a *Fiction* , as ſome Learned Men think ; yet this is very certain, the Ancients imagin'd, that it was neceſſary in order to *Divine Inſpiration*, to become *furious*, and to be in ſuch a *conſternation* , that the Hairs of their Head
ſhould

should stand on end , the Members of their Body should quake, and their Words should be ill-sounded; at least the People believ'd this. Neither ought this to appear surprizing, for these People who live without any *Principles* , and have no Assistance from any *Light* , but what their own *Wit*, and an *ungovern'd Fancy* furnishes, seek always after that which appears most extraordinary, and have an high Opinion of every thing they do not understand; nay they seem to take a Pleasure in that which provokes their Fury, like *Children*, who love to hear sad and doleful Stories of *Spirits*, or *Witches*, altho' they make them afraid.

But if the Common People greedily hunt after such kind of *Tales*, and highly esteem the *Predictions* of the *Diviners*, yet Rational Men give no heed to them; nay they do not scruple publickly to mock at them. Thus the Poet *Ennius* , for instance, speaking of these *Diviners* and *Prophets*, treats them very coarsly; for he calls them *superstitious* , *impudent*, *Fools* and *Beggars* : He says , that they know not how to *take* the *right Way* themselves , while they pretend to *shew* it to others ; and that while they *promise* others great Riches , they ask a Peny for an Alms.

Superstitiosi vates, impudentesque harioli ;
Aut inertes, aut insani , quibus egestas imperat ;
Qui sibi semitam non sapiunt, aliis monstrant viam;
Quibus divitias pollicentur, ab his drachmas ipsi petunt.

ARTI-

ARTICLE XXVII.

Of *their* ENCHANTMENTS.

WE fee in the Book of *Exodus,*, that *Pharaoh* had his *Enchanters*, who could by their Art counterfeit many of the *Miracles* which *Mofes* wrought in the view of this *Prince.* The Time of doing thefe great *Prodigies* is now paft, and fo we are not any longer to expect that we fhall meet with the like: And if we fhould find any fuch, I believe it would be the wifeft Courfe to conceal them; for thefe kind of Stories are mightily fufpected, efpecially when they come from a far Country. Neverthelefs, fince I am refolv'd to fet down even the fmalleft things, wherein I can perceive an Agreement between the *Indians* and the Ancients, I hope I may be pardon'd, if I fay fomething of the *Enchanters.*

Their *Enchantments*, at leaft fo far as they are come to my knowledge, are confin'd within a very narrow Compafs; for they confift only in taking *Serpents*, and making them *dance* at the Sound of the *Flute*: They commonly carry many forts of them, which they keep in Hampers, and go with them from Houfe to Houfe, and make them *dance*, when any body will give them any thing.

When they meet with any of thefe Animals in their Gardens or Houfes, the common way of making them come out of their Holes, is by playing upon the *Flute*, and finging fome *Songs*; and then they take them up in their Hands, without receiving any Hurt; but they take great heed not to kill them: And when they have drawn them out of the place where they were, they carry them into the Fields, where they keep them with the reft, to make them *dance* upon Occafion.

It

It happen'd once where I was, that one of them appear'd, that had lain conceal'd in a Guard-House, and a Soldier kill'd it, which threw the pretended *Enchanter* into a strange Consternation; who took it, and Buried it with a great deal of Veneration and Ceremony, and put into the Hole where it was interr'd a little Rice and Milk, as it were to expiate the Injury that had been done to the Race of the *Serpents*.

The *Egyptians*, *Phœnicians*, *Grecians* and *Romans*, in ancient times ador'd the *Serpent*. The Figure of this Animal upon their *Money*, and in their *Pictures*, is the *Hieroglyphick* of *Health* and *Good Fortune*; and when it held its Tail in its Mouth, it signified in the first place *Eternity*; and secondly, the *World*; because by a General Law, all Men are oblig'd to return to the Place from whence they came: And thus perhaps, to make the *Jews* think of having Recourse to GOD for *Health*, and the *Cure* they wanted, *Moses* lifted up the *Brazen Serpent*, which, as he might have seen in *Egypt*, was the *Hieroglyphick* of both these.

It would be difficult to assign the Reason of this universal Veneration which almost all Nations have had for *Serpents*, which are otherwise frightful Animals, and can do nothing but Hurt. Perhaps it was done upon the same Account, that the *Negro's* of *Guinea* do still offer *Sacrifice* to the *Devil*; *i. e.* for Fear left they should do them some Mischief; which is the Reason they endeavour by their Submission and Worship to pacifie them. Perhaps this was a Consequent of the History of *Eve* and the *Serpent* related by *Moses'* in *Genesis*, which was known to other Nations: But after what Manner, and upon what Account soever, this *Worship* was at first establish'd, this is certain, that it was most General, and there is scarce any Nation in which it has not been us'd.

I have

I have heard of several Persons who have related astonishing Stories of these *Indian Enchanters*; but for my part, as in such an *Article* I can scarce believe what I have seen, so I cannot think fit to weary my *Reader* with a long Narrative of these *Prodigies*; and therefore I shall only add, That it appears to me very probable, that this kind of *People* in Ancient Times, were the first and the only *Enchanters*; and that perhaps the Inconvenience which Men suffer'd from *Serpents* or other Animals, occasion'd some to seek out the way of mastering them. And so we find, that *Egypt*, which was the Country that abounded most in *creeping things*, was also the most Famous for this kind of *Mysteries*.

But whether this be done by the help of the *Devil*, or meerly by some *secret Causes* in *Nature*, is a Question that I dare not enter upon; for whatsoever Side I should take, I shall certainly meet with a great many Adversaries.

I shall only observe, that the Name *Incantator*, and that of *Epodos*, which both signifie the same thing, and are the Names that the Ancients gave to all those that did extraordinary things, do sufficiently justifie this Conjecture about the first *Inchanters*; for both of them signifie a Man that Sings about any thing, or upon the account of any thing; as the *Indians* do at present, when they have a mind to bring forth the *Serpents*, or to make them Dance.

The *Jews*, who continued a long time with the *Egyptians*, might very well learn to practise these Tricks of the *Egyptians*, for they are often mention'd in *Scripture*; but supposing that they did not make use of them, yet at least they knew them, and understood after what manner other Nations took those *creeping things*; for *David* compares the Madness of *Sinners* to a *Serpent*, or an *Adder*, that will not hearken to the Voice of the *Inchanter*. *Their Poison*

is

is like the poison of a serpent; they are like the deaf adder that stoppeth her ear, which will not hearken to the voice of the Charmer, charm he never so wisely, Pf. 58. 45.

'Tis most certain, that Men have always talk'd of the Power which Inchanters or *Magicians* had over these creeping things; and that they have always said, that they could allure, and kill *Serpents* by their Songs. *Virgil* speaking of *Poetry*, (which was the common Style of these *Diviners* and *Inchanters*, whence both of them are indifferently call'd by the Name of *Vates*) says, that it could fetch down the *Moon* to the *Earth*; that *Circe* by singing certain Verses, chang'd the Companions of *Ulysses* into *Hogs*, and that by the same means the *Serpents* were kill'd in the Meadows.

> *Carmina vel cælo possunt deducere lunam,*
> *Carminibus Circe socios mutavit Ulyssi,*
> *Frigidus in pratis cantando rumpitur anguis.*
>
> Virg. *lib.* 8.

Ovid in his *Amours* speaks of them in the same terms, and expresses the manner of taking *Serpents* in these words, *Rumpere vocibus angues.*

Silius also relates the same thing, speaking of the *Marmarides*, who were a People of *Africa*, whose Power he admir'd; and says, that by their *singing* they found out the way of taming *Serpents*, and making them docible :

> *Ad quorum cantus serpens oblita veneni,*
> *Ad quorum cantus mites jacuere Cerastæ.*

In fine all the Ancients agree, that there were some People, who by certain *Verses* or *Words*, did *wonderful things.* There were some, according to *Ovid*, who could *kill the Fish, dry up the Fountains,* and make the *Fruit fall off* the *Trees;*

by

by pronouncing only some Verses, or singing some Songs.

Carmine læsa Ceres sterilem vanescit in herbam;
Deficiunt læsi carmine fontes aquæ,
Illicibus glandes, cantataque vitibus uva
Decidit, & nullo poma movente fluunt.

ARTICLE XXVIII.

Of their PRIESTS, *call'd* BRACHMANS.

SINCE I have lately mention'd the ancient *Brachmans*, I think my self oblig'd to say something more particular upon that Subject, and to give som Account of the Figure which the Successors of these Great Men make at present. The *Brachmans* were so Famous in Antiquity, that some have come as far to hear them, as the Queen of *Sheba* did formerly to hear the Wisdom of *Solomon*.

St. *Jerom* writing to *Paulinus*, and giving him an Account of the Learned Men, who out of a desire to improve themselves, have travell'd thro' several Countries, and have gone even to the utmost Borders of the *Earth*, that they might find out some Able Men, for increasing their Knowledge, tells us, that the Famous *Apollonius* travell'd thro' the Country of the *Scythians* and *Massagetes*, pass'd over the famous River *Phison*, which is *Ganges*, and at last arriv'd among the *Brahmans*, where the Learned *Hiarchas*, being seated on a Throne of Gold, taught some select Disciples, the Secrets of *Nature*, the Motion of the *Stars*, and the Computation of the *Years*.

As to the Throne of Gold, give me leave now a second time to remark, That 'tis very strange, S. *Jerom* should so much magnifie the Quantity

of

of *Gold*, which is to be found about *Ganges*, and on the Coast of *Coromandel*; that *Quintus Curtius* should also tell us of greater Quantities that are in the Lands water'd by the River *Indus*, whereas now at this Day there is so little of it to be found, in comparison of what they have told us; the greatest Riches of the *Indies*, from the *Ganges* to the *Sinus Persicus*, being the Mines of *Diamonds* in the Kingdom of *Golconda*; but all the *Silver* that is brought thither by Strangers, and almost all the *Gold* that is there, comes from the Isle of *Sumatra*, or else from *China*.

To resume the Matter a little higher, with respect to *Apollonius*, we observe with some Authors, that after he had pass'd the River *Indus*, he entred into a Country where formerly the Famous *Porus* reign'd, who had to do with *Alexander*; and that he was at the City *Taxilis*, which some have pretended, but without sufficient ground, to be *Cambaia*, a City of *Guzerat*. This Kingdom was then govern'd by *Pharaates*, who was a very mild Prince, and greatly belov'd by his Subjects; so that he entirely trusted to the Love and Fidelity of his People, and never kept any Guards about his Person. He shunn'd all the Pomp and Grandeur which consists in a Numerous and Magnificent Retinue; and his Court, tho' very decent, had nothing in it, but what was very plain: Next to his House, there appear'd a splendid Temple dedicated to the *Sun*; and this was that Magnificent Structure, that was chiefly admir'd by all Travellers. Every thing there, was so well order'd, that a Stranger could neither take the *Palace* of the King for the House of G O D, nor the *T E M P L E* for the House of a *Man*; because the *Temple* had all the Magnificence, becoming the Habitation of a *G O D*, and the Palace all the Plainness that was agreeable to that of a *Mortal Man*.

Apol-

Apollonius, after he had refted fome Days at the Court of King *Pharaates*, went towards the River *Hyfpafis*, near to which he found a *Monument* erected by *Alexander*, on which the following Words are to be read in *Greek*:

A
MONUMENT
CONSECRATED TO MY FATHER
HAMMON:
TO MY BROTHER
HERCULES:
TO
MINERVA:
TO
JUPITER OLYMPIUS:
TO THE
CABIRES
OF SAMOTHRACIA:
TO THE
INDIAN SUN:
TO
APOLLO
OF DELPHOS.

He pafs'd this River, and after four Days Journey, he arriv'd at laft to the City of the *Wife-Men*, where the Famous *Hiarchas* prefided, whom we have already mention'd. There he was entertain'd by the *Brachmans* with a Difcourfe about *Tranfmigration*, and the *Production* of the *World*. Thefe Learned *Indians* admit Five *Elements*, of which they fay all things were made. The firft was a kind of Etherial Matter, but very thin and fubtil, and of this they pretend were made what they call the *Gods*, or the *Celeftial Genii*; which agrees very well with

H 2 the

the *Theology* of the Learned *Chinese*; if it be true, as many pretend it to be, that at the bottom they are *Atheists*, and hold, that after Death the Soul is refolv'd into an Etherial Matter; and this was properly the Philosophy of the Famous *Phoe*, of whom we have given an Account in the *Article* of *Metempsychosis*. The other Four *Elements* which they admitted, were *Fire*, *Air*, *Water* and *Earth*; and they believ'd, that of their Mixture all *corruptible Creatures* were compos'd.

I shall not here stop to make uncertain Reflexions upon the *Etymology* of the Name of *Brachmans*, who at this Day are call'd *Brahmans*, whom some will have to be descended from *Abraham*; so that according to them, *Brahmans*, is as if one should say, *Abrahamites* : Nor upon the Three *Wise-Men*, that came from the *East* into *Judea*, to Worship J E S U S C H R I S T; who as *Jac. Boiffard* pretends, were *Brachmans*; for all these Conjectures which are founded only upon similitude of *Words*, or some resemblance in *Customs*, cannot satisfie the Mind : For if a Man would reason exactly, and infer none but good Conclusions, he must have good Principles, and more solid Proofs : And therefore without enquiring whence the *Brahmans* are descended, and what was their Original, I shall only compare what they are now, with what they have been formerly, at least so far as I could learn.

The *Brahmans* at present have preserv'd some very good Remains of the Learning of the Ancient *Brachmans*. They are well-skill'd in *Arithmetick*, and Calculate the *Eclipses* of the *Sun* and *Moon* as exactly as the best *Mathematicians* of *Europe* : They Work the hardest Rules of *Arithmetick* without a Quill, or Lead-Pen, and do it with wonderful ease. Besides this, they have many Books of *Morality*, and some others that are stuff'd with the Fabulous History of the *Gods* : And these are all that they study, for as

to

to *Chronology*, they are moſt ignorant of all Mankind, and an Age with them is an Antiquity ſo remote, that it is impoſſible for them to explain it. All their Books, which ſpeak of the preceding Times, are nothing but a Miſcellany of the Stories of their *Gods* and their *Ancient Kings*, in which they have no fix'd *Epocha*; or to ſpeak more properly, the *Brahmans* are at this day, ſuch as the moſt Learned Men in every Nation were formerly, who unhappily neglected the Study of *Time*, which is ſo neceſſary for *Hiſtory*, without troubling themſelves much about the Difficulties, which ſuch a Negligence muſt create to their Poſterity.

The *Chaldeans* applied themſelves only to ſtudy the Motion of the *Stars*, and the Interpretation of *Dreams*. The Overflowing of the River *Nile*, gave Occaſion to the Study of *Geometry* among the *Egyptians*: The *Aſſyrians* and *Perſians* ſought after the means of knowing *Nature*, and penetrating into her Secrets; and the *Grecians*, at the beginning of their Politeneſs, were wholly taken up with the Care of their own Satisfaction; they wrote little, or if they did, they wrote only what was agreeable to their own Inclination, and ſcarce mention'd any thing but the Amorous Intrigues of their *Gods*; as if it were by this means to excite Men to imitate them in their *Pleaſures*: Excepting only ſome Books of *Morality*, and ſome Advices for a *Juſt* and *Quiet Life*, ſuch as *Heſiod* has written; and even the greateſt part of his Works, give an Account of the *Generation* of their *Gods*, and conſequently are a confuſed Heap of all ſorts of *Fables*. From whence it comes to paſs, that the beſt Things, and the moſt certain Accounts we have about the Firſt Times of *Greece*, are founded almoſt wholly upon Conjectures, which perhaps may have been taken from ſome Ancient Monuments: For when, after ſome Ages were paſt, Men would have applied themſelves ſeriouſly to

H 3　　　　Hiſtory,

History, they were oblig'd either to omit many things, or to invent, or make, as I may say, a *Chronology* out of their own Brain; there being as many Opinions about the *First Ages* of the *World*, as there are *Historians*. Thus the *Following Ages* would run the same Hazard as to *Our Times*, if all Nations were so negligent about them, as the *Indians* are. The principal, or to speak more properly, the only School of the *Brahmans*, is at *Benares*, which is a City situate upon *Ganges*.

I have already said, that the *Indians* attribute much to *Talismans*, and the *Secret Properties* of the *Celestial Bodies*, to *Figures* and *Numbers*; but those among the *Brahmans*, who pass for Men of the greatest Ability and Experience, keep these pretended *Mysteries* to themselves, and the Common People know nothing of them. 'Tis said, that they were formerly very much vers'd in Occult Sciences; and indeed all those who apply themselves to the Study of these *Ænigma's*, go into the *Indies*, to improve by their Skill, and to discover there the Secrets of *Natural Magick* in all their Purity and Extent; such as are, for instance, the *Combinations* of certain *Numbers*, or certain *Letters*, and some odd *Figures*, by which they think they can discover *Things Future*.

'Tis pretended, that the *Cabala* has taken a great part of its Follies from the Philosophy of *Phoe*, which we mention'd in the Article of *Metempsychosis*: And in this confus'd Heap of *Rabbinism* and *Magick*, something is discover'd, that comes near to the Doctrine of the Learned *Chinese*, concerning the Heaven and the Etherial Matter, into which *Phoe* said that the Souls were resolv'd, after their separation from the Body: For if this Philosopher believ'd, that our Souls are dispers'd in the Air, of which according to him they are a Part, the *Cabalists* had no less strange *Idea's* about the Matter of which the Heaven was fram'd; they believe this

Matter

Matter to be animated, and pretend that the Queen of Heaven, *Regina Cœli,* mention'd in *Jerem.* c. 44. is the Soul of this Material Heaven which appears to our Eyes. 'Tis thought alſo, that the *Cabala* deriv'd many things from *Plato*'s Philoſophy, which is deduc'd from that of *Phoe.*

If I ſhould judge of the pretended *Magick,* and Occult Science of all the *Indians,* by that of an Old *Brahman,* whom I ſaw at *Pondichery,* I ſhould have no great Opinion of it. This Good Man, who paſs'd for one of the moſt Learned, and at the ſame time for one of the moſt Formidable in the Country, upon the account of all the Miſchief he ſaid he could do by his Art, came many times to my Lodging, and promis'd to ſhew me ſtrange things, and to teach me great Secrets; and he told me that for this end he was oblig'd to cut the Throat of a Cock, but that this muſt be done in ſecret; becauſe, as I have elſewhere obſerv'd, it was forbidden to offer Bloody Sacrifices to their Gods: Yet I was reſolv'd not to ſuffer him to go on any farther, if I once ſaw that he would proceed to Invocation. I perceiv'd that *Nature* had no ſhare in what he was doing; for I had only a deſire to ſee, how far the Confidence he had in his Art could carry him, and whether his Preparations had any thing in common with thoſe that the Ancients made uſe of upon the like Occaſions; but he ſpar'd me the trouble; for whether it were that he perceiv'd, that I gave no great credit to all that he told me about his *Inchantments,* or whether he had only the Reputation of being an Able Man, without being truly ſo, he would never come to a Concluſion, or make the Experiment; but always found for an Excuſe a thouſand Inconveniences: Sometimes it was not a proper Time, ſometimes he could not find a Cock that was well-condition'd, and ſuch as it ought to be, to make a Sacrifice of, in ſhort, there was always ſome

Impe-

Impediment or other. Perhaps alfo he would not fo far debafe his fublime Knowledge, as to commu-nicate it to a Prophane Man, and one that was never initiated into their *Magical Myfteries*. How-ever, he never went farther, but only gave me great Promifes; which confirm'd me in my firft Opinion, and the Notion I always had of their Follies.

ARTICLE XXIX.

Of the Averfion *they have for all forts of* WINE.

I Do not know to what we can attribute the Averfion which the *Indians* have for all forts of *Wine*: For firft, it cannot be faid, that they derive it from the *Mahometans*, fince the *Moors* have been but a fhort time Mafters of their Country; befides, that they liv'd in this Abftinence a long time before *Mahomet*, who did not begin to publifh his Doctrine till the beginning of the feventh Century.

He would certainly carry this Matter too high, who fhould fay, that fome Men after the Deluge, in imitation of thofe who liv'd before that general Inundation, and who having never known *Wine*, had never drank of it, did afterwards wholly abftain from it; and that perhaps the Indecent Pofture, in which *Noah* was found by drinking of it, contri-buted thereto; for this would be to fuppofe a thing of which there is no manner of Proof, befides that this *Hypothefis* would not agree with the Teftimo-nies of fome Authors, whom I fhall prefently cite.

I believe that the moft probable reafon that can be given of this Cuftom, is the Vertue of fome ancient *Brachmans*; and that it may be affirm'd, the Aver-fion which the Ancient *Brachmans* have for every thing that might diforder them, made them look

upon

upon this Drink as a pernicious thing, which made a Man lofe that for which he is moft to be valued, I mean his Reafon; which at laft induc'd them to inftil thefe Sentiments into the People whom they govern'd.

The fame Abftinence was alfo had in Veneration among the *Jews*, and the *Nazarens*, not only thofe who were born fuch, as *Sampfon* and St. *John Baptift*; but alfo all thofe who made a Vow to continue in that State for a certain Number of Years, were to abftain from *Wine* and all forts of Liquors that might make them drunk, and alfo from *Raifins*, whether new or dry; as is commanded in *Numb.* 6.3. *He fhall feparate himfelf from wine and ftrong-drink, neither fhall he eat moift grapes nor dried.* We have alfo an Inftance in the *Scripture*, of the *Rechabites* defcended from *Jonadab* the Son of *Rechab*, who likewife abftain'd from all forts of *Wine*: And 'tis well known, that the *Mahometans* drink no *Wine*, but as to *Raifins*, they eat of them without any Scruple.

Let no Man fay that the *Indians* do not drink *Wine*, becaufe they have it not; for I am perfuaded that it is in their Power to make it, fince the *Vines* which the *Europeans* plant there thrive very well; and I my felf have eaten good *Grapes* there: and I am affur'd, that in the Country about *Golconda*, which is not very far from the Sea, there is great abundance of *Vines*.

I know that the *Brahmans* drink much of melted *Butter*, and am alfo affur'd, that they are guilty of ftrange Excefs among themfelves, and that this *Liquor* gets into their Heads, and makes them drunk, which appears to be very extraordinary; and I could have wifh'd to have feen the Experience of it; but thefe Gentlemen know fo well how to take their Meafures for doing it fecretly, when they have a mind to indulge their Pleafures, that 'tis impoffible to furprize them at any time.

The

The *Romans* always drank *Wine*, but of old the the Ufe of this Liquor was forbidden to the *Women*; for fear left (as *Valerius Maximus* fays) it fhould make them fall into fome Extravagance: *Vini ufus olim Romanis fœminis ignotus fuit, ne fcilicet in aliquod dedecus prolaberentur*, Valer. Max. *l. 2. c. 1.* They were fo exact and rigorous in the Obfervation of this Law, that *Egnatius Meceninus* underftanding that his Wife had drank *Wine*, kill'd her without being punifh'd for it; which happen'd under the Reign of *Romulus*, as *Pliny* tells us, *l. 14. c. 13.* This Rigour was the Effect of their Jealoufy; for they did not believe, that a Woman, who had drank it, was capable of defending her Chaftity, and refifting the Solicitations of a Gallant; and in this they were not miftaken. *Ovid* knew very well, that *Wine* makes Men debauch'd; but he feems to propofe exceffive Drinking as a Remedy againft Love; which is little better than the Evil he pretends to cure by it:

Vina parant animum veneri, nifi plurima fumas.
　　　　　　　　Ovid. *de Remed. Amoris.*

The *Egyptian* Priefts continued a long time without drinking *Wine*, and becaufe their Kings were Priefts, they were alfo oblig'd to live in the fame Abftinence. 'Tis obferv'd that *Pfammetichus* was the firft King that drank of it, about 640 Years before Chrift; which probably he learn'd among the *Syrians*, to whom he fled, when *Sabachus* King of *Ethiopia* march'd into *Egypt*. But altho' this Liquor was made ufe of in his Reign, and under the Reign of his Succeffors, yet they always us'd it with moderation; and there were Laws, which prefcrib'd the Quantity that their Kings and Priefts were to drink of it. And they did not only abftain from drinking *Wine* before this Prince, but alfo from offering
　　　　　　　　　　　　　　　　　　Sacrifices

Sacrifices of it to *God*, as many other People did ; becaufe the *Egyptians* believ'd that this Liquor was hated by the *Gods* ; the *Wines*, according to them, having been made fruitful by the Blood of thofe Wicked Men, who in ancient times rebell'd againft Heaven. I relate this from *Plutarch*, who in this place makes ufe of the Teftimony of *Hecatæus*. The words of his Tranflator are thefe : *Reges quoque ex facrarum præfcripto litterarum certa menfura vinum bibebant, ut fcribit Hecatæus, quia & ipfi effent facerdotes. Bibere cœpit Pfammetichus, cum neque bibiffent ante, neque diis libaffent vinum, non id gratum diis rati; fed fanguinem eorum, qui aliquando bellum diis intuliffent; ex quorum cadaveribus terræ permixtis, putant vites effe ortas.* Plutarch. *de* Ifide *&* Ofiride.

'Tis manifeft, as I have already faid, that the *Indians* drink no *Wine*, and that the *Brahmans* particularly have an Averfion for that Liquor. Yet I have read the quite contrary in *Athenæus*, who from the Relation of *Chares* of *Mitylene*, treats the *Indians* as a People addicted to Drinking. The Occafion was a Drunken-Bout, or a Match of Drinking for a Wager, which *Alexander* appointed between the *Indians*, after the Death of *Calanus*, who was one of the Wife-Men of the City of *Taxilis*, or *Taxila*, and one that follow'd this Prince into *Perfia* ; where he was publickly Burnt, with a great deal of Ceremony, only to deliver himfelf from the Inconveniences of Old-Age, which he began to feel. To this purpofe I fhall fet down the very words of the Tranflator of *Athenæus* : *Chares Mitylænus in fuis de Alexandro hiftoriis, cum de Calano Indo philofopho narraffet, illum in accenfum rogum fe projeciffe, & ita obiiffe, refert Alexandrum ad ejus tumulum gymnicos ludos edidiffe, ac muficos, & qua laudaretur funebrem orationem haberi præcepiffe: tum etiam quoniam Indi bibaces erant, meræ potionis certamen propofuiffe, cujus præmium effet primario victori talentum; fecundario minæ triginta; tertio decem; eorum autem qui tum vinum avidius biberunt, triginta quinque perfrigeratos mox expiraffe ; in tentoriis autem fex , exiguo poft intervallo periiffe, victoriam obtinuiffe quendam nomine Promachum, epotis meri congiis quatuor.* Athenæus, *Deipnofophift. lib.* 10.

The Text of *Quintus Curtius* does not relate the Hiftory of *Calanus*, and it is not to be found, but in his Supplement , *Quint. Curt. lib.* 10. But there is no mention made of thefe Famous Drinkers, nor of the Reward which *Alexander* gave to the Conqueror; which furprizes me ; for fuch a Hiftory as this was curious enough to find a place , among an infinite number of other Transactions which this Author relates of his *Heroe* , and which were not near fo extraordinary as this. Yet in one place he fays, that all the *Indians* were ftrongly inclin'd to *Wine* , and drank very much of it. *Ab iifdem vinum miniftratur, cujus omnibus Indis largus eft ufus. Id. lib.* 8. He is fpeaking there of the *Curtizans*, who fill'd Drink for the *Indian* King, and carried it to his Bed , where he drank plentifully. I wonder alfo that *Arrian*, who defcrib'd largely enough all the Particulars of the Death of *Calanus* , has faid nothing of this terrible *Bacchanal*, at which he who obtain'd the Prize drank four *Congius*'s of *Wine* , *i. e.* 192 *Pints*; and then Died within a few Days after his Victory.

I know not how to reconcile thefe two Paffages of *Quintus Curtius* and *Athenæus* , with the Way of Living that the *Indians* ufe at this Day. If the Paffage of *Quintus Curtius* were not fo general, it might be alleg'd, that fome of them who were next Neighbours to the *Perfians* were addicted to *Wine* , for the *Perfians* drink very much ; but this Author fays exprefly, that all the *Indians* us'd the fame Cuftom, -- *Vinum -- cujus omnibus Indis largus eft ufus;* as I have remark'd before. And this does fo much the more furprize me , becaufe they then made Profeffion of the Philofophy of the Famous *Phoe* , which is the fame same that they still follow to this Day, and the *Brahmans* who govern'd them at that time, were accounted the wisest and most knowing Men in the World; for I cannot conceive how they could authorize such Excesses; how *Alexander* made so many People burst themselves by intemperate Drinking, and all this to celebrate the Funeral of a Man so modest and vertuous as *Calanus* is represented to be; and lastly, how this Prince employ'd such Fools to honour the Memory of so Wise a Man.   From all which we may conclude, That if the *Indians* were in Ancient Times such as these two Authors describe them, there must have been a great Change made among them; since of great Drunkards they are now become very sober, and mortal Enemies to *Wine*, which is a very rare *Metamorphosis :*   For commonly whosoever has been us'd to drink much, will always drink. Who can think, for instance, that those who live upon the Banks of the *Rhine*, can resolve but for one Day to drink nothing but Water.

Some doubtless will enquire when this great Change commenc'd, for such an *Epocha* deserves very well to be observ'd: But this is a Question to which I believe no Man can answer; because it appears that the *Indians* had at all times this Aversion to *Wine*, and as I have already said, 'tis scarce credible that they could ever be without it: Besides, if such a Change had been really made, it must have been done by some Famous *Law-giver*, who had an absolute Power over all the *Indies;* but since the Days of *Alexander* it was never heard that the *Indians* had any Person of this Character.   But I perceive, that by relating these Reasons, to prove that the *Indians* were never Drunkards, or at least to start Difficulties against that Opinion, I lie open to this Objection, That by this means I do expresly oppose the Testimony of *Chares* of *Mitylene* and *Quintus Curtius ;* and I must confess, that I can hardly grant
what

what they relate of the *Indians*; and tho' I do not wholly reject what they have said about them, yet I muft at leaft fay, that I believe the Paffage of *Quintus Curtius* is too general, and that the Vice with which he accufes them, reach'd only to fome little particular Cantons of the *Indies*; which probably, as I have already faid, are thofe that border upon *Perfia*. We muft alfo remark, that in the *Indies Alexander* went but a little way from *Indus* and *Hydafpes*, and fo confequently it was not very difficult for him to have *Perfian Wine*; and particularly the *Wine* of *Schiras*, which is upon the Confines of *Perfia*. This *Wine* is famous throughout all the *Indies*, and that which is moft commonly drank. There are many Ships that go to fetch it, and bring it to be fold in all Places, where the *Europeans* are fettled.

ARTICLE XXX.

Of their Traffick, *and their* Diffimulation.

THEY apply themfelves very much to *Traffick*, and have very Good Succefs in it; but you ought to be upon your Guard, when you make any Bargain with them; for if they do not cheat you, 'tis certainly becaufe they cannot. Whatever unreafonable Offer you make in driving a Bargain, tho' you fhould fet a Price upon any thing more by half than it is worth, they are never in a Paffion, but by their Mildnefs they often get the better of the *Europeans*. 'Tis in vain for you to be angry with them, for you cannot move them to give you any Anfwer but what is civil, and they will fuffer you to vent all your Paffion, without giving you any difobliging Word: Tho' you fhould offer them but five *Sous* for a thing that is worth ten *Piftoles*, they would not fly into a Paffion, nor exclaim

bitterly

bitterly againſt you for making ſuch an unreaſona-
ble Propoſal; but they would only tell you very
calmly, that this is not enough; but ſtill they
would inſenſibly entice you to come up to their
Price. They love alſo to have to do with People of
a ready Wit, and ſay, that theſe, for the moſt part,
are more eaſily brought to their Price than the
Phlegmatick; wherein they are not miſtaken.

They are beſides great *Uſurers*, particularly with
reſpect to *Strangers*; and perhaps 'tis among them
a Point of *Religion*, or at leaſt a thing permitted by
the *Law*, as it was formerly among the *Jews*; to
whom God permitted, that they might take *Uſury*
of all other Nations beſides their own. *Thou ſhalt
not lend upon uſury to thy brother; uſury of money, uſury
of victuals, uſury of any thing that is lent upon uſury; unto
unto a ſtranger thou mayeſt lend upon uſury, but unto thy brother thou ſhalt not lend upon uſury,* Deut. 23. 19, 20.

ARTICLE XXXI.

Of the Eſteem they have for ARTS: *And, of the
Opinion of the* Ancients, *as to* SILK.

ARTS are not eſteem'd among the *Indians*,
but only in proportion to their being neceſſary to Humane Life. Thus the Art of *tilling* the
Ground, and that of *keeping* the Flocks, are eſteem'd
the principal; whereas that of a *Goldſmith* is reputed
moſt vile and deſpicable.

They are very ignorant in *Graving* and *Deſigning*;
but all the World knows their Way of Working in
Silk and *Cotton*, and for many Ages they have been
renown'd for the Finery of their Works in theſe
Materials.

Father *Petavius*, after many others, relates, that
about the twenty-fifth Year of the Reign of
Juſti-

Justinian, *i.e.* about the Year 562 of CHRIST, some Monks that came from the *Indies* to *Constantinople*, brought thither some *Silk-Worm's* Eggs, and taught there the Way of Working *Silk*.

This Learned Chronologer, and all that have said the same thing with him, intend nothing else by it, but that nothing was made of *Silk* in the *Eastern Empire* until the Reign of *Justinian*; but they do not mean that it was not us'd there, for it was known and made use of there a long time before him.

We read in *Scripture*, that when *Ezekiel* (deploring the Miserable State to which the Famous City of *Tyre* would shortly be reduc'd) relates every thing that contributed to its Grandeur; he says that it *traffick'd* with the *Syrians*, and that, amongst other things, it *fetch'd* thence *Silks*. *Syrus negotiator tuus; —— & sericum proposuerunt in mercatu tuo.* Ezek. 27. 16. which the *Syrians* could easily have from the *Indies*, going down the River *Euphrates* into the Gulf of *Bassora*.

The *Persians* also anciently made use of it, and the Habits of *Silk* were esteem'd among them one of the Signs of the highest Dignity; upon which account, one of the Honours that *Ahasuerus* did to *Mordecai*, was to give him a Cloak of *Silk : Coronam auream portans in capite, & amictus serico pallio.* Est. 9. 15.

We must not therefore imagine, that the Distance between the People that border'd upon *Palestine*, and the *Indians*, hinder'd these People from *trading* with them, and *knowing* what fine things they had. The Author of the Book of *Job* was not ignorant of their Way of Working *Painted Linen*, and generally all sorts of *Colour'd Stuffs*; for when he would shew that Wisdom is above all things, how precious soever they be; he says, that *the colour'd Cloth of the Indies is not to be compar'd with it : Non conferetur tinctis Indiæ coloribus*, Job 28. 16.

Per-

Perhaps it may be objected, That what the Ancients call'd *Sericum*, was not the fame thing with our *Silk* ; and confequently the *Monks* who came from the *Indies* to *Conftantinople*, did not only teach the manner of working it , but alfo were the firft that brought it thither , and that before them, they did not make ufe of any fuch *Silk* as we have now.

Many Authors are ftill of this Opinion, and pretend that there was a great difference between the *Sericum* of the Ancients , and the *Silk* we have at prefent; but I do not fee that their Opinion is founded upon any folid Reafon, for they ground it only upon what has been faid by fome , as to the manner in which *Sericum* was made , which has no affinity with our way of making it ; which in my Judgment concludes nothing , for proving that it was not the fame thing. with the other : For 'tis very poffible , that the *Jews*, *Greeks* and *Romans* having in effect the fame *Silk* which we now have, affign'd it another Original than it really had ; becaufe they knew not the manner of making it, nor from whence it was taken , being very far from the Country where it was wrought.

Many , for inftance , thought that is was taken from the Bark of a Tree, that they found out a way for Combing and Spinning it, as *Strabo* relates, *l.* 15. and *Paufanias in Eliacis.*

Pliny, and with him many of the Ancients, faid that it was made of a kind of Wool that grows upon Trees in the *Indies* ; which at firft view may appear to be a vain Fancy, and altogether improbable ; but if it be more narrowly examin'd, it will be found, that *Pliny*, and thofe who follow'd his Opinion, were not fo far miftaken as fome think , or at leaft that what they have faid was not altogether groundlefs ; for tis very probable , that before Men knew the way of feeding *Silk-Worms*, and making them work,

I   that

that there were of these Infects upon Trees, that they made choice of such Trees as had the moſt tender Leaves, and ſpun their *Silk* about the little Branches, as the *Palmer-Worms* do at this day, whom they do upon other accounts very much refemble. Thus Men finding theſe little Balls upon the Trees, and ſeeing nothing in them but a kind of Bean, imagin'd that this ſort of Trees naturally produc'd both the one and the other, and that they had no other Original: And this Opinion however falſe, yet at leaſt had ſome ground, and was more defenſible than that which ſuppos'd the *Silk* to come from the Bark of a Tree.

Ovid in his *Metamorphoſis* ſpeaks of certain Worms, which encompaſs'd the Branches of Trees with ſlender Threads, and afterwards aſſum'd the ſhape of *Butterflies*:

> *Quæque ſolent canis frondes intexere filis*
> *Agreſtes tineæ, res obſervata colonus,*
> *Fatali mutant cum papilione figuram.*

Perhaps by this the Poet meant the *Palmer-Worms*, who Spin like the *Silk Worms*, and are chang'd alſo into *Butterflies*: Perhaps alſo he meant the *Silk-Worms*, who at that time were diſpers'd in the Trees, as the *Palmer-Worms* are; eſpecially ſince no uſe was then made of them, and conſequently no Care was taken about them. It may indeed be objected, That the Threads mentioned by *Ovid* were White, *canis filis*, which ſeems not to agree with the *Silk* that our *Silk-Worms* commonly make, which is almoſt always Yellow; but I believe, that to this it may be anſwer'd, That the Dew and Airineſs of the Place, might perhaps give it that Colour: Yet in this I will not be poſitive, but only propoſe it as a Conjecture.

Almoſt all Writers agree as to the *Etymology* of the Word *Sericum*, which they derive from a certain

People

People call'd *Seres*; but fince many Nations have had this Name, 'tis difficult to difcover from which of them the *Silk* took its Name.

There were in *Inner Ethiopia*, and towards the Source of the *Nile*, a People call'd *Seres*; another People of the fame Name poffefs'd the Lands which are between *Ganges*, *Hydaspes*, and the River *Indus*; and thefe at prefent compofe the Empire of the *Mogol*, and part of that of *Persia*: And laftly, there is a third of that Name, which lies to the North of *China*, and is bounded to the Eaft by the *Oriental Ocean*, and to the Weft by *Scythia*, which compofed the Kingdom of *Tangut* and *Niuche*, and a part of Great *Tartary*:   Their Capital City was call'd *Iffed*, or *Serica*, which many think to be the fame with that which is now call'd *Suchur*.

If I were to derive the *Etymology* of the Word *Sericum* from one of thefe three People, I think it fhould be derived from that People which lie between *Ganges*, *Hydaspes* and *Indus*; this Country abounding in *Silk*, and it being eafy to Traffick from thence into *Palestine*, by means of the *Gulf* of *Persia* and the River *Euphrates*.   But without going fo far off, to feek after it, I believe that *Sericum* may very well refer to the *Syrians*, who as I have juft now remark'd, Traded in *Silk* with the Merchants of the City of *Tyre*, who carried it all over *Palestine*.   In fine, however this be, almoft all the *Oriental Nations* are agreed in the Name they have given to *Silk*; the *Hebrews* call it *Sericot*, the *Syrians Seriaca*, and the *Greeks* exprefs a Garment of *Silk* by the Word *Sericos*:   And fome have thought that it was deriv'd from the *Arabic* Word *Sarac*, which fignifies to be *refplendent*.

ARTICLE XXXII.

Of the Manner in which the Indians *WRITE, and of what they make use of instead of PAPER.*

THE *Indians* write upon the Leaf of a Tree, which is call'd *Latanier*, and is a kind of a *Palm-Tree*, but whose Leaves are not so long as those of an ordinary *Palm-Tree*; they are strong and thick, and they Write upon them with a Pencil. When their Letters are drawn, some rub over all the Leaf with Black, and so fill up the Characters that are written; but the greater part do only draw the Letters with an Iron-Pencil. These Leaves require no great labour to prepare them, it being sufficient to dry them, and then lay them by the side of one another, for they are shap'd like a Fan. When they are dried sufficiently, they have the Colour of Straw, but by length of time they grow very bright.

The Ancients mention'd these Leaves on which the *Indians* wrote, and they call'd the Tree that bore them *Talos*, taking *Talos* in all probability for *Latos*, and betweeen *Latos* and *Latanier* there is no great difference. 'Tis true, this Word has not an *Indian* termination; but coming from far, probably it was thought fit to make it look like a *Greek* Word, by giving it a termination in *os*, agreeable to their own Language: Yet it appears by the description they have given of this Tree, that they knew it not at all; for they say that its Leaves were six Cubits long, wherein they were much mistaken, for the Leaves of the *Latanier* are seldom so long as two Cubits. It may very well be, that they took the *Bananier* for the *Latanier*, for the former has often Leaves ten or twelve Foot long; but they are so thin, that
the

the leaſt blaſt of Wind tears them in pieces, ſo that it were impoſſible to Write upon them.

One may eaſily imagine, that at the beginning, when Writing was firſt found out, it was not ſo common as it was afterwards; and therefore it was not indifferently us'd for all ſorts of things, but only for thoſe which deſerv'd eternally to be remembred by Men; ſuch as the Beginning of the World, the Special Favours that Heaven had beſtow'd upon Men; the Foundation, Splendour, and Fall of Empires, and the Names of the Heads of the Principal Families.

Since then they Wrote ſo ſeldom, and when they did, it was deſign'd to laſt till Future Ages, Stones were probably the firſt Matter that Men made uſe of for that end. 'Tis affirm'd, for inſtance, that *Enoch* engrav'd upon two Obeliſques the Hiſtory of the Creation of the World. The firſt and ſecond Tables, on which were written the Commandments of the Law, which God gave to his own People by the Hand of *Moſes*, were of Stone; *Exod.* 31. 18. and 34. 4. *Joſhuah*, after taking the City of *Hai*, wrote *Deuteronomy* round about an Altar which he erected to the Lord: *Et ſcripſit ſuper lapides, Deuteronomium*, &c. and we need not wonder, that all *Deuteronomy*, containing thirty-five large Chapters, ſhould be written in ſo ſmall a compaſs, altho' then the Stones were not poliſh'd nor ſmooth'd with Iron-Tools, and the Characters muſt have been very great; for then they wrote every thing in Abbreviations, and for the greateſt part of the time in *Hieroglyphic Marks*, after which manner the *Iliads* of *Homer* might be written upon a *Serpent*'s Skin; and all the *Acts* of the *Martyrs* were collected and written, even to their Laſt Words; ſuppoſing in the mean time, that they have given in ſuch *Words* as they *ſpoke*, and not ſuch as were *proper* for them to ſay. This cuſtom of Writing only in Abbreviations,

was

was the cause that they Wrote with wonderful Swift-
nefs. *Aufonius* fays, there were certain People,
whofe Hand was fwifter than another's Tongue,
and wrote fafter than others could dictate, and
finifh'd a Sentence, before another fpoke it.

> *Currant verba licet, manus eſt velocior illis;*
> *Nondum lingua ſuum, dextra peregit opus.*
>
> Mart. *Epigr.*

In the following Times, they made ufe alfo of
Metals to write withal; and *Job* in his Mifery
wifh'd he had fomebody who could write with a
Pen of Iron what he fpoke, and engrave it upon
Plates of Lead, or on a Fiint-Stone: *Quis mihi
tribuat ut ſcribantur ſermones mei? quis mihi det ut ex-
arentur in libro ſtylo ferreo, & plumbi lamina, vel celte
ſculpantur in ſilice!* Job 19. 23, 24. When *Judas
Maccabæus* fent an Ambaffador to the *Romans*, the
Articles of the *Offenſive* and *Defenſive League*, which
that *Commonwealth* made with the *Jews*, were engraven upon Tables of Brafs, and fent to *Jeruſalem.
Et hoc reſcriptum eſt, quod reſcripſerunt in tabulis æreis, &
miſerunt in Jeruſalem*, &c. 1 *Maccab.* 18. 22. The
Spartans alfo being inform'd that *Jonatas* was dead,
and that his Brother *Simon* had fucceeded him in
the *High-Prieſthood*, and the *Government* of *Judæa*,
wrote to him likewife, on Tables of Brafs: *Scripſerunt
ad eum, in tabulis æreis.* In fine, their *Treaties, Leagues*,
and all their *Publick Acts*, were commonly written
upon this Metal.

Tables of Wood were alfo made ufe of to this
purpofe, whereof fome were cover'd with Wax, but
commonly they wrote what they had a mind to
upon the bare Wood. Sometimes alfo they us'd to
this purpofe Tables of Cedar, which preferv'd their
Works for a long time: Sometimes alfo they us'd
indifferently all forts of Wood, which they only
rubb'd

rubb'd with a certain Water drawn from Cedar; and this Liquor hindred Worms from breeding in it. *Pliny* says, that they made use of the same Juice in *Egypt*, to preserve Bodies from Corruption.

The *Arabians* anciently made use of the Shoulder-Bones of Sheep and Camels to Write upon, and many of these Bones tied together, made a Book; from hence we may judge that they Wrote not much, for it would require a great quantity of these Bones to make a Volume of a middle size. Thus in the Beginning of *Mahometanism,* and of a long time before, they were not accounted very Learned Men. *Pocock* says, that *Othoman,* and the first Followers of *Mahomet,* made use of the same Bones of Sheep and Camels, to Write the Follies of their False Prophet. By this we may perceive how great their Dulness was, which still continued until they Traded with the People of *Medina,* who were much more refin'd than the Inhabitants of *Mecca,* whom I last mention'd.

At last *Papyrus* was found in *Egypt*, which is a kind of Flag, from which a Skin was taken, that was first well beaten, and then gumm'd. All other Nations came thither to fetch it; and from that time the number of Books began to increase very much, this Plant requiring no great Preparation, and being of a less Volume than the Tables they were formerly oblig'd to make use of; but the *Egyptians* being jealous of the multitude of Books that were made by Strangers, and vex'd to see that that they had succeeded in that Way as well as they, forbad the Exportation of *Papyrus* any more out of *Egypt*. This Prohibition gave occasion to the Inhabitants of *Pergamus* so to prepare a Sheep's-Skin, as to make of it what we call at this day *Parchment,* upon which account it had the Name of *Charta Pergamena.* Yet *Herodotus* affirms, that the *Ionians* found it out a long while before.

'Tis

'Tis almost impossible to tell exactly who were the first that invented Characters, and the Way of expressing our Thoughts by Figures; neither is there any certainty about it: Yet the *Phœnicians* flatter themselves, with the conceit of being the first Inventers of them; and *Lucan* in his *Pharsalia* tells us, that they were commonly reputed so to be:

Phœnices primi (famæ si credimus) ausi,
Mansuram rudibus vocem signare figuris.

which Mr. *Brebœuf* has so happily and elegantly translated in these four Verses;

From them did come to us that Art ingenious,
Of Painting Words, and Speaking to the Eyes;
And by divers Shapes of Figures drawn,
Of giving Colour and Substance to our Thoughts.

But if be true, as we have already said, that *Enoch* wrote upon two Obelisques the History of the *Creation of the World*, it may be alleg'd, That the *Phœnicians* were not the first who made use of *Writing.*
Nevertheless I think that 'tis very possible, that the *Phœnicians* were truly the Inventers of *Letters,* altho' before them there were Monuments erected, of Histories describ'd upon Stone or Metal, which was then done only by Hieroglyphick Figures; which signified something by themselves; and not by Characters, which in themselves had no relation to what they signified; such as in following Times the Letters of the *Phœnicians* were, and our Letters are at this Day.
The first Men therefore found out the Way of Expressing their Thoughts by Hieroglyphicks, and the *Phœnicians* by Characters; which if they require more Place than the Hieroglyphicks, were more easy to be made: For the former were made
of

of all forts of Figures of Plants and Animals; fo
that to Write well, it was neceffary to know how
to Defign well.

Altho' Hieroglyphicks were no longer us'd for
Writing, the Ufe of them was ftill retain'd in
Coats of Arms and Seals; and as *Clemens Alexandrinus* advis'd the Chriftians of his Time, to take
the Figures that had any Relation to Chriftianity,
for Emblems, fo he allow'd them the Ufe of many
others, that were common among the *Pagans*. The
words of his Tranflator are thefe : *Sint autem
vobis fignacula, columba, vel pifcis, vel navis, quæ curfu
voloci a vento fertur; vel lyra mufica, quâ ufus eft Poly-
crates; vel anchora nautica, quam infculpebat Seleucus;
& fi fit pifcans aliquis, meminerit Apoftoli, & puerorum
qui ex aquis extrahuntur.* Clemens Alexandrinus *in
Pædagog.*

The *Grecians* alfo pretend, that the Art of
Writing firft began among them, but without any
Ground; for all the World is agreed, that *Cadmus*
brought it from *Phænicia* into *Greece*. 'Tis true
indeed that the *Grecians* invented a different Character, but it was many Ages after they had receiv'd one from the *Phænicians*; and for a long time
they made ufe of it only for *Scholia's* and *Annota-
tions*, which they wrote at the Bottom of the Page,
or in the Margin : Yet becaufe the Great Letters
took up too much fpace, and being for the moft
part four-fquar'd, requir'd more Exactnefs, they left
them at laft, to follow the prefent Running-Letters,
and never made ufe of them more, but for Publick
Infcriptions, for Titles, and the Beginnings of
Chapters, whence they were call'd *Initial Letters.*
'Tis certain alfo, that the *Rabbins* alfo us'd thefe
Running-Letters, in which they wrote their *Commentaries.*

The *Papyrus* of *Egypt* gave the Name to our
Paper, which is one of the moft ufeful and convenient
                                                    things

things that the Wit of Man hath invented. But altho'
nothing is more common among us than Paper,
yet it is not certainly known when it first began,
and to whom we owe the Invention of it. Some
have affirm'd that it was in use in the time of *Titus
Livius*, who died in the Fourth Year of the Reign
of *Tiberius*; but 'tis very probable they are mistaken, and that altho' this Famous Historian speaks
of *Tela Lintea*, yet by it he understood some Cloth,
upon which something was Painted; for 'tis evident, that Paper was very far from being so Ancient.
Melchior Inchoffer, a *German-Jesuit*, who flourish'd in
the beginning of the last Century, has carried this
Matter into the other Extream, and says, that Paper
has not been known for above Two Hundred
Years. But I cannot understand, how such a Man
as he, who was no Novice in Antiquity, could be
ignorant, that we have many Manuscripts which
are older than Three Hundred Years', and yet are
written upon Paper, such as we use at this Day.
Father *Mabillon, in Re Diplomatica*, says, that Mr. *He-
rouval* communicated to him a Letter, which the
Lord *Joinville* wrote to St. *Lewis*, upon ordinary
Paper; and from hence concludes, that Paper
might safely be allow'd to be 500 Years old.

It is both wonderful and grievous, that such
Useful Things as these should be Buried in Obli-
vion; so that we cannot Reason about it, but only
by Conjecture.

ARTICLE XXXIII.

Of their ARMIES, *and Way of* FIGHTING.

I Do no longer wonder at the Histories we are
told, of the Numerous Armies of *Xerxes* and
Darius, since I saw near *Balassor* a Camp of the
Moors;

Moors ; tho' indeed this Kind of Aſſembly does not deſerve the Name of an Army, but ſhould rather be call'd a Confus'd Multitude ; for it is a Crowd of all ſorts of People , among whom there is ſcarce any Order to be found.

In the firſt place , every Horſe-Man has always at leaſt Two or Three Servants, and as many Wives ; and the *Omrah's,* who are Commanders, and the General-Officers , have of each proportionably ſo many more : Thus in an Army wherein there are 100000 Souls, there will ſcarce be found 10000 Fighting-Men : Whence any one may judge, what Confuſion they muſt be in , when being weaker than the Enemy, they are forc'd to retreat ; and how much they are embarraſs'd by their Wives, and Children , and vaſt Loads of uſeleſs Baggage ; upon which account , they ſeldom make a good Retreat.

If the *Indian-Pagans* have not as many Wives as the *Moors* , yet they have no fewer Servants , and other uſeleſs People. Among the reſt , the *Faquirs* there are intolerable, who are alſo very Numerous in the Armies of the *Mogol,* and have nothing elſe to do there , but only to Beg an Alms ; nay oftentimes they determine what they will have from you, according to your Rank and Quality, and will not bate you a *Sous* of it ; but will ſtand for Four or Five Days before a Tent-Door , crying Night and Day with a loud Voice ; *Give me ſo much* , *Give me ſo much :* So that the readieſt way to purchaſe your Eaſe, is to give them what they deſire.

When the *Moors* and *Indians* fight, they know not what it is to draw up in Squadrons, and every one fights as he pleaſes. So that if there were a Squadron well-order'd, it would be eaſy for a ſmall Number of good *Horſe-Men* to put them in Diſorder ; yet there are ſome among them that are very Stout and Brave, but they are not many ; and almoſt all thoſe that

that are moſt reſolute among them, take *Opium* before they engage in the Battel; which makes them furious, and inſenſible of Danger.

The Infantry are few in Number in the *Indies*, neither do they know their Duty better than the Cavalry. When they are engag'd in Fighting, the greateſt part of them get behind a Buſh, and from thence fire upon their Enemies: Some others, who have a mind to come to cloſe Fighting, wear nothing commonly but a little pair of Drawers, that they may be the lighter; and they who run beſt, are moſt eſteem'd: For we muſt not imagine, that two Bodies of Men being very cloſe, and in good Order, will come ſo near as to break one another, which they will find very dangerous; but every one there charges on his own Side, as he thinks fit; and when they are in Action, one would often think they are Running Races.

For my part, I believe that the *Jews* Fought much after the ſame manner, by the Praiſes which the *Scripture* gives to *Aſahel* the Son of *Zerviah*, and Brother of *Joab*, who was kill'd by *Abner*; of whom it ſays, that he ran as faſt as a wild *Roe*: *Perrò Aſahel, curſor velociſſimus, quaſi unus de capreis quæ morantur in ſylvis*, 2 Sam. 2. 18. Which Activity would not now be much eſteem'd among us, eſpecially in the Brother of a General.

'Tis very well known, that the *Jews*, quite contrary to the *Moors*, had but very few Cavalry, and that almoſt all their Forces conſiſted of Infantry; perhaps becauſe the Country was more full of Woods than that of the *Mogol*: Upon which account, they were reputed by their Enemies to be very bad Horſe-Men, and were commonly ſcoff'd at by them. This was the Reaſon why *Rabſhekah*, when he exhorted *Hezekiah* to yield, and ſubmit to the Power of *Sennacherib*, and to put no Truſt in the Aſſiſtance of *Egypt*, offer'd him, on his Prince's part,

part, 2000 Horfe, if he would acknowledge him for his Lord, and fubmit to him; adding in Raillery, that he could not find among all his People, fo many Men fit to ride upon them. *Now therefore, I pray thee, give pledges to my mafter the King of Affyria, and I will give thee two thoufand horfes, if thou be able on thy part to fet Riders upon them,* Ifa. 36. 8. Neverthelefs in the Days of *Solomon* they had a confiderable Body of Cavalry; and the *Scripture* obferves, that this Prince had 12000 Horfes in his Service, 2 *Chron.* 1. 14. But it does not appear, that they had fo many either before or after his Time; and fo this Number lafted only during his Reign: Yet I do not think that they were altogether deftitute of them; and 'tis very probable, that *Rabfhekah* carried his Raillery a little too far; tho' 'tis very plain, that they were no ways excellent for their Cavalry. They commonly rode upon Affes, and therefore we are not to wonder, or look upon it as a thing extraordinary, that *Chrift* making his Entrance into *Jerufalem*, made ufe of an Afs for this End, fince it was the common Cuftom of that Nation to ride upon Affes. Nay a Man was not efteem'd there Powerful and Great, unlefs he had his Stables full of thefe Animals: And therefore the *Scripture* defcribing the Riches and Magnificence of *Jair* the *Gileadite*, who after *Tola* judg'd the People of *Ifrael*, fays, that *He had thirty fons, who rode upon thirty affes*: *Habens triginta filios, fedentes fuper triginta pullos afinarum,* Judg. 10. 4. And it tells us the fame thing a little after of *Abdon*, who was alfo one of the Judges of *Ifrael*, *Judg.* 12.

The *Indians* have alfo *Elephants* in their Armies, as we read of the *Perfians*, and almoft all the *Eaftern* Nations had in former times. Thefe are a fort of furious Animals, for befides that they are cover'd all over with Iron, to defend them againft the Arrows and Mufquets, which are let fly at them on all hands,

hands ; their Trunk alfo is arm'd with a great Chain , which they turn about very fwiftly , and make a ftrange Havock wherefoever they go ; efpecially when they are conducted by skilful *Cornacs*, as they call them, who govern the Elephants.

The *Romans* experienc'd in former times the Fury of thefe Animals , who kill'd them a multitude of People, and put them in Diforder, in the firft Battel they gave to *Pyrrhus* King of *Epirotes* ; neither did they learn, till after they were defeated, after what manner they fhould defend themfelves from them ; which was by fhooting at their Trunk ; for that being the moft fenfible Part of their Body, whenfoever they find themfelves wounded there, inftead of advancing againft thofe who attack them, they turn back againft their own People , who are then no longer Mafters of them.

The Cuftom of making Ufe of Elephants in Armies among the *Indians* is very ancient, for they us'd them in the Days of *Semiramis* : This Queen, who carried a War into the remoteft Parts of the *Indies*, obferving the Deftruction which thefe Animals made, according to the Relation of *Diodorus Siculus*, caus'd many of them to be made of Wood, and to be plac'd at the Front of the Army, in the time of Battel ; whereupon the *Indians*, who thought there were none of them in the Army, feeing on a fudden fo great a Number of them , were very much aftonifh'd, and their Horfes were no lefs frighted, than if they had been real live Elephants , they were fo exactly counterfeited ; the *Indians* gave way at firft, and the *Affyrians*, feeing them in Diforder; purfu'd them briskly ; but the others perceiving at laft, that inftead of real Elephants, they had only brought againft them great Maffes of Wood, took Courage, rallied again, and fell in upon the Forces of *Semiramis* with fo much Bravery, that they defeated them.

History

Hiſtory alſo informs us of certain People call'd *Gandares,* dwelling upon the Bank of the River *Ganges ,* whom *Alexander* would not attack becauſe of the great Number of *Elephants* they had, or perhaps becauſe the *Grecians* oppos'd it, as *Quintus Curtius* ſays : and indeed they had great reaſon to fear theſe *Animals,* which being few in number, but well guided, made a horrible havock in an Army.

You may ſee in *Quintus Curtius,* how much the *Elephants* in *Porus's* Army, confounded the Troops of *Alexander ;* and what trouble the *Grecians* had to defend themſelves at firſt againſt them.   The ſame famous *Hiſtorian* informs us, what Love the *Elephant* ſhew'd to *Porus,* which he rode upon in the day of Battel, how it lifted him up with its Trunk, and plac'd him upon its back ; and laſtly, how it defended him even to the laſt extremity, until the Blows which the *Grecians* gave him on all ſides, beat him down upon the Ground.   It may perhaps be affirm'd, that if all the Captains and Soldiers of this unfortunate Prince, had ſhown ſo much Affection and Conſtancy to him, as this poor Animal did, *Alexander* had never advanc'd his *Conqueſts* farther.

ARTICLE XXXIV.

Of their Sweet-ſcented WATERS.

THE *Indians,* among their Pleaſures, have preſerv'd the Cuſtom of the Ancients, with reſpect to Flowers and Sweet-ſcented Waters, and generally as to every thing that gratifies the Smell. When Perſons of Quality viſit one another, thoſe who receive a Viſit, have long Bottles of Silver, which throw out Roſe-water thro many Holes, almoſt like our Watering-pots ; and this is ſprinkled
upon

upon the Face and Head of those whom they have a mind to complement; to whom, at the same time, is presented a cover'd Box of *Powder* of *Sandal*, which is a very odoriferous Wood, wherewith they perfume their Cloaths; and because this Powder is yellowish, and their Cloaths for the most part are made of very fine white Cloth, this produc'd such an effect, as at first seem'd very odd, and surpriz'd me: But, recollecting my self, I remember'd, that we have many People in *France*, who have White Powder upon Black Cloaths, down to their Breast, and then I condemn'd my former Surprize.

The common Employment of Women of Quality in their Retirement (for they scarce stir out of their Houses any more than the *Turks*) is, to make Chaplets, Garlands, and Crowns of Flowers, such as the Men carry publickly on their Heads on their Marriage-day; wherein they follow the Ancient Custom of the *Grecians*, who were a little nice in their Pleasures; who, not only on the Day of Marriage, as may be seen in all their *Epithalamiums*, but also during all the mild Season of *Spring* and *Summer*, took great Care to have always Crowns made of Flowers, such as were fairest and fresh-gather'd.

ARTICLE XXXV.

Of *their* OINTMENTS

ALL *Nations* almost have look'd upon *Oil* as one of the things they can least be without; for they fancy that 'tis impossible to preserve themselves from *Megrims*, and many other Pains, without rubbing their Head every day with *Oil*, or putting it upon the part disaffected: But this Custom, which at first was introduc'd by a kind of Necessity, became in process of time, one of the chief Instruments

ments of *Luxury* and *Effeminateneſs*, which corrupted the Manners of Men.

I ſay, that this Cuſtom was begun by a kind of Neceſſity, for as I have now obſerv'd, it was look'd upon as a ſovereign Remedy againſt *Megrims*, and eſpecially in hot Countries: This is moſt certain, that thoſe who take care to rub their Heads with *Oil*, ſcarce ever become Bald. We ſee in Scripture, how much the *Jewiſh* Women, among others, were addicted to this kind of *Anointing*, which they often preferr'd even before ſuch things as are neceſſary to Life. Thus the *Widow* of the *Prophet*, which addreſs'd herſelf to *Eliſha*, tho' ſhe was very poor, and wanted all things elſe, yet had ſtill ſome *Oil* wherewith to anoint herſelf. *Non habet ancilla tua quiddam in domo mea, niſi parum olei quo ungar*, 2 Sam. 4. 2.

The *People* of the *Indies* are no leſs addicted to this Cuſtom, but eſpecially the *Women*; and it would be one of their greateſt Troubles, if they ſhould not have their Heads always ſhining with *Oil*; but becauſe they have not *Oil* of *Olives*, they make uſe of that from *Coco*.

Anointing was us'd among the *Ancients*, not only againſt *Pains* of the *Head*, and to cure *Wounds*, but alſo to ſtrengthen the *Nerves*, and make the *Members* more ſupple, eſpecially after ſome laborious Exerciſe. Thus we ſee in the *Iliads*, that *Ulyſſes* and *Diomedes* being return'd from the Army of the *Trojans*, whither they had gone to enquire what had paſt, waſh'd themſelves, rub'd themſelves with *Oil*, and then ſat down to Breakfaſt; *Hiq; loti, & uncti pingui oleo, jentaculo aſſidebant, Iliad. l.* 10.

The *Indians* alſo uſe it after their Journies, and in general after any Action that fatigues them, for then they neither take reſt nor eat, until they have waſh'd and rubb'd themſelves with *Oil*.

K

In ancient times the *Wrestlers* us'd it also, not only those who were design'd for Wrestling, to hinder the Enemy from taking hold of them, but also all others to make themselves more supple and strong.

At first, Men considering only the Usefulness of these Anointings, employ'd plain *Oil* without any Scent, but by degrees mingling things pleasant with such as are useful, they join'd sweet Scents and Spices to it: Thus that which was at first only a Preservative or a Remedy, became at last one of the most sensual Pleasures; for then every one that would appear fine and genteel, must have his Hair wet with Essence, and be such as *Anacreon* represents *Bathillus* to us, who for drawing the Picture of this *Samian Beau*, order'd the Painter to draw him with moist Hair : *Nitidas comas fac illi. Anacr. Od.*29. *Virgil* describes *Turnus* to us after the same manner, and says that his Hair being frizled with a hot Iron, was all moist with *Myrrhe*.

Crispatos calido ferro, Myrrhaq; madentes.
                                     Æneid l. 12.

This *Luxury* proceeded so far, that they made no Scruple, to get their whole Body anointed with *Essences*. This was done by *Telemachus* and *Pisistratus*, as wise as they were, after they had visited the Palace of *Menelaus*, and before they sat down at Table, as *Homer* relates ; *Hos autem postquam ancillæ laverunt & unxerunt oleo. Odyss. l.* 4.
Others, immediately before they went to Bed, anointed the whole Body with odoriferous *Oils*; and this was also done by many *Christians* of the first Ages, but was condemn'd by *Clemens Alexandrinus* in the *Christians* of his time. *Coronarum autem & unguentorum usus, non est nobis necessarius, ad libidines enim & voluptates impellunt, maxime cum nox prope est.* Clem. Alex. *l.* 2. *c.* 8.
                                                    The

The Women made moſt uſe of them, and *Arabia* did not furniſh *Perfumes* ſtrong enough to ſatisfie fully their Smelling. 'Tis not very long ago ſince we *Europeans* had alſo the ſame Faſhion, but now the Mode being chang'd, 'tis abſolutely neceſſary for People of Faſhion to conform to the Cuſtom of the Time, and ſhe that twenty five Years ago would have continu'd without any Trouble in the midſt of a dozen of moſt odoriferous Boxes, and who carried always Sweet-ſcented Gloves about her, is now ready to faint, if ſhe does but ſee certain Flowers, or come near the leaſt Perfume. *Altro Tempo, altro Guſto.*

Among the *Jews*, when any one entred into the Houſe of one of his Friends, *Eſſences* were preſented to him to anoint his *Head*; and it was a want of Civility, or a mark of the little Eſteem they had for a Man when they did not offer them to him. Thus the *Phariſee*, at whoſe Houſe *Jeſus Chriſt* din'd, being diſpleas'd, that a *Woman*, and a *Woman* that was a *Sinner*, ſhould come to anoint his Feet; our *Saviour* rebuk'd him, and ſaid, That the *Woman* had done no more, than what he himſelf ſhould have done: *Mine Head with Oil thou haſt not anointed, but this Woman hath anointed my Feet with Ointment,* Luke 7. 46.

The *Pſalmiſt* intending to ſignifie, that he would never have any Familiarity with a *Sinner*, ſays, That he ſhall never make uſe of his *Oil* to anoint my *Head, Oleum peccatoris non impinguet Caput meum; i. e.* That he will never viſit him, and conſequently, he ſhould have no occaſion to receive any Civility from him.

The *Ancients* did not only make uſe of *perfum'd Oils* and *Eſſences*, for their own uſe, but they alſo anointed *Birds*, as may be ſeen in that Amorous Ode, wherein *Anacreon* brings in two Doves ſpeaking, whereof one carried a Letter to the Beau

Ba-

Bathillus, and the other wishes her Joy upon having her Wings perfum'd, which scatter'd every-where such an agreeable Smell :

>*Tot unde nunc Odores*
>*Huc advolans per auras*
>*Spirasq; depluisq;*   *Anacr. Od. 9.*

The *Greek* expresses it much better.

The *Indians* commonly present those that visit them only with *Rose-water*, as I have observ'd in the preceeding *Article* : But when any stay with them for some days, they never fail to offer them *Oil* every Morning.

ARTICLE XXXVI.

Of their affected External BEHAVIOUR.

WE may truly affirm of the *Indians* in general, That they behave themselves very decently ; they take great Care to wash themselves, and I'm assur'd, that as to frequent Washings, they may dispute with the most scrupulous *Pharisees*, with whom they agree in many things besides this, as in their Prayers which they affect sometimes to make in publick, but more especially in their external Behaviour, which is serious and grave.

Passion is with them a sign of a mean Soul, and they have an extraordinary Contempt of those who have no command of themselves, but grow quickly angry. When one does them any Wrong or Injury, they seem to take it very patiently, but nevertheless they meditate Revenge ; and when once they are resolv'd to do a Mischief to any Man, they do it most certainly ; and the Danger is so much the greater, because they keep their Temper, and use

all

all their Confideration about it.   They conceal fo well the Refentment, that alfo among themfelves they are always upon their guard, and chiefly when they have do with thofe, whom they know to be difcontented upon good Reafon ; yet they are every day tricking one another, and often find the fatal Blow given by the Hand of thofe whom they look'd upon as their deareft and moft faithful Friends ; and when they find themfelves thus deceiv'd, they never think of him who has gull'd them, but only accufe themfelves of their Misfortune, for trufting to a Man whom formerly they had juftly provok'd, and confefs that they have very well deferv'd it at his Hands ; for they are of this Principle, that an Injury is never to be forgotten. Altho' in private they are the Men of all the World moft addicted to Debauchery, yet in publick they are very referv'd, for then you never hear the leaft obfcene Word come out of their Mouth, and their external Behaviour is always very modeft : In fine, they may be propos'd as Patterns of Moral Perfection, if they thought as they fpeak, and liv'd in the fame manner as they profefs'd to do.

ARTICLE XXXVII.

After what manner the Mogols *divide the Days, and reckon the Hours.*

THE *Mogols* divide the whole Day, *i. e.* 24 Hours into 8 Parts or Quarters, and each of thefe Parts are divided into many other, according as the Days are long or fhort.   Thofe for inftance, who are near the Line, and with whom by confequence the inequality of Days and Nights is not very great, have very little difference in their Divifions and Quarters ; but the Difference is more fenfible sible under the *Tropics*, and is always increas'd proportionably as it is distant from the *Equinoctial Line*.

For knowing what a Clock it is, they have a *Horologium* of Water, but very different from the *Clepsydra*; and they say it was invented by one *Ctesibius* of *Alexandria*, about the Year 634, from the Foundation of *Rome*. The *Clepsydra* consisted of two Concaves join'd to one another, whereof one was full of *Water*, and the other was empty. The undermost had a piece of *Cork* which almost quite fill'd the bottom of it, leaving only so much Room as was necessary, for its rising and falling with ease. Upon this *Cork* was plac'd a little *Image*, which held a little *Wand* in its Hand, with which it mark'd the Hours upon the Lines, that were drawn upon a little *Pillar*, fasten'd to the Sides of the *Concave*, which was rais'd higher than it. There was a little Hole by which one *Concave* had Communication with the other, and that which was full, emptied itself gently into that in which the *Cork* was: And as the *Water* rose by degrees, proportionably the *Cork* ascended, and the little *Image* that was plac'd upon it mounted up also, and thus it mark'd the *Hours* with its *Wand*.

That which the *Megols* make use of, and which they call *Gari* or *Gadli*, is more plain, but then it requires greater Care, for there must always be a Man to look after it. It is a *Concave* full of *Water*, into which is put a little *Goblet* of *Copper*, which has a little Hole in the Bottom; thro' which the *Water* enters by little and little into the *Goblet*, and when it is full, so that the *Water* within it begins to mingle with the *Water* in the *Concave*, then it goes to the Bottom, and the time which it takes to be fill'd is call'd a *Gari*, which according to the Observation I made of it, amounts to 22 *Minutes* and 50 *Seconds*; So that when the Day is just 12 Hours long, each

Quarter

Quarter contains eight *Gari's*, which make 180 Minutes, *i. e.* 3 Hours. When the Days are ſhorter, the Quarters of the Day contain fewer *Gari's*, and thoſe of the Night have ſo many more; for we muſt always increaſe the one in proportion as we take from the other; ſince the Day and Night ought regularly to make between them 64 *Gari's*, *i. e.* 1440 Minutes, and according to us, 24 Hours. As ſoon as one *Gari* is paſt, he that looks after the Hours, ſtrikes with a Hammer ſo many Blows upon a Table of Copper, as there are *Gari's* pàſt; after which he ſtrikes ſtill more, to mark in what Quarter it is, whether of the Day, or the Night.

Some, as *Aben-Ezra* relates, have pretended, that the *Teraphim*, ſo often mention'd in *Scripture*, were nothing but the *Horologia* of *Water*, much like the *Gari's* of the *Moors*; but this they have affirm'd without any Proof, and even without any probable Reaſon: For the *Gods* which *Rachel*, for inſtance, ſtole from her Father *Laban*, are call'd in the Text *Teraphim*; and 'tis no ways probable, that it was an *Horologium* which ſhe took from her Father; for this was not a thing ſo precious, as to be ſtole away, and to be ſought after ſo carefully, as *Laban* ſearch'd for this in all the Tents of *Jacob*. Theſe *Teraphim* were the Gods *Penates*, and not *Horologia*; but it is an Error to affirm that theſe *Images* did ever Speak; and that *Rachel* took them away, only to hinder her Father from conſulting them, as to his Flight.

ARTICLE XXXVIII.

Of their Principal TEMPLES.

THE *Jews* had Reaſon to look upon the *Temple* of *Jeruſalem* as the Houſe of the LORD, and a Place truly Holy, where GOD would be eſpecially Worſhipped.   K 4   The

The *Mahometans* do falsly imagine the same thing of *Mecca*, and the *Indian Pagans* of the *Pagod* of *Jaguernat*, which is a great Structure built by the Sea-side, and near to *Balaffor*; which is said to be very Rich, and among other things, to have a large Statue, which has two great Eyes of *Emeralds* : But since I was never there, and never met with any *European* who knew the certainty of it , I can say nothing positively about it , whether it be so, or no.

The *Mogol* has caus'd it to be shut up, (at least I was told so) and this he did to hinder the Concourse of an Infinite Number of *Pagans*, who came thither from the remotest Parts of the *Indies* ; from whom the *Brahmans* drew a great quantity of Silver.

THese are the Principal Points, wherein I obferv'd that the *Indians* agreed with the Ancients, and particularly with the *Jews*; but one that would Reafon like a *Pagan* , would find a far greater Refemblance between thefe two Nations. A *Roman*, for inftance, who under the Reign of *Titus* had known them both , would have defcrib'd them after fuch a Manner as this which follows.

The People of *Judæa* , and thofe who dwell in the remoteft Countries of the *Indies*, agree very well in their Temper, the Cuftoms and Manner of Governing.

Firft , Both of them liv'd in a hard Bondage , to which they were fo much the more fubject, becaufe they lov'd it , and even ador'd their Captivity ; I mean that of the Law, which was the hardeft Slavery.

Both thefe People are fo fcrupuloufly addicted to Antiquity, that they cannot make any Progrefs in the Sciences ; but are oblig'd to continue in the Ignorance of their Forefathers; for every thing
that

that has the leaſt Appearance of Novelty, frights them; and 'tis a Crime among them to improve the leaſt in the World, above what the Ancients ſaid.

The Learning of both conſiſts only in getting by Heart, what they ſay the Gods have done for them; beſides, the Books of *Morality*, whoſe Precepts they take care to learn, and which they repeat every Moment with an affected Gravity; which is no leſs a Sign of their Ignorance, than of their Preſumption.

They do not make War but by ſudden Heats, neither do they Conquer but by the ſame Means; or to ſpeak more properly, they are only *Machines*, which are mov'd by their *Prieſts*; who inſpire them either with Boldneſs or Fear, according as they aſſure them of gaining or loſing a Battel.

They Fight ſometimes in Defence of their Religion with great Obſtinacy, which being founded upon ſome Promiſe of their *Diviners*, cannot proceed but from a Furious Rage : And theſe Miſerable Wretches do not perceive, that they do but ſtrengthen their Fetters, and increaſe the weight of their Chains, while they give the *Prieſts* occaſion, by their Victories, to confirm the *Law*, or rather their own *Tyranny*.

Beſides, ſince they treat all other People as *Profane*, and refuſe any familiar converſe with *Strangers*; and ſince in general they deſpiſe all the World, 'tis not to be wondred, that they are equally deſpis'd by others.

The Forefathers of the *Jews* look'd upon their Subjection to the Yoke of the *Romans*, as the greateſt Miſery, which yet might have turn'd very much to their Advantage; for the Commerce they were thereby oblig'd to hold with the moſt Polite and Learned People in the World, having open'd their Eyes, ſet them at Liberty for the future to

Think

Think for themselves, and help'd them to shake off the Slavery, of following blindly the Sentiments of their Fathers: And so indeed some of them since that time have applied themselves to the History of other Nations, and the Study of Good Arts, which before were unknown to them.

The Chains of the *Pagans* continue still whole and entire; and it would be likewise a Happiness for them, if some Civilized Nation could ever break them off, and subject them to its Empire.

They thought in the Days of *Alexander*, that they should have been deliver'd from their Captivity, and if the *Grecians* had made a longer stay in the *Indies*, they had certainly communicated to them the Politeness of Fine Learning: But this *Heroe* had a mind to overcome so many People, that he might be able to flatter himself with having the Power of Subduing any other, and making them embrace the Laws of the *Conqueror*: For scarce did he appear to have march'd into a Country, but he was presently gone out of it again; like those Torrents, which leave so much the less Footsteps in any Place, because they have past thro' them with so much swiftness.

An Antiquary, or an Austere Man, would talk quite otherwise of the *Jews* and *Indians*, tho' he should not make any Distinction between their Religions, but look upon them both as standing upon the same Foot: And I believe the few Remarks I have made upon these Two Nations, may furnish us with the following Reflexions.

The *Jews* and *Indians*, have preserv'd, at least in a great measure, the Simplicity of the Primitive Ages of the World; which they make appear in their Food, their Cloaths, and their Pleasures; wherein they always seek after that which is most Natural; for they love that most, which most readily
dily

dily offers itſelf to their Thoughts, and moſt Naturally gratifies their Fancy.

The Fear of Erring, makes them follow the *Coun-
ſels* of the moſt Wiſe and Learned among them ;
becauſe they conſider, how dangerous it is for all
Men, but more eſpecially for thoſe who have no
Experience, to govern themſelves by their own
Knowledge of Affairs.

They practiſe very punctually all the *Rules* which
the *Religion* they profeſs preſcribes ; and conſider
ring that no Man can live independently, but is in
a manner Born for Subjection, they love rather to
ſerve their Gods, and ſubmit blindly to their Law,
than to be Slaves to Caprice and Ambition, as almoſt all other Nations are.

They neglect all *Sciences* which are not neceſſary
to Life, and look upon them only as ſuch Accom-
pliſhments, which make Men indeed more Learned,
but oftentimes alſo more Miſerable, and almoſt always more Vain.

They know that Vice ſpreads much more eaſily
than Vertue, and therefore they avoid all Familiarity with *Foreigners* ; for fear leſt they ſhould make
their Evil Cuſtoms and Vices alſo become familiar
to them : And therefore they have ſometimes made
ſtrange Efforts, to prevent their being oblig d to
Live with them, by hindring them from entring
into their Country, or driving them out of it.

They never trouble their Heads about *Novelties,*
but follow their *Traffick,* or exerciſe themſelves in
that *Trade* which they have learn'd from their Fathers ; and herein they differ very much from the
People which we call *polite* and *civiliz'd,* for they
are never ſatisfy'd with what was left them by their
Forefathers ; but are continually ſtudying to invent
ſomething new, and to put a Force, if I may ſo
ſay, upon Nature ; and the more they can ſtrike
out of the Common Road, and depart from the

Cuſtoms

Customs of their Anceftors, the greater Reputation they acquire.

Thus we have two very different, and even contrary Views of the fame Object: The *Roman* reprefents to us the *Jews* as a very ftupid People; the *Auftere Man* defcribes them to us, as a People full of profound and true Wifdom; and each of them follows the Inclination he has either to *Novelty*, or *Antiquity*.

Thus all things in this Life, are fuch as Men do commonly praife or blame, according as they are agreeable or contrary to their Inclination; there being few things fo bad, but fome will approve them, and yet fewer fo good, but they meet with fome Cenfure.

ARTICLE XXXIX.

Of the INDIES *in General, and their Manner of Living there.*

I Believe the Reader will eafily pardon me, if notwithftanding the Refolution I have taken up, of defcribing only the Agreement of the *Indian* Cuftoms with thofe of the Ancients, I do now quite lay afide *Antiquity* in this laft *Article*, and affume the ordinary Style of Relations, by giving a fhort Account of the *Indies*, fuch as Travellers have given: For fince I cannot hope to fay any thing New upon this Subject, but only the fame that has been faid by many others before me, I fhall infift upon it but a little while, and only touch upon fome few things, to fhew that I am not fingular, and too much wedded to my Firft Notions.

All Men almoft, that never travell'd out of their own Country, frame to themfelves the fame
Advan-

Advantagious *Idea* of diftant Countries : They imagine , that there is abundance of every thing there that is neceffary for Life , and that they are free from the Defects and Inconveniences which they meet with in their own : Nay they look upon them as Delicious Places, becaufe the greateft part of Travellers have defcrib d them as fuch in their Relations , who always give agreeable Defcriptions of the Countries they have feen.

Before I went out of *Europe*, I read many Relations of Foreign Countries : Thofe Relations reprefented them to me as Inchanted Places; every thing there was fine, and every thing was lovely ; abundance of Innocent Pleafures prefented themfelves to me , and there wanted nothing to thofe who liv'd in thefe Happy Climates , but to live for ever, that they might be eternally happy. And fo I believ'd, becaufe fo I read ; but I am now undeceiv'd fince I have feen thofe Places, whereof I had fuch Advantagious Profpects : And have almoft always obferv'd, that the greateft part of thofe who have written about them, have too much magnified their Pleafures , but faid very little of the Inconveniences that are to be met with there, and of every thing that was grievous to be endur'd.

The Author of Nature has very equally diftributed his Favours to all the feveral Countries of the World ; each of them hath fomething Good, and fomething Bad ; and when a Man has feen many of them, 'tis difficult to ftay long in one, without defiring to be in another; becaufe there is none of them that does not want fomething, that may eafily be found elfewhere. Thus a Man ought to lay afide all Prejudices, which he may have about this *Article* , and never to imagine , that there is any Place in the Univerfe, where there is nothing to be defir'd , and where a Man does not meet with fome Troubles mingled with the Pleafures that are there.

The

The Coaſt of *Coromandel* is in the Torrid Zone, and ſo it is expos'd to terrible Heats, which reign there for a certain Time of the Year, and then the Winds which are call'd *Land-Winds*, becauſe in effect they come from the *Land*, are the moſt troubleſom in the World: They commonly laſt from Nine or Ten a Clock in the Morning, until Three or Four a Clock in the Afternoon; and a Man muſt be well ſeaſon'd for the Climate before he can venture to go out during that time; for each Step that you take, you would think that one is throwing *Fire* in your Face, eſpecially between Ten a Clock and Two. This *Land Wind* is follow'd with a *Wind* from the *Sea*, which riſes quickly after the other is ended; and is ſo much the more pleaſant, as the Heat of the Day has been greater; and one may very eaſily enjoy the Pleaſure of a Walk.

It is commonly look'd upon as the greateſt Pleaſure in Hot Countries, to ſee the Trees there always Green; and yet 'tis pleaſant to ſee them otherwiſe; and I do not know but the Variety of the Seaſons which we have in *Europe*, has ſomething in it more agreeable; for if we do not feel there the Cold of our Winters, yet there is nothing to be ſeen that that comes near the Beauty of our *Spring*; there it is a perpetual *Summer*, but a *Summer* ſo hot, that it burns up all the Herbs, and parches the Fields; ſo that both keep not their Verdure, ſave only for Two Months after the Rainy Seaſon.

The Rains there are regular and conſtant, and commonly laſt from the middle of *June* to the middle of *September*, and ſcarce ever ceaſe during that time: They are leſs troubleſom at *Pondichery*, than elſewhere, becauſe the Country being nothing but Sand, they do not ſpoil the Roads there, which in the Kingdom of *Bengala* are almoſt impaſſible during that time, becauſe the Ground there is very Fat. Theſe Rains are abſolutely neceſſary in the *Indies*, and

and when they fail, there certainly follows a Famine, because the Rice-Grounds require much Rain.

The Rice is the common Food of the Country: After they have dress'd it, they put Butter and Saffron upon it, with some Herbs, and others put Meat or Fish to it, which they call *Caris*; they always take care to season it highly with Pepper: However, these *Ragous* relish very well.

They use Hunting very much, and have great store of Game; for there is the Wild-Boar, the Wild-Goat, the Hare, the Partridge, the Wild-Pigeon, a multitude of Snipes, or Wild-Ducks, and of Teal, and of all other forts of Water-Birds; I never saw a Coney there.

One can hardly eat better Fish, than is at *Pondichery*; among the rest, there is one fort which is call'd *Pampre*, and is a flat Fish, much like our Turbat, but that it is not altogether so thick; but the Flesh is as firm, and has as delicate a Taste. They eat also there good Mullets.

There is great plenty of Fruit, but all of them different from ours. The *Mango* is most esteem'd there, and comes near to our Peach, but that it is commonly higher, and the Stone of is not near so hard; its Leaves also resemble very much those of the Peach-Tree. When they are of a good kind, they are excellent; but excepting these, all the rest are very stringy. It were needless here to set down the Names of all the other Fruits which are to be found there; for besides that this would lead us into too long a Digression, 'tis impossible to give a just *Idea* of them, to such as have never seen nor tasted of them.

Citrons are there very common, as well as *Oranges*; but as to their Numbers, this Country falls far short of *America*, which is doubtless the Country that abounds most in this kind of Fruit: Yet I have
seen

seen in the Isle of *Moeli* a kind of little *Oranges*, which I never saw in *America*. They are no bigger than our *Quinces*, and have a Skin all over Red; the substance of them is more watry than that of common *Oranges*; and as they grow ripe, their Skin by degrees opens almost like that of *Pomgranates*.

There are in the same Isle a great quantity of *Cassiers*, which are the Trees that bear *Cassia*. 'Tis well enough known in *Europe*, how these Canes are made, which contain this kind of Purging Gum: When they are ripe, they are long and dry; and when there arises a Wind, these Trees, which are commonly very heavy-laden, clash and dash one another to pieces; which makes such a Noise, as at first hearing astonishes those who know not the Cause of it, especially when they happen to be in the Middle of the Forest; where without seeing any *Cassiers* near them, they hear this rattling Noise a great way off.

If a Man does but set a Foot in the *Indies*, he must hear of *Bethel*, for next to *Rice*, it is the thing that is most used, and which the *Indians*, and also many *Europeans* can be least without.

This *Bethel* is a Plant that grows almost like our *Virgin-Vine*, and there is commonly assign'd to each of these Plants a Prop about 15 Foot high; its Leaf is almost like an Ivy-Leaf, but it is not so thick; and this is the Leaf of which the *Indians* are so greedy, but they never eat it alone: For first, they mix a little Lime with it, made of Shells, and then they wrap up within it little Slices of *Arreca* cut very small. This *Arreca* is a Fruit that is altogether like a *Nutmeg*, and differs nothing from it, save that it has no smell. This Mixture of the Leaves of *Bethel*, *Lime*, and *Arreca*, they call *Bethel*. Those that are rich, mingle also with it *Cachou*, which is well enough known in *Europe*, tho' it comes from the *Indies*. All these Drugs mingled together, make their Lips and Teeth as Red as Blood 'Tis

'Tis certain that *Bethel* is a Plant of great Vertues, for it is very good for the Stomach, and it was never known, that thofe who eat it regularly, do any ways offend the Stomach by it, any more than they do the Teeth, which it preferves found, tho' they lofe their Colour, and become Red.

The People of the Country do commonly prefent one another with *Bethel*, (as we prefent one another with *Tobacco* in *France*) and wherefoever they go, they have always fome Stock of it with them. 'Tis reputed dangerous to take it from the Hand of *Women*, at leaft unlefs they know them well; becaufe 'tis pretended that they make ufe of it in ftead of *Philtres*, and that they mingle Drugs with it proper for that purpofe. As to this I can fay nothing, but only that I faw once one of our Soldiers, who having continued more than two Days without any Defire to Eat, deferted the Company, to follow a *Woman*, who, as I was affur'd, gave him fome *Bethel*; tho' 'tis certain the *Woman* was not worth the Trouble, being very old and ugly; whereas the Soldier was a young *Man* of 30 Years of Age, very well-fhap'd They make ufe alfo fometimes of thefe *Bethels* to poifon their Enemies.

I had almoft forgot to tell you, that when the *Indians* are wounded, they caufe one to chew the Leaves of *Bethel*, and then apply them to the Wound; and this Remedy has almoft as quick an Effect, as *Baulm*.

The Lands of the *Indies*, generally fpeaking, are much deferted, for one is often oblig'd to travel a great way to find out fome poor Cottages, or fome wretched Villages, which they call *Aldees*, whereof the greateft part is alfo abandon d. This Defolation was a Confequence of the War with the Great *Mogol*, who began with Ruining the Country of the *Indians*, that he might make himfelf Mafter

of

of it; and who, upon a Politick Account, continues still to keep them under Oppression and Misery, lest they should have a mind to shake off the Yoke; for notwithstanding all the Losses they have suffer'd, they are still much more numerous than the *Moors*. A Man cannot but be affected with Compassion, when he reflects upon the Slavery of these People, and the entire Desolation of their Country; and compares their Present State, with what they were about 100 Years ago.

The *Asiaticks* have always been look'd upon as a Soft and Effeminate *People*, and this Observation is very just; for indeed they do not care for Labour, but on the contrary are wholly addicted to Ease; and even when they do take Pains, they do it with so much Indolence, as plainly discovers they are toss'd off from their Center. For my part, I attribute it to the Heat of the Climate; for I have seen some *Europeans*, who in a little time contracted the same Disease, and it was very difficult to preserve one from it.

This Indolence and love of Ease, makes them neglect nothing which may contribute to it; and they have commonly good Success, if they take never so little Pains for it. 'Tis true, there is not here that great Multitude of *People*, and that Enjoyment of *Society*, wherein consist the chief Charms of *Europe*: But then we must always confess, that this way of Independent-Living is extremely gratifying; for there, as one may say, a Man is less entangled than elsewhere; their Liberty is very great, and every Man Lives as he thinks fit: Besides, that the Great Lords there Live at a Small Expence, chiefly as to what concerns the great Number of *Servants*, which in this Country are very easily maintain'd.

The People of the *Indies* are divided into *Moors*, *Pagans*, and *Topases*. The *Moors*, as I have already
said

said, are Lords of the Country, the *Pagans* are Slaves, and the *Topases* are properly neither the one nor the other.

These *Topases* or *Mesti's* are descended of the *Portuguese* and *Indian* Women, and their common Profession is to carry Arms ; and tho' they have neither the *Riches*, nor the *Complexion* of their Fathers, (for they are Tawny and Black) yet they preserve at least their *Gravity*. I believe that the Name of *Topas*, was given them because they all wear Hats, for the *Moorish* Language *Topica log* signifies the *People* of the *Hat*. The Great *Mogol* has a great number of them in his *Armies*, and they commonly serve as *Gunners* : The *French*, *English* and *Dutch* are also in their Pay. They speak a kind of broken *Portuguese*, which is the Trading Language of the *Indies* that all Traders are oblig'd to learn.

'Tis very well known, that the *Portuguese* were formerly Masters of the *Indies*, and that they made all the *Potentates* in them to tremble. *Francis Almeida*, Viceroy of the *Indies* for *Portugal*, defeated in a Naval Fight *Campson* the *Sultan* of *Egypt*, at the beginning of the 16 *Centrury* ; and the famous *Alfonsus Albuquerque* is no less commended for the taking of *Goa*, and the many other Victories he obtain'd over the *Indians*. But since that time, they have very much declin'd, and almost all the other Nations of *Europe* which at present are in the *Indies*, are settled there only upon their Ruines ; especially the *Dutch*, who are at present what the *Portuguese* were formerly there.

They have not only Business with the *Europeans*, but also with the *Indians*, who growing weary of the Cruelty and Tyranny wherewith they had been treated by them, rose up in Arms against them in many places. The Inhabitants of the *Isle* of *Moeli* who are all *Mahometans*, and (as 'tis said) came out of *Arabia*, were of the Number of those that re-

L 2   volted,

volted, who Maſſacred the *Portugueſe*, and made themſelves Maſters of the *Iſle*. In it I ſaw a *Moſque* which had formerly been a *Portugueſe* Church.

Beſides theſe *Meſti's* who are really deſcended from the *Portugueſe*, there are others who alſo aſſume the Name of *Topaſes*, as the *Paria's* whom I mention'd in Article 15. When they become *Chriſtians* they put on the *Hat*, and preſently in an inſtant they are chang'd from the moſt contemptible State that is among the *Indians*, to the Quality of *Senhor Soldad*, which is no ſmall Title among the *Chriſtians* of the Country. But the *Indians* always deſpiſe them, and can tell them, that none but the *Beggars* embrace *Chriſtianity*, whom for that reaſon they call *Chriſtians d' Aros*, i. e. *Chriſtians* of *Rice*; meaning by this, that they do not become *Chriſtians*, but only that they may live more at eaſe, and to ſecure *Rice* to themſelves, for in this Country there is no mention made of *Bread*. And in effect I do not find that the *Chriſtians* take it much amiſs, for theſe *Paria's* are commonly the moſt deſpicable *People* that can be imagin'd in the *World*, and tho' they turn *Chriſtians*, yet they are never the honeſter Men for all that. They are very much addicted to Stealing, and when they cannot make uſe of their Hands to take any thing away, they very dextrouſly uſe their Feet. What I ſay here may at firſt view appear ſurprizing, yet there is nothing more certain; for if you let fall any *Silver*, a *Knife*, or a *Fork*, and do not preſently reflect upon it, they, becauſe they commonly wear no *Shoes*, take up very dextrouſly with their *Toes*, that which is fall'n, and then putting one Hand behind them, they find a way, by bending the *Leg*, to put into their Hand that which their Foot hath taken up: And all this Contrivance is perform'd, while you do not ſee them ſtoop in them leaſt; nay, they will be talking to you all the time they do the
Trick,

Trick, efpecially when it happens to be in the Night.

It feems, that as foon as they turn *Chriftians,* they count it below them to work.   To this purpofe I have heard from a Perfon worthy of Credit, that one day finding a young Woman Arrefted, who practis'd a Trade very common in the *Indies,* and probably did fomething elfe, for which no fuch Perfon is punifh'd, fome body ask'd her, why fhe did not work for her Living ; and that the young Woman being much furpriz'd with the Queftion, anfwer'd him, That fhe was a *Chriftian :* A very fine Anfwer indeed !

I fhall add no more of the *Indians,* and the little I have faid, was only to fhew that I had no mind to appear fingular.   Thofe who have a mind to be fully inform'd of every thing that concerns the *Indies,* its *Inhabitants,* its *Trees,* its *Fruits,* its *Plants,* and its different forts of *Animals,* may confult a great many Writers in our Days who have given a particular Account of them.

RE-

REFLEXIONS

UPON

TRAVELS

TRAVELS are like other things, which may be either profitable or hurtful to thofe who undertake them, according as they know to make a good or bad ufe of them.

There is not in Nature a better School for Vertue, and underftanding the World, than *Travels* are to thofe that are fo happy as to undertake them with good Principles, and after they have made ferious Reflexions ; but then there is nothing more dangerous to thofe who have the Misfortune, to be entangled in vicious Inclinations.

If a *Traveller* has only the Pleafure to fay, I have feen the Country, and to relate fuch things as appear extraordinary, that he may be look'd upon as an *Oracle* in the Country where he lives, he has taken a great deal of needlefs Pains, and travell'd to very little Purpofe.

Some leave their Native Country to go into another, they change *Climates*, go over the Seas, and this they call *Travelling* ; many things pafs thro' their Fancy, but nothing remains in it, either thro' their Incapacity or Negligence, and they return home juft as wife as they went out, *i. e.* very ignorant. It would be an affront to ask them of the different *People* they have feen, or the chief *Antiquities*

ties of the *Cities* thro' which they pass'd, since very often they scarce remember so much as their Names.

Such People cannot modestly pretend to the Title of *Travellers*, since they are nothing, as I may say, but *Looking-glasses*, which have receiv'd the Images of many Objects, but have kept none of them.

Others remark in a Country, even to the smallest Particulars, the Fruitfulness of the *Soil*, the different kinds of *Fruits* that are there, the *Traffick* and *Profit* that may be made in it; and this kind of common Observations, which are so pleasant to some People, appear insipid to others   One wou'd think that nothing had escap'd their Curosity, but they go no farther than these things; and about them they write Books, wherein a Man may learn in two Hours time what they have taken a great deal of Pains for many Years to collect together: In fine, they sacrifice themselves for the Publick, who should have a great Regard to them, since they labour so much for it, without doing any thing for themselves.

The principal Design of a *Traveller*, ought to be to improve himself by every thing that he finds among Foreigners, either in their Sciences or their Customs: But since in all places of the World, there is scarce any Good to be found without a mixture of Evil, he should use no less Precaution to avoid the one than to improve the other.

The first *Travellers*, who were all *Philosophers*, and People of ripe Years, left their Country only upon this Prospect; and their sole Design in visiting Foreign Countries, was to make themselves wiser and better. They did not go from Home until they had made serious Reflexions upon their Undertaking, and had for a long time studied Vertue, that they might the better avoid splitting upon these Rocks wherewith the World is fill'd, which are so much

the

the more dangerous, the less they are known. And these wise Precautions, made them reap from their Travels, all the Improvements and Advantages they could naturally hope for.

But now in other times there are other manners: All Men at present make Voyages, and the greatest part of them do it without troubling themselves much about the Danger they run, nay without knowing any thing of it; and because they seldom endeavour either to govern their Affections, or to inform their Minds, it very often happens, that they grow worse by their Travels, and if they retain any thing, 'tis commonly that which is bad.

When one is Rich, and has good Bills of Exchange, and strong Recommendations to all the Places thro' which he is to pass, he naturally thinks that he has all things necessary for Travelling; and yet he has but the least of those things that are necessary for such an Undertaking.

'Tis very true, that in order to the seeing of other Countries with Pleasure, and improving by the Good we find in them, we must not want *Money*; yet supposing a Man who had otherwise taken Care of every thing that was necessary to his Conduct, should at last fall short of *Money*, he could easily leave the Country to return Home, and the Misfortune would go no further: But when one Travels without any other Provision but that of much *Money*, he runs the Hazard of doing himself so much Mischief, as can very hardly be cur'd afterwards.

When one would see *Foreign Countries* without Danger, and pretends to make such Reflexions upon his Travels, as may serve him for Rules all the rest of his Life, he should begin with laying a solid Foundation of *Religion*, which nothing is able to shake; for when one travels without this Precaution, thro' many People of different Religions, it

grows

grows fo cuftomary to hear People mention *God*, and the Worfhip that is due to Him, after fo many different ways, that it is very dangerous, left by this Means he fall into a kind of Indifference about Religion, which borders upon *Deifm* : And upon this Account, an able Man in our time, *viz.* Mr. *Bruyere*, has faid, That commonly a Man brings home from his long Voyages, much lefs of *Religion* than he had before.

The fecond thing that a *Traveller* ought to endeavour, is, to poffefs himfelf with a teachable Spirit, and to follow the way of living well with other Nations ; and for this end, the general Rules of Civility which he learn'd at home are not fufficient, but he muft alfo have Reafon and good Senfe, and befides that offer Violence to his Mind, by forcing himfelf to follow the Cuftoms of others, and comply with their way of living ; for to follow always the Cuftoms of their own Country would be a Defeƈt in Civility.

Every one that follows only the firft Motions of his own Heart, is apt to condemn among Strangers, what he finds there contrary to the Cuftoms of his own Nation ; and this Cenfure is founded upon the good Opinion which almoft all Men have of themfelves, and of every thing that relates to them.

It feems to me, that the further we are from our own Country, her Interefts become proportionably dearer to us, and we find ourfelves the more inclin'd to defend them. Hence arife Difputes and Complaints between People of different Countries, and oftentimes fomething worfe. This is a fatal Rock upon which many *Travellers* fplit, and which every one ought carefully to avoid.

And this he ought to do fo much rather, becaufe he can always with Honour refrain from fpeaking about his own Religion and Country ; and if one

would

would have the People, with whom he lives, to entertain a good Opinion both of the one and the other, the beft way of recommending them is by his own good Conduct.

There is in a certain State, that ftands by itfelf, a voluntary Affembly of free People, at leaft of thofe who pretend to be fo ; and there the People take upon them to determine Affairs of State, to fpeak publickly of them, and openly to condemn or approve the Proceedings of their Kings ; which in effect is the only thing wherein the Fantome of Liberty, that makes fo great a Noife, confifts : 'Tis certainly very dangerous there for any one to e-1poufe too warmly the Interefts of his own Coun-try ; for the Impunity wherewith the Common People ufually flatter themfelves, upon fuch-like Occafions, renders this Liberty more troublefom there than in any other place of the World.

A *Traveller* ought to fhun as much as is poffible making Love in the Places thro' which he paffes, he muft erect a ftrong Rampart about his Heart, a-gainft this Paffion ; for if he fuffers himfelf to be but a little affected by it, he will quickly find all his Meafures broken, which he fhould have taken for reaping fome Advantage by his Travels ; he will affect Solitude, and have his Mind fill'd with nothing but the Idea of the Perfon whom he loves : He will be infenfible to all things elfe, and confequently be incapable of making all thofe Re-marks, which he might have made if he had the Command of his own Heart.

Some perhaps will object againft this Advice, and fay, that it is impoffible to learn Civility and the good Manners of a Country without feeing the Women that are there ; and in this I agree with you : But then I fay, that you muft not entertain a Paffion for any particular Woman ; for when you are once thus engag'd, all witty Difcourfes and external

ternal Civilites are neglected, to leave room for the inward Motions of the Heart; and then the only thing you can know, is the Person whom you love, which is no great Discovery; and as to the Heart, 'tis very probable that Women of all Countries are alike.

'Tis true, that in mix'd Companies made up of Men and Women, one may better learn what is the way of living in a Place, than elsewhere; for the Emulation and Desire of outshining others, makes every one study to appear in all the Finery which is counted most fashionable and genteel in his own Nation; but all this Care and Precaution vanishes, when once Love insinuates itself, especially in the Minds of witty Men.

I believe 'tis hardly necessary to advise a *Traveller* to forbear Gaming, for none can be ignorant of the Extremities, into which this Folly does often throw a Man.

A Man who is far from his own Country, who has lost his Money, and has no Friend to resort unto, is in great Danger of committing some Crimes under his Necessity, which he would have blush'd to have done before his Loss. The first Advances he makes in going out of the right way, do indeed cost him some Trouble, but when once he is well-entred in his sinful Course, he acquires insensibly such a Habit, that he neither blushes, nor thinks any more of it, except it be to divert himself. Thus a Man sometimes, merely by want of Prudence, throws himself into an *Abyß* of *Miseries*, from which he can very hardly extricate himself.

But supposing he has Vertue enough to restrain himself from doing a mean thing upon such an Occasion, yet it cannot be deny'd, but it is at least a great piece of Imprudence, to hazard the losing of what he has, for the sake of gaining what he has not, and to venture what is certain upon the

Prospect

Profpect of that which is uncertain.   For my part, I compare fuch a Man to the Dog in the *Fable*, who fwimming, and holding a Piece of *Flefh* between his Teeth , let it go to lay hold of a *Shadow*; and by this means was fruftrated both of that which he poffefs'd, and of that which he hop'd to catch.

There are fo few *folid Friendfhips* in the *World*, that a Man ought generally to be very cautious how he engages in any ; but more efpecially in *Foreign Countries* , where you may meet with fuch People, who court *Acquaintance* with every body, and in fpite of your Teeth will pretend to be your *Friends*.   From your firft *meeting* , they will put a *Confidence* in you, or expect to be *trufted* by you; they *fwear*, that they will *open* their *Heart* to you, becaufe they find in you a certain *Je ne fcay quoy*, which encourages them to do it ;   and they affure you , that you are the *only Perfon* to whom they have *difcover'd themfelves* fo *frankly* ; but what they tell *you*, they have faid like-wife to a *Thoufand others*.

We ought therefore carefully to fhun fuch kind of *Wits* ; fince their *great Civilities* can proceed from nothing elfe, but either a great *Lightnefs*, or a defire to find out *Cullies*.

Many have been *undone* by making fuch *Friendfhips* , without reflecting upon what they did , or knowing the Perfons with whom they engag'd ; while they follow'd them , and were infenfibly ruin'd with them.   Others have forfaken them at an eafier rate , and have loft nothing but their *Silver* ; but both the one and the other are very much to be blam'd.

It were to be wifh'd, that a *Traveller* fhould carry a *Friend* along with him, but a *Friend* that is fincere, and one whom he has throughly known, before he proceed to put *Confidence* in him :   For when one paffes thro' the Country all alone , there is danger, left for want of *Company* , he engage in that which is *bad :*   And 'tis very difficult for one that is alone, to Remark all things Obſervable as exactly, as when he has one with him, who endeavours to do the ſame thing; for this occaſions a kind of *Emulation,* who ſhall *diſcover* moſt, and make the moſt ſolid and *learn'd Reflexions* upon what they ſee.

When two Friends *Travel* together, and both of them are govern'd by Good Principles, the one can ſupport the other in caſe of a Fall; for ſome have been entic'd to commit certain Extravagancies, and have yielded to certain Follies, which they would have reſiſted, if they had had a true Friend with them, who could have open'd their Eyes, to ſee the Danger to which they would be expos'd.

The Good Diſpoſition of the *Heart,* is indeed the chief Qualification that is neceſſary for one that would *Travel* without *Danger,* and to *Good Purpoſe;* but this is not ſufficient, unleſs he have alſo the Improvements of the *Mind;* of which the moſt neceſſary are, the Study of *Hiſtory,* and a moderate Knowledge at leaſt of *Geography.*

Every one ſhould at leaſt know the chief Points of the *Hiſtory* of the *Kingdom* thro' which he is to paſs, for without that he will be wholly at a Loſs; when he hears others continually ſpeaking about late *Tranſactions,* of which he knows nothing, and ſo is oblig'd to be ſilent. And beſides, he is utterly incapable of *Improving* himſelf by the *Antiquities,* the *Monuments,* the *Pictures* and *Inſcriptions* that are to be met with there; which never deſcribe things but by halves; and conſequently cannot inſtruct a Man, who has otherwiſe no *Idea* of the Thing deſcrib'd.

Geography is alſo neceſſary to a *Traveller;* for certainly one ought to know where he is, whither he is going, and under what Prince's Dominion he lives: And it would be a ſhame, when one is about to leave a Country, to be ignorant of that into which he is to enter.   *Lan-*

Languages are also a great Help in *Travels*, but 'tis very difficult for a Man to know so many of them, as to be understood all over *Europe*:   Yet I believe that the *French*, *Italian*, *German* and *English* Languages would carry a Man very far, for as to the *Latin*, 'tis very well known that it is not us'd but only among Learned Men, and consequently that it is of no Use for carrying on the Trade of the World.

The *Advantages* that may be made by *Travelling*, are different, according to the several Countries thro' which you pass.   As for instance, we may learn much in *Europe* as to the Ways of Living, as to Good Arts and Politicks; the *Oriental Countries* are very barren as to these things; and we could not make use of their Ways and Customs without appearing ridiculous, they are so contrary to ours : Good Arts are there very much neglected, and their Policy is altogether Bloody.   But on the other side, we find there an infinite Number of the Remains of *Antiquity*, because generally all the *Eastern People* change much less than the *Europeans*. By these Remains of *Antiquity* I do not mean the Ruines and Fragments of Palaces, which are doubtless more frequent in *Europe* than in *Asia*; but I mean the Customs of the People, and their Ways of Living, which are in effect the Remains of the most remote *Antiquity*.

I believe that one who would take fit Measures, before he begins to *Travel*, might find there a multitude of curious Remarks which would conduce very much to the Improvement of *Learning*, and the Explication of *Holy Scripture*.

To this end he should for some time prepare himself, by making, for instance, a Collection of all the Passages of *Scripture*, which appear most difficult, and wherein it seems necessary to have recourse to *Allegories* : These *Memoirs* a *Traveller* must have

have always ready at hand, and never fail to set down every thing that may any ways have Reference to them.

These *Remarks* will not only be useful for Explaining *Scripture*, but will serve also to Justify many Places of the *Ancients*, which appear to us either ridiculous or suppositious, but on the other hand, they may also undeceive us as to many things we admire in some *Authors*, and which we believe to be very true.

From all this let us conclude, That he who knows how to *Travel* as he should, will reap great *Advantages*: He will *improve* his *Mind* by his *Remarks*, *govern* his *Heart* by his *Reflexions*, and *refine* his *Carriage* by *Conversing* with *Honourable Persons* of many Countries; and after this, he will be much better *qualified* to Live *Genteelly*, for he will know how to *accommodate* himself to the *Customs* of different People, and so in all probability to the different *Humours* of those he is oblig'd to Visit: By this Means he will never do any thing to Others, which he knows to be contrary to their *Inclination*; which is almost the only Point wherein consists what we now call, *The Art of Living.*

THE END.

Books Printed, and Sold by Will. Davis.

A New and Accurate Defcription of the Coaſt of *Guinea*, divided into the *Gold*, the *Slave* and the *Ivory-Coaſts:* Containing a Geographical, Political, and Natural Hiſtory of the *Kingdoms* and *Countries.* With a particular Account of the *Riſe, Progreß*, and preſent *Condition* of all the *European* Settlements upon that *Coaſt* ; and the juſt Meaſures for improving the ſeveral *Branches* of the *Guinea-Trade.* Illuſtrated with ſeveral Cuts. Written originally in *Dutch*, by *William Boſman*, chief Factor for the *Dutch*, at the Caſtle of St. *George d' Elma* ; and now faithfully done into *Engliſh.* With an exact *Map* of the whole *Coaſt* of *Guinea.*

A Hiſtorical and Geographical Defcription of *Formoſa* ; an *Iſland* ſubject to the Emperour of *Japan.* Giving an Account of the *Religion, Cuſtmos, Manners*, &c. of the *Inhabitants;* together with a Relation of what hapned to the *Author* in his *Travels:* Particularly, his *Conferences* with the *Jeſuits*, and others, in ſeveral Parts of *Europe.* Alſo, the Hiſtory and Reaſons of his *Converſion* to *Chriſtianity* ; with his Objections againſt it, (in Defence of *Paganiſm)* and their Anſwers : By *George Pſalmanaazar*, a Native of the ſaid Iſland. Illuſtrated with *Cuts.*

The Ingenious and Diverting *Letters* of a *Lady's Travels* into *Spain.* Defcribing the *Devotions, Nunneries, Humours, Cuſtoms, Laws, Militia, Trade, Diet*, and *Recreations* of the People. Intermix'd with great variety of modern Adventures, and ſurprizing Accidents : Being the trueſt and beſt *Remarks* extant on that *Court* and *Country.* The Sixth Edition ; with the Addition of a Letter of the *State* of *Spain*, as it was in the Year 1700.

AN
ESSAY
UPON
LITERATURE:
OR,

An Enquiry into the Antiquity and
Original of LETTERS;

PROVING

That the two Tables, written by the Finger of
God in Mount *Sinai*, was the firſt Writing
in the World; and that all other Alphabets
derive from the *Hebrew*.

With a ſhort View of the Methods made uſe of by
the Antients, to ſupply the want of Letters before, and improve the uſe of them, after they
were known.

LONDON;

Printed for Tho. Bowles, Printſeller, next to the
Chapter-Houſe, Sr. *Paul's* Church-Yard; John Clark,
Bookſeller, under the Piazzas, *Royal-Exchange*; and
John Bowles, Printſeller, over-againſt *Stocks Market*,
M.DCC.XXVI.

AN ESSAY

On the Original of

LITERATURE, &c.

T is fomething ftrange, that among the abundance of Writers in the World, and the multitude of Authors who have publifh'd their Labours for the inftruction of Mankind in this Age, not one has thought it worth while to give any fignificant Account of the Art by which all their Works are perform'd; and by which indeed all manner of Science is convey'd from Age to Age, and handed down from our Anceftors to this Day; I mean that of Writing.

B

P R I N T I N G and the Knowledge of Types impreſſing their Forms on Paper by Punction, or the work of an Engine (*for ſuch is the Printing-Preſs*) is a Modern Invention born of Yeſterday ; and *however advantageous to the World*, is what the World it ſeems, made ſhift without, and was wholly ignorant of for above 5000 Years, and it is not yet full 300 Years old ; that Art being the Invention of a Soldier, as that of Gunpowder and Guns was of a Scholar, the *Dutch* affirming that *Lawrentius Coſterus*, of *Harlem*, was the firſt Author of Printing ; tho' others ſay, that *John Fauſtus* of *Mentz* invented it, and from thence was taken for a Conjurer, and gave Birth to the Stories we have going under the Name of the Famous Doctor *Fauſtus.*

But W R I T I N G, is of a very ancient Date, and has been the moſt uſeful of all Arts in the World, as it has been the preſerver of Knowledge, and has handed down the firſt Principles of Science in the World, from one Generation to another ; by which we, to this Day ſtand, (and all the Ages before us, for many hundreds, nay, ſome thouſands of Years, have ſtood) upon the Shoulders of our Fore-fathers Learning, and have improv'd upon their Invention ; carry'd on progreſſive Knowledge, upon the foot of their Diſcoveries, and brought experimental Knowledge both in Arts and in Nature, to that Prodigy of Perfection to which it is now arriv'd.

I F there was ſuch a Time when Men had not the Knowledge of Letters, as no doubt there was, tho' ſome queſtion it to this Day : I ſay, if there was ſuch a Time, Knowledge and Diſcoveries in Philoſophy, or in Mechanick Arts, with Hiſtory and the Knowledge of
Things

Things paft, had great Difficulties attending them, and particularly this, that they were preferv'd only in the Repofitories of thofe undecay'd Memories when Men were living Records of a Thoufand Years ftanding; which by the way, is full as long as moft Writings or ftanding Regifters remain in the World ; at leaft fuch as are of any fignificance to us ; the facred Records of the Scriptures, and fome part of the *Roman* and *Grecian* Hiftories excepted; which yet (the latter efpecially) leave Things very uncertain and ill attefted to us, and fo as fills us rather with Difputes about what was, or was not Genuine, than with a true Account of things. But in the *Antediluvian* World, if they had not the ufe of Letters, and a written Chronology, which yet I will not affert ; yet *Oral Tradition,* had fo juft an Authority, the Authors living fo many Years to perfect their Pofterity in the Particulars of what they related to them, that we have no Reafon to doubt the Truth of what was handed down from Father to Son; when MOSES, the firft *Hiftorian that we know of,* was not fo remote from the laft Days of *Noah,* as that the Particulars could be loft, but being convey'd from Father to Son, he might be well able even without the help of Divine Infpiration, to write the whole Hiftory of the ftate of things before the Flood, *Noah* having without doubt, made a perfect Relation of them to his Sons.

As to *Writing,* and the knowledge of Letters, the firft we meet with in Scripture, and *Scripture is the oldeft as well as the trueft Account of thefe Things in the World,* was the two *Tables of Stone,* written by the Finger of GOD himfelf; containing the written Law of God, the fame

which

which we call the *Decalogue*, or Ten Commandments.

I know it will be anſwer'd, that tho' it was written by the Finger of GOD, yet there muſt certainly have been ſome Writing among Men before that, how elſe could the Children of *Iſrael* read it? But to this it may be as reaſonably objected, if there had been any ſuch thing as *Writing*, or the uſe of Letters before, what need had there been for GOD himſelf to have written the Ten Commandments with his own Hand? And what need had *Moſes* to carry two New Tables up into the Mount, to have the ſame Words written again? Why cou'd not *Moſes* have written the ſame Words over again, which 'tis very likely were left legible enough, notwithſtanding breaking of the Stone. It is true, neither of theſe Arguments are Concluſive; but I think, both of them weigh much in the Caſe, and import, that thoſe Tables were the firſt *Writing*, or written Language that was ſeen in the World.

BUT further, Tho' the *Ægyptians*, were eſteem'd, and juſtly too, the *Magi* of the Earth at that time; and had made Diſcoveries in many uſeful Parts of Science, in whoſe Wiſdom *Moſes* is ſaid to be very Learned, we yet know of no knowledge of Letters among them, but that they wrote all by a Way particular to themſelves, *(viz)* by *Hieroglyphicks* or paintings of Creatures and Figures, which at beſt, and however Ingenious the *Egyptians* were in ſuiting thoſe *Hieroglyphicks* to their own Underſtanding, it muſt be allow'd that it was but a poor Shift, compared to the preſent improvement of Letters, and the Writing and Printing thoſe Letters in Books as is ſince practis'd in the World. AND

AND ſo ignorant has the World been of the uſe of Letters, even ſince thoſe Times, that we find upon the Diſcovery of any of the Unknown Parts of the World, and particularly in *America*, they had not only no knowledge of Letters, but they had no Notion of forming Speech into any intelligible Deſcription, but by meer Sound and ſpeaking with the Mouth, which by Cuſtom they learn'd from one another; and hence it was, that they had ſuch an infinite variety of different Languages (if it be proper to call them Languages) or rather differing Dialects of the ſame Language, that you were no ſooner paſs'd from one Tribe to another, but you found they underſtood little or nothing of the other's Speech.

NAY, ſo ignorant were the *Americans* of the uſe or meaning of Letters, and writing Words upon Paper, which ſhould be intelligible at a Diſtance, that they tell us the following Story, which happen'd at our firſt planting of *Virginia: Viz.* Captain *Smith*, one of the firſt Adventurers, happening to be taken Priſoner among the *Indians*, had leave granted him to ſend a Meſſage to the Governor of the *Engliſh* Fort in *James Town*, about his Ranſome; the Meſſenger being an *Indian*, was ſurpriz'd, when he came to the Governor, and was for kneeling down and Worſhipping him as a GOD, for that the Governor could tell him all his Errand before he ſpoke one Word of it to him, and that he only had given him a piece of Paper: After which, when they let him know that the Paper which he had given the Governor had told him all the Buſineſs, then he fell in a Rapture the other Way, and then Capt.

Smith

Smith was a Deity and to be Worſhipp'd, for that he had Power to make *the Paper ſpeak.*

Nor was the reſt of the World one jot wiſer than theſe People, as to this particular of having Letters form'd to expreſs their Speech, except that which the *Egyptians* attain'd to, who were accounted the wiſeſt People in the Earth, and thoſe by their utmoſt Wiſdom arriv'd to little more than this, that they were ſenſible of the Defeét, had a Notion of ſomething wanting, that when they had ſpoken to one another Face to Face, they cou'd know nothing more : They cou'd not preſerve the Memory of things but in their own Minds, or ſend any Intelligence from one to another in remote Places, but by expreſs Meſſengers retaining the whole Meſſage they went about in their Memories.

But the Knowledge of the Defeét, or the Senſe of the want of ſuch a thing as a legible Charaéter, did not at all put the *Modus,* or Manner of doing it into their Thoughts, they had no Notion of expreſſing Sounds by Words without Speech, or that any Charaéter to be form'd, cou'd ſignify, and direét to the Repetition of the Words ſpoken ; it wou'd have been as Eaſie for a Man deaf and Dumb, to entertain a Notion of what ſound Meant, or of what it really was to ſpeak, as of having any Set of Figures, to direét the Tongue to the ſound of Words from them.

But thoſe *Ægyptians* being cunning and ſtudious Artiſts, and Receiving their Knowledge from the *Arabians,* who they ſay were the firſt Aſtronomers ; they invented a way of Writing by *Hiroglyphicks,* that is to ſay, by figures of Beaſts, and painting of the Creatures, which they were ſpeaking of, ſo as thereby to underſtand the
Thing

Thing they intended : For Example, if they had order'd a Perſon to carry a Sheep to ſuch a Town, they would paint a Man with a Sheep on his back going into the Gates of the City, or Town, and the like, if a Man would ſay in *Engliſh*, I ſaw an Ox upon a Bridge, the writing was an EYE, a SAW an *Ox* upon a BRIDGE and the like.

IT cannot be deny'd, but that they carried this Art of ſpeaking a great length, and abundance of Ingenious things were done that way ; but all was Circumlocution, going round the Buſh, and round the Buſh, and indeed to very little Effect, for the World was not able to form any Method fully to Expreſs themſelves to one another at a Diſtance.

IT might be very well worth while to enquire here whether they had any Commerce in thoſe Days, and how that Commerce was carry'd on? How they kept their Accounts, and what Equivalent they had for writing to maintain Correſpondence, which to us in theſe Days would ſeem impoſſible ? Nay, I do not ſee, I Confeſs that they were able to ſend a Meſſenger of an Errand, tho' it were but into the Market, or from one part of the Town to another, for more Buſineſs, or with more partic lar Orders, than the Bearer could carry in his Head; as to keeping Accounts, tho' Figures indeed are a kind of univerſal Character in tl e World, and underſtood a like, over (at leaſt) all the Chriſtian World, yet we do not read that Figures were in uſe before Letters, or that Arithmetick, (tho' now an eminent Part of Mathematick Knowledge) was known or underſtood any ſooner than Letters ; or that the forming them, and Numbering things by them, was known before writing was known : All the ways that I meet with, by which Men caſt up Numbers of

things

things, were prefcribed by pointing to their Fingers, and confequently reach'd only to the Decimal Point, to Number Ten, which they could
tell upon their Fingers ; if they went any farther, they did it by telling the fame Fingers
over again, and fo making two Tens, and three
Tens, and four Tens as they had Occafion ; and
by this Means they cou'd caft up tho' with Difficulty as far as Ten Tens, which we call a Hundred, but which they knew no Name for, till many Ages of the World were run off.

Some are of Opinion that this Numbering upon
the Fingers was the true original of all Arithmetick,
and that from thence it was that the firft Invention of Numbers and Figures ftop't at Number Ten,
and carry'd on all Ennumeration by Repetition
of Decimal Periods, from Ten to *Twenty*, *Thirty*,
Forty, *Fifty*, which is no more or lefs than as above
Two-tens, Three-tens, Four-tens, Five-tens, and
fo on to a Hundred, and then as the Things to be
Numbered, or added encreafe, Counting thofe
Hundreds, up by Tens, as One Ten Hundred
which they call a Thoufand, and then by Two
ten Hundreds, and Three ten Hundreds, and the
like to a Hundred, ten Hundreds, that is a Hundred Thoufand, and ftill keeping to the firft way
of Numbering every Ten : Of thefe Hundred
Thoufands, Ten was call'd a Million, and fo over
and over again, *ad infinitum*, and ftill every Tenth
of one or another Denomination or kind, had a
new Denomination, fo that by Doubling, and
Redoubling, all kinds of Numbers may be reckon'd, at leaft all that are practicable, to Men ; there
being a kind of Infinity in Arithmetick beyond
human Capacity of accounting, or leaft of ex-
prefling ; no Number of any thing being fo great,
but that it may be doubled, or reckon'd over a-
gain

gain to a Tenth of thofe Doublings, and fo on again till every Ten adds Ten-fold to what went before, 'till we come to Innumerable, and even then to ten Hundred Thoufand Millions of Innumerables, if fuch a Term was agreeable to Senfe.

W H A T Method the wife *Egyptians* had to fupply this Defect of Numbers by their Hieroglyphicks, I can by no Means meet with in any Author ; but what Notions they have of it themfelves, and which they muft entertain from the Traditional Relicksof their Fore-fathers, is this, *(viz.)* They us'd certain Bundles of Reeds, which lay open in fome publick Place in every City, each Bundle confifted of ten Reeds, which Reeds, excepting thofe of the firft Bundle, had each of them ten Knots like a Bamboo Cane, and perhaps was made of fome Cane that grew in Joints, like that we call a *Bamboo* ; the Reeds cf the firft Bundle, only ftood for Units, and when reckon'd over, number'd but Ten, whereas, the other Reeds which had Knots in them, ftood every one for Ten ; and the Number of one of thofe Bundles was equivalent to our Hundred. There was a Mark placed to feparate betweeen the Reeds that were in Tale, from the others, for in reckoning any Number, they removed the Reeds one by one from the Right to the Left Side of the Mark, (counting their Knots) till they had compleated the Number their Bufinefs requir'd.

B U T with all their reckoning, it feems they had no Numeral Sounds ; they had no Numerical Letters, or Words, fuch as One, Two, Three, Four, and fo on to Ten ; no Words for a Hundred

dred or for a Thoufand, much lefs had they any Figures to exprefs them by.

A s to their *Hieroglyphicks*, which were their Types of Expreffion, we have nothing confiderable, extant that ever I have met with ; what is pretended to of that Kind I fhall fpeak to by it felf : There have been Obelisks and Monuments difcover'd indeed in the antient *Thebes*, that is to fay, in the Ruins of it, or in fome fuch Remains of Antiquity, which have been found among the *Ægyptians*, on which various *Hieroglyphick* Figures have been found ; but we have no Rule left, by which to interpret them, or to underftand in the leaft what they fignify'd ; fo that the Art of Writing by *Hieroglyphicks*, if there was ever fuch an Art, I mean to write intelligibly one to another at a diftance, is fo entirely Loft, that it remains a Queftion, whether ever it was really Intelligible in the fame manner as our Writing is, or no ; that is fo Intelligible as to furnifh Miffives from one to another ; and if not, we need not fet fo much by the Wifdom of thofe Ages, and of the People in thofe Countries as we have done, or think it fo much a Lofs to the World, that the Memory of them, and ufe of them is not preferv'd ; feeing they were not able to find out by all their Penetration a Method to convey the Mind, without fpeaking, much lefs able to hand Words from one to another, by fuch an Equivalent to Speech as we do now by Pen, Ink, and Paper.

N e x t to the *Ægyptians*, the *Phenicians* are efteem'd the antienteft People in the World, who were of any Fame for Wifdom, and Knowledge ; and they are fam'd for two Things, in which they certainly did out do all the reft of Mankind, at that time ; thefe are (*firſt*) the Knowledge of

Na

Navigation (2.) Of Commerce : The *Syrians* and *Sydonians*, and the Inhabitants of all that Coaſt, which was then call'd *Phenician*, and extended from that we now call *Scandaroon*, almoſt to *Alexandria* in *Ægypt*, were all Merchants, and very great Merchants too, as we find in the Propheſies of the Ruin of thoſe Cities by *Iſaiah*, *Ezekiel*, *Zephania* — — and other Prophets, where it is ſaid that their Merchants were Princes, *that is* very conſiderable Merchants, Trading to *India*, *Æthiopia*, and as we may ſuppoſe, to all the Coaſts of the *Red* Sea, and by Land over the Deſerts, to the Gulph of *Perſia* ; I ſay we may ſuppoſe this from the ſaid Prophets, who in reckoning up the prodigious Wealth of their Merchants deſcribe the Countries they Traded to, by the ſeveral Sorts of Merchandizes, they Traded in, and which they had it ſeems vaſt Stores of always by them ; ſuch as Gold, and precious Stones, which they are ſuppos'd to have from *Ethiopia*, on the Weſtern Bank of the *Red* Sea, and which came by Shipping to *Ezion Gebar*, or *Baalzephon*, and from thence by Land Carriage, or as they now call it by Caravan, to the ſaid Ports of *Tyre, Sidon, &c.* Then the Silks, the Purple, the Scarlet, and fine twin'd Linnen ; theſe denote their Trading into *Perſia*, which as it was, and is to this Day, the Country of the World, where the beſt Silk is naturally produc'd ; ſo were the *Perſians* fam'd for their rich Manufactures of all kinds, the Workmanſhip of which was, and is to this Day, admirably fine ; and this we read of far back as the *Babyloniſh Garment*, which *Achan* found among the plunder of the City of *Jericho* and which he thought of ſo much value, that next to the Wedge of Gold, he was

tempted

tempted by it to run the hazard of his own Life, and of God's Curfe, pronounced by *Jofhua* his General.

THESE Things, I fay, prove the *Pheni-cians* to be a kind of univerfal Merchants, and that they correfponded with the whole World in Trade; for befides their Trade to *Africa* and the *Eaft-Indies*, and to the Iflands which the Scripture fpeaks of, we find in our own Hiftories that they traded to this very Ifland of *Britain*, which was at that time fteem'd the utmoft Bounds of the Earth.

AND yet even thefe expert Merchants, thefe skilful Navigators, knew nothing of Letters; their Money, which was fouud here many Ages after, had no Infcription upon it, but confifted chiefly of Rings of Copper, and Brafs, and Iron, with only a Stamp of an old Tower or Caftle, which, 'twas fuppos'd, reprefented the ftrong Caftle of *Sidon*, faid by the Prophet *Ifaiah* to be built in the midft of the Sea, and on which her Pride of the ftrength of her Situation was founded.

NEXT, the *Arabians* claim to be not only a more Ancient Nation than the *Ægyptians*, or than the *Phenicians*, but to have taught them all their Knowledge, as particularly their Skill in the Art of Navigation to the *Phenicians*; and the motions of the Heavenly Bodies; with the know-ledge of Aftrology, and Judgment in hidden Caufes in Nature to the *Egyptians*; whence the Wife Men were call'd *South-fayers*, the People of the (South, which were the *Arabians* by their Situation, being efteemed the Author's of all that kind of Knowledge; and thefe *Arabians* pretend to have Peopled *Egypt*, and even *Ethiopia* itfelf, by Collonies tranfported
over

over the *Red Sea* from *Arabia*, which lies extended on the Eaſt-ſide, as the other do on
the Weſt-ſide of that Sea ; for which Reaſon it
is to this day call'd the *Arabian Gulph*.

YET theſe *Arabians* themſelves, ſo far as
we can learn, had not the uſe of Writing, or
the leaſt knowledge of Letters ; nor do we find
any remains of ſuch a thing among them, or
any Pretences to it, tho' their Pretences to
their being Originals of all Learning in the
World, run very High in the Writings of
their antient Authors, and higher by far than
we have Reaſon to believe they have any Authority for.

YET theſe I ſay, had no knowledge of
Letters, and cou'd never form to themſelves
an Idea of Writing, or marking a Sound of
Speech down in legible Characters, or as that
poor *Virginian* expreſs'd it, to make a piece of
Paper ſpeak.

WE have indeed an Account of the Inventors of Muſick and Muſical Inſtruments in the
Scripture, even much antienter than *Noah's*
Flood, but we do not know any thing of the
invention of Muſical Notes by that ſame Ante-
Diluvian Artiſt ; for as the Notes by which we
prick down, *as it is call'd*, our Tunes, are a kind
of Univerſal Character, being underſtood alike
by all Nations, who underſtand Muſick, ſo the
doing it was a kind of Writing, and will unde-
niably be ſo eſteem'd, *of which hereafter*.

BUT we have reaſon to believe, that this particular piece of Knowledge alſo is much more
Modern, and even more Modern than *Orpheus*
himſelf, to whom ſome will give the Honour
of that Invention, and had it not been Modern,
the ſame Hand who had found out the Way to
make

make Marks upon Lines ſpeak in the Language
of Muſick, and ſing or ſay, *FA, LA. SOL &c.*
would certainly have ſeen it poſſible to have
form'd other Words upon the ſame Foot, and
have brougʰt the World to a Method of underſtanding one another much ſooner than they
did.

THE pricking down of Tunes therefore by
Marks which we call Notes, and to which we
give Tones, or Sounds of Art, is certainly a Modern Invention; as indeed the Names of the
Figures or Notes do evidently imply, which are
Latin Originally, and moſtly now *Italian*, a
Speech which, we know is but the Baſtard-child
of the Latin. *Some ſay the Emperor* Nero, *who as
much a Tyrant as he was, is allowed to be the greateſt* Maſter of Muſick of the Age he liv'd in;
was alſo the Inventor, or at leaſt the Finiſher,
of that Part of Muſical Knowledge which relates to the pricking down the Notes of Muſick
upon Paper; and particularly, that tho' the
whole Notes might be mark'd before, and that
many Ages, even back to *Apollo* himſelf, or
to *Orpheus*, yet that the Diviſions of Notes in
which our Modern Maſters ſo much excell, were
the Work of that Emperor; and that he brought
them to the great Perfection which they remain in to this Day. I do not affirm this, nor
am I enclined to Compliment ſuch a Monſter
of Nature as that Emperor was, at ſo high a
rate, as to advance the Probability beyond
what it ought to be: That *Nero* was a good
Fidler may be true, and he was certainly ſo;
but that he had any thing elſe good about him,
I never heard, except this, of improving the
muſical Notes.

I ſee

I fee no part of the World, which we can apply to, *farther than we have*, for the original of this Art of writing, except to *China* and *Japan*, whofe claim to Knowledge of Letters, and to the Art not of writing only, but even to that of Printing too, is as extravagant, as that of the World's being created 11000 Years ago, and their Claim to a Chronology of their own Monarchy for 7000 Years paft.

THESE People pretend to have known Letters, and have had a written Character for many thoufands of Years ; and perhaps before that account of Time, when according to our Regifter, the World was created ; what Authorities they have, they beft know, nor is it at all worth our inquiry ; we are well affur'd that we have Divine Authority for our Account of Time, from its Beginning to this Day, and that by Confequence their pretences to fuch Antiquity are Fictitious, and to the laft degree Ridiculous, and on the fame Account, their pretended Knowledge of Letters muft be fo too.

I know it is fabl'd of *Cadmus* that he invented Letters, and others fay the *Phenecians* were the Authors, but thefe are uncertainties, and have little more than what I juftly fay is fabl'd of them, for even who this *Cadmus* was, is a doubtful thing, and whether really there ever was fuch a Man, in the World, or no ; but of that hereafter.

UPON the whole, as we are fure the two Tables of Stone, were written by the Finger of God, that is to fay, Divine Power imprefs'd, by what Method we know not, thofe Words on the two Tables of Stone, and at the fame time no doubt inftructed *Mofes* in the reading of them, and in the Knowledge of their Sounds; fo we have an unqueftion'd Authority to affign the

Know-

Knowledge of Letters, and the Art of writing them to a Divine original; that is to say, that the Knowledge was immediately dictated from Heaven, and that *Moses* was enabled to Inſtruct the Children of *Iſrael* in the Knowledge of them, by an immediate Divine inſpiration.

No w if we look upon the Face of the World for ſo many Ages, and how notwithſtanding ſo many Arts were known to them, and diſcover'd by their own ſearch, that yet they had no Notion, nor ever could have of Letters, and Writing; I ſay, if we look thus on the real difficulty of making any Diſcovery of that kind, we may depend upon it, that if God himſelf in Favour to his Creatures, and to his own People of *Iſrael* in the firſt Place, had not inſpir'd them with this Knowledge, all the Power of Invention that was ever beſtow'd on Man before, could not, nor would to this Day have been able to do it.

Mankind had no Idea of ſuch a thing among them, it was not in them to make a peice of Paper ſpeak, and to ſtamp a Voice and Words, which were neither more or leſs than meer Sounds to ſtamp them on a Paper, and empower other People to ſpeak over again, by the help of thoſe dumb Figures, the ſame Words that the firſt Perſon had uttered at a hundred or a thouſand Miles diſtance; no Man could imagin ſuch a Thing feaſible, nor did it ever as I have Reaſon to believe; enter into any Man's Thoughts to contrive any thing of ſuch a kind.

But God from Heaven giving Laws to Men, gave not an oral, but a written Law, and it was from him, that Letters were cloathed with Sounds, to be convey'd to any diſtance, and by the ſight, and upon any occaſion that requir'd it repeated Articulately as often as was requir'd, by which the

Senſe

Senſe of things was convey'd from Man to Man, and from Age to Age, it was his own doing, and from him alone it deriv'd.

HERE I place the true Original of Writing, and indeed of all Literature if there was any thing known before this, 'tis more than we have any Account of in Hiſtory or Monument among the Antiquities of the moſt antient Buildings: The Ruins of the moſt antient Cities ſhow no Inſcriptions, the old *Babel*, part of which remains to this Day has no appearance of any thing Written ; the *Ægyptian* Pyramids the next peice of Antiquity to *Babel*, at leaſt that we know of, which are Fair, and preſerv'd entire, have yet no Figures or Semblance of Letters left upon them.

THE great Men of thoſe Ages frequently erected Columns and Pillars to preſerve the Memory of their Actions, and to preſerve their Names ; but without any Letters to ſignifie whoſe they were. Oral Tradition preſerv'd their Names from Generation to Generation. The great *Nimrod*, the mighty *Semiramis*, *Jupiter* himſelf, however, deify'd for great Actions ; I have great Reaſon to believe of them, what would be very ſcandalous to ſay of a great Monarch in our Days, that none of them could write their own Names.

NAY, to carry it farther, had Writing been in uſe, had the World known Letters, and could thereby have written down a true Hiſtory of the Lives of the Great Men of the firſt Ages of the World, as well the Poſt Deluvian Heroes, as thoſe before the Flood, their Tyrannies, the horrid Deſolations, the inhuman and unnatural Luſts, the Murthers, and other Crimes

C they

they committed, would have recommended
them to Posterity in other Figures, and shown
them in different Colours from what the next
Ages saw them in ; Instead of placing them
among the Stars, and worshipping them as
Gods, they would have been rank'd among
the blackest Devils ; their Memory would have
been the Abhorrence and Terror of future
Ages, and not the Subject of their Admira-
tion first, and at last of their Adoration.

What should we have understood of *Jupiter*,
who is said to have made War upon, deposed,
and murthered his Father *Saturn*, but as an
accurs'd Paricide, justly doom'd to a Station
in eternal Darkness, for one of the first Usur-
pers and King-killers in the World ? How
would *Noah*'s Drunkenness, of which it pleases Heaven, by the help of Writing, to give
us a Part, (at least) of the truer History, been
abhorr'd and detested by the Ages following,
and recorded to his Shame, if a true Account
of it cou'd have been written down and pre-
served to Posterity ? Instead whereof, he is by
the Miss-understandings of the People carrying
the Story but from Tongue to Tongue, made the
God of Wine, extoll'd as a Patriot to the World,
by furnishing them with so excellent, so delicious a Liquor as the juice of the Grape ; and
hence he is made the Idol of all the Revels of
Mankind, Father of Drunkards, and has Temples rais'd to him where the *Bacchinalia* or Feasts
to this drunken good Man, are celebrated with
all manner of Excesses, Lewdness, and infinite Debaucheries ; and all this for want of
the knowledge of Letters, and the skill of
writing a true Account of the first Crime of
Noah, which he good Man afterwards repented

pented of ; had he known the abuſe that wou'd have been put upon the World in his Name, he wou'd no queſtion have left ſome Monument of his abhorrence of it, tho' he cou'd not write it down. *N. B.* He is ſuppoſed to be the *Bacchus* of the Antients.

I T is the Opinion of ſome, and the *Jews* had ſuch a traditional Notion, whether True or not, that *Noah* did not ſtop at once drinking Wine to exceſs, as is ſignify'd in the Text; but that he grew a grievous Drunkard, a kind of habitual Sot ; and that he expos'd himſelf by it in the vileſt manner, to the Contempt of his Poſterity ; that eſpecially his Son *Ham,* and his Grandſon *Canaan,* made a Sport of him, and ridicul'd and expos'd him for it, which is ſignify'd, ſay they, by his being Uncover'd in his Tent, and by their ſeeing his Nakedneſs ; and that he continu'd in this habitual Drunkenneſs a Hundred Years : But that *Shem* and *Japhet* being religious, ſober good Men, left not their Father in this Exceſs and Extravagance, but by their Prayers and Entreaties to him, and to God for him, convinc'd him at length of his Sin, and brought him to be a moſt ſincere Penitent : Thus they cover'd his Nakedneſs, concealing his Infirmity as much as poſſible, and reſtoring him by Degrees to his Senſes ; for which he afterwards gave them his Bleſſing, and on the contrary, heartily Curs'd his Son *Ham* and all his Poſterity ; but eſpecially young *Canaan,* who, 'tis ſuppos'd, had a great Hand in expoſing and making Sport with his Grandfather's Infirmity and Wickedneſs : But this is a Digreſſion ; I ſhall not affirm that this Story is true in Faſt, but rather adhere to the Letter

C 2

of the Text, which feems to point it out as a fingle Offence.

EITHER Way it ferves to the Purpofe in hand : 'Tis moft certain that the want of Letters, and the World not being able to collect and write down the true Lives, (or Hiftory of the Lives) of thefe firft Great Men, has been the main Reafon of their Names and Memories being fo grofly abus'd, and the World fo much more abus'd about them, as to exalt for their Adoration the vileft of Men, call the Stars by their Names, build Temples to their Honour, and Worfhip them as Deities, who were here on Earth the worft of Men, meer incarnate Devils, Monfters not fit to live, and who had nothing but flagrant Wickednefs to recommend them; as *JUPITER*, a Paricide, King-killer and Ufurper of his Father s Throne. *MARS*, a Fury and outragious Monfter for Murther and Rapine, and therefore made the God of War. *MERCURY*, a Sorcerer and notorious Wizard, a Fortune-teller, and dealer with the Devil. *VENUS*, a beautiful Woman, but an everlafting Whore, an infatiate impudent Strumpet, an infamous notorious She-Devil, the vileft and worft of her Sex. *BACCHUS*, (if *Noah* really was the Man) the firft of Drunkards, tho' otherwife, and afterwards, a good Man and a Penitent, which they that Worfhip'd him never heard of; or if they did, never plac'd that Part among the Vertues, for which they ador'd him. O! had they known the Ufe of Pen and Ink in thofe Days, and had they had a *Juvenal* to have Satyriz'd and Recorded the immortal Crimes of thofe Wretches, who they call'd the Immortal Gods, how would they ha'

been

been set forth in their True Colours ! and how wou'd the World have made their very Names a Curse, and an Execration to Posterity, rather than Idoliz'd them for Vertues and for Hero's? But all this mistaken Opinion of these Men, is owing, under the Disposition of Providence, to the want of the Use of Letters, and of Faithful Writers, to have recorded the Histories of those Times, free from Fable and Romance, and to have set the Actions of those Men in a true Light.

Since the use of Letters, since Writing came into the World, and since History has preserv'd the true Account of the Actions of Men, we have had no new Gods set up; no Statues have been nick-nam'd, nor infamous Men exalted after their Death to the Rank of Deities : Some of the *Roman* Emperors indeed aspir'd to the Title, and impiously accepted of what, in those Times, they call'd Divine Honours; even *Alexander* the Great had the Vanity to approve of it, being fond of being stil'd the Son of *Jupiter* But History has done Heaven Justice, and the Ages when these Men liv'd having had the blessing of Pen, Ink and Paper, or the Equivalent to them, (of which I shall speak presently) have branded the Names of these Men with a just Mark of Infamy for the Attempt; and by leaving the Memory of their Deeds upon Record, have register'd their Names amongst the worst of Men; the Great Sir *Walter Raleigh* hints this, when speaking how the most Wicked among mortal Men, were made Immortal among the Heathen, He says, it is not to be wonder'd at that ' *Alexander Magnus, Tiberius, Nero, Ca-* ' *ligula,* and others, ought to be number'd a-

among

' mong them, being as Deform'd Monſters as
' any of them ; and he adds, how cou'd the
' ſame Honour be deny'd to *Laurentia* and
' *Flora*, which was given to *Venus*, ſeeing they
' were as famous Harlots as ſhe. *Vid. Sir*
' *Walter Raleigh's Hiſt. of the World*, fol. 52.
This is one of the Benefits of Hiſtory ; we
have now no more dependance upon Tradition or the oral Hiſtory of Men and Things, the
Writings of the Antients are our Foundation
to fly to for the Characters of Things, and of
Men ; and tho' it is true, that even ſince the
uſe of Letters and of Writing, there has too
much Fiction and Fable enter'd into the
Writings of the Learned, eſpecially their Poe-
tical Works, as *Homer* in particular, who has
ſung the Wars of the *Greeks*, and the Siege of
Troy from a Reality, into a meer Fiction ; yet
even among theſe we find Room to pick out
Fragments of Truth, enough to make a Judgment both of the Times, and of the Actions of
Men performed in them.

P A R T II.

HAVING thus advanc'd a Propoſition in
Honour of the Subject I am upon, namely, that Writing and the uſe of Letters is of
divine Original, and that there was no knowledge of Letters, much more of Writing, before that of the two Tables of Stone written
by the Finger of God in *Mount Sinai :* It ſeems
needful that I ſhould examine Antiquity a
little

little and fee vhat Pretences are made in the World to the original of Letters, the knowledge of Sounds in form of thofe Letters, and the writing or impreffing them upon the Materials prepar'd for that purpofe, of all which in their Order.

THE Time when *Mofes* brought the Children of *Ifrael* out of *Egypt*, and Encamp'd them at the Foot of *Mount Sinai*, was the Year of the World 2515, *Mofes* being then 80 Years old, for he was born in the Year 2434.

IF we look back, we fhall find this was fo fhort a Time, even after the Flood itfelf, or efpecially after the Death of *Noah*, who died in the Year of the World 2005, that as firft, it is not likely that Letters came into the World fo foon, being by the general Opinion of all Writers, not above 500 Years after the Confufion of Languages. So (2.) It is more Antient, and far beyond all the famous Men, to whom Hiftory, or even Fable itfelf, would give the Honour of being the Authors of Learning, and of bringing the knowledge of Letters into the World.

CADMUS is the moft antient of thefe, and who, *Pliny* fays, brought the knowledge of Letters into *Greece*, from whence others have ignorantly enough made him the Inventer of them : But all we have of *Cadmus* is, that he brought 16 Letters of the *Greek* Alphabet into *Peloponefus*, that is, into *Greece*, where he built the City of *Thebes*, and from whence all the Learning and learned Writings of the *Greeks* had their beginning. Some would have us believe this *Cadmus* to be a Great Grandfon of *Noah*, and to have come directly from *Affyria* foon after the Confufion of Languages : But

this

this is all Fiction, and we find by more authentick Accounts, that *Cadmus* was not born till after the Year 2600. or thereabouts, which was Eighty-six Years after the Tables of Stone were written in *Mount Sinai*, and that he was a *Phenician* born, being the Son of *Agenor*, a King of the *Phenicians.* ✳

Now, as the *Phenicians*, who were *Canaanites*, might easily learn the use of Letters from the *Hebrews*, and make some improvement in that Knowledge in 86 Years, Forty of which was after the *Israelites* were planted in *Canaan*, before *Cadmus* was born, and Sixty Years more before he went into *Greece:* This is not improbable at all.

THIS *Cadmus*, Fame tells us, carry'd with him 16 Letters of the *Greek* Alphabet into *Greece, to-wit,* α β γ δ ε ι η κ λ ν ο ϖ ζ σ τ υ. Four more, 'tis said, were added by *Palamedes*, but not till the time of the Siege of *Troy*, which was not till 220 Years after. This *Cadmus* also lived some time in *Egypt*, at a Town call'd *Thebes*, from whence it seems his Ancestors came to *Tyre*, a City of the *Phenicians*.

Now, after the Children of *Israel* had by the Finger of God, been instructed in the knowledge of Letters, for *Moses* inspir'd from Heaven, no doubt taught them first to Read, and then to Imitate that Heavenly Scripture the Law, otherwise it had been of no Use to them: I say, after this, and after it came to be look'd into by other Nations, who Convers'd with the *Israelites*, it is no Wonder that those Nations form'd Letters also of their own making, and gave them Sounds proper to their own speaking, after the manner of the *Hebrews*, with whom they Convers'd.

IT

✳ *Ovids met; Vol 1st Book 3d P 85*

I T is also to be obferv'd, that this feems con-firm'd (at leaft to me) in that the firft Nations which we read of, who had the ufe of Letters after the *Hebrews*, were thofe who were the near-eft to them in their Habitations ; fuch as the *Egyptians*, FROM WHOM they came, and who at the firft Time of appearance of this Heavenly Art, liv'd not above two Days Journey from them, and the *Phenicians* TO WHOM they came, that is, when they (the *Ifraelites*) Con-quer'd *Canaan*, and who then liv'd not *near them* only, but even *among them*, for the *Phe-nicians* were the very *Canaanites*, which the *Ifraelites* fhou'd have deftroy'd, but did not.

T H E *Phenicians* then having made a begin-ning, (for 'tis apparent they had then form'd but Sixteen Letters of Four-and-twenty) *Cadmus* with what Knowledge was then in the World, went into *Greece*, and there taught his Citizens of *Thebes* the ufe of thofe Sixteen Letters, which for that Reafon they pretend he Invented : But 'tis evident, that he only brought them with him into *Greece*, but did not invent them in *Greece* ; the *Phenicians* having the Ufe of them before the *Thebans* ; and thus alfo other Writers not allowing themfelves to think, *or perhaps not knowing the Hiftory* of the Tranfactions at Mount *Sinai*, and of *Mofes* his inftructing the *Ifraelites*, give the Honour of the firft know-ledge of Letters to the *Phenicians* ; and others again to the *Egyptians*, both which bring it fo near to the *Ifraelites*, as ftill confirms the Pro-bability of what I have here advanc'd, and which, I think, ftands now almoft beyond the reach of Contradiction.

W E

WE ought then a little to enquire what kind of People those were, to whom all the Great and Wise Actions of those early Ages of the World are ascribed, that we may see when they liv'd, and whether they assumed to themselves any thing that may contradict our present Thesis, or entitle those Men to the Honour of introducing this Knowledge into the World.

APOLLO, a Name understood in various Manners by the Antients, in the Heaven he is call'd the *SUN*; in Hell *PLUTO*; on Earth *APOLLO*; and who was indeed but a Minstrel, or Fidler, in English a Ballad-singer, a Tumbler, or a Merry-Andrew, or Mountebank, or what you please; yet is said to be a teacher of Science, and judge of Wit, and rectifier of the Understanding among the People.

ATLAS, the Brother of *Prometheus*, was rather Prior to *Moses*, tho' he liv'd in some part of the time of *Moses*, but *Prometheus* himself was King of *Armenia*, and reign'd in the time of *Moses*. This is that *Prometheus* of whom so many Fictions are made by the Poets, as of his making a Man of Clay; stealing Fire from *Jupiter*; as also of his being Chain'd on the Top of Mount *Caucasus* by the Hands and Feet, and a Vulture all the while devouring his Bowels.

ALL these Fables are Construed to signify no more than the Greatness of his Wisdom and Knowledge, as that of his Brother *Atlas* carrying the World upon his Shoulders, was, to signify that he supported the Government of the whole World, by the Wisdom and Justice of his Laws.

(a) St.

(*a*) St. *Auguſtine* ſays, That *Prometheus* was feign'd to have form'd Men out of Clay ; that is to ſay, he formed the Minds of Men, by inſtilling Principles of Knowledge, and of Wiſdom into them, and was an excellent Inſtructor of Mankind. So *Theophraſtus* and others interpret him ſtealing Fire ; or as it was called by ſome, the invention of Fire, whereby he gave Life to his Men of Clay, or of Wood, which he had made ; that is, ſays he, that he inſpir'd the Minds of Men, or fir'd their Minds with earneſt Deſires after Knowledge : And that whereas, before him, Men were but ſilly ignorant, and blind, he enlighten'd their Minds with Knowledge : And by that Vulture gnawing his Bowels on Mount *Caucaſus*, is ſignify'd the gnawing, earneſt, anxious Deſire, he had to compaſs the Syſtem of Aſtronomical Knowledge, and the Motions of Heaven'ly Bodies, not then attained to by any of humane Race.

A L L this I mention, (tho' ſomething remote) for this Reaſon, and ſo I bring it down to my Purpoſe, (*viz.*) That ſome have made this *Prometheus* the firſt inventor of Letters in the World. But this is evidently contradicted ; for that before him, *Moſes* had the written Law in the Mount, as above ; ſo that whatever *Prometheus* had, he muſt, or at leaſt might have from *Moſes* many Years after.

(*b*) Dr. *Goodwin*, in his Collection of the *Jewiſh* Antiquities, agrees with my propoſed Article, (*viz.*) That *Moſes* firſt taught the Uſe of Letters to the *Jews* ; that the *Phenicians* learn'd

---

(*a*) *Auguſt.* de Civit. Dei. *lib.* 18.
(*b*) *Goodwin,* Civil. & Eccleſ. Rites, *p.* 275.

learned them from the *Jews*, and the *Grecians* from the *Phenicians*; that *Mofes* learned them by Infpiration, having the firft writing of them from the Hand of God himfelf, this the Scripture pofitively afferts; and thus my deriving the knowledge of Letters from a divine Original is, I think, fufficiently fupported.

THE next Perfons who Authors would entile to the Invention of Letters, are, 1. (a) *Palamedes*, who the *Greeks* talk very much of; but this *Palamedes* lived no fooner than the Siege of *Troy*, 163 Years before *Homer*; whereas the written Law of God was given to *Mofes* Sixty Years before the City of *Troy* was built, (*viz.*) *Anno Mund.* 2514, and *Troy* was built, *Ann. Mund.* 2574, and was deftroy'd again by the *Grecians*, *Anno Mund.* 2870. 2. *Memnon*; the fame Author tells us, this *Memnon* brought the ufe of Letters into *Egypt*. But again, as above, even *Memnon* is by Others faid not to be the Inventor of Letters to the *Egyptians*, only of forming a kind of Intelligence, by Figures, or *Hieroglyphicks*; and knew nothing of an Alphabet of Letters to form Words from by Prolation. As for the other *Memnon* he was too Modern, being kill'd by *Achilles* at the Siege of *Troy*: And as to the *Egyptian* Figures or Hieroglyphicks, I fhall fpeak of 'em afterwards.

THE *Arabians* are the next who claim the Invention of Letters; but they who pretend to it in their behalf, can bring no Authorities

---

(a) *Servius*, L'b. 2. *Goodwin*, Pag. 275.

for it ; nor do we meet with it in any Hiſtory, but ſome Writings of the *Sarazens* and *Turks*, whoſe Credit is too low with me, to give any thing for Authentick, upon their Authority.

ANTIQUITY then gives us no Light into any thing, at leaſt, that I ever met with, to weaken, much leſs to contradict the Propoſition I have advanc'd, namely, That the written Law of GOD, gave the firſt appearance of Letters in the World ; the progreſſion of Knowledge, and the uſe of Letters I ſhall account for afterwards ; thus, (*viz.*) That from *Moſes* the uſe of Letters were taught the *Iſraelites*, and by them communicated to the reſt of the World, namely, to the *Phenicians* on one Hand, and by them to the *Greeks*, and on the other Hand to the *Egyptians* ; and by them to the *Ethiopians*.

THAT the *Egyptians* ſhould learn it from the *Ethiopians* (for *Memnon* was an *Ethiopian*) is ſtill more unlikely, the *Ethiopians* being never fam'd for communicating Knowledge to the World, or indeed retaining any valuable Degree of it among themſelves : Beſides, had *Memnon*, who liv'd in the Year of the World, 2233, been the Inventor of Letters, and had brought thoſe Letters in Uſe among the *Egyptians*, How came it to paſs that the *Egyptians* uſed the lame unintelligible ænigmatick Method of Figures and Hieroglyphicks, *&c.* and that for ſeveral Hundred Years after the ſuppoſed Time of *Memnon*'s Life.

THESE Hieroglyphicks had various Significations, according to the receiv'd Uſage of the Country ; as by a Circle was meant the *Sun* ; by a Semi-circle, the *Moon* ; the Image of a
Hawk,

Hawk, being the King of Birds, fignified the King of *Heaven* ; by the Figure of a Man, *Wifdom* ; a Horfe Harnefs'd, *Strength* ; a Lyon, *Courage* and *Fortitude* ; a Horfe Un-bridl'd, fignified *Liberty* ; by a Crocodile, *Impudence* ; by a Fifh, *Hatred*, and the like. And thefe Figures with many other, were ufed till after the Children of *Ifrael* went out of *Gofhen*.

ALL thefe Things concur to confirm, *as far as a Thing of this Nature, and fo very Antient, can be expected to be confirmed*, that the World had not the ufe of Letters, till the exhibiting of the written Law of GOD at Mount *Sinai*.

I fhall add but one thing more, and that is the Improbility that Letters could be in ufe in the World much fooner than that time, as the World was then ftated ; The Nations were not fo fettled as to be very well Improved, or indeed very Populous at that time : Sir *Walter Raleigh* obferves, That even fome Ages after this, Men were advanced to the Government of Nations upon the meaneft Terms of Excellence that could be imagin'd. *Atlas* was chofen King of *Mauritania*, becaufe he had knowledge of Heavenly Bodies. *Hercules*, becaufe of his great Strength was Deify'd : *Mercury* for Magick and Cunning : *Pelafgus* was chofen King of *Arcadia*, becaufe he taught the People, but how to build fimple low Cottages, to defend them from Storms and Rain, and learned them to grind Acorns, and make Bread of them for their Nourifhment, who liv'd before upon Roots and Herbs. Is it likely that thefe rude Ages, when Wit and Knowledge was at fo low an Ebb, fhould invent fo Noble, fo fublime a Thing, as the ufe of Letters ?

Form-

Forming Sounds by the help of Characters which should speak, and be repeated from Mouth to Mouth.

How falsely then have the *Grecians* boasted of their antient Learning, and of the antiquity of their Knowledge, their Philosophy, and *the like*, when this was the poor Ignorant People who inhabited the *Arcadian* Plains, where afterwards all the Learning of this Part of the World sprung up.

THEN as to the time of *Moses*, let us consider that *Moses* gave this Knowledge to the *Israelites* before the planting of any of the *Grecian* Common-wealths ; consequently, it must be long before the antient Learning of the *Greeks* began ; for as I have observ'd, it was long before the building of the City of *Troy*, above 146 Years before the Building of *Thebes*, and still more before the first using of Letters among the *Greeks*. I say,

AGAIN, Let us go back to the time of the Flood itself, and of *Noah*, who Re-peopled the World by the Posterity of his three Ante-Diluvian Sons. The Flood was in the Year of the World, 1656. being the next Year after the Death of *Methuselah :* After the Flood, According to Sir *Walter Raleigh*'s Account, it was 170 Years to the beginning of the building of *Babel*, This Building having been begun upon the most ignorant Notions of things, that could be supposed to come into the Heads of rational Creatures, and shews an immense Dulness in the People of that Time, to think that a human Building could resist an universal Deluge ; *but that by the way.*

THIS Building, with the digging the Foundation, which must be a prodigious Gulph for so vast a Fabrick, which was some Miles in Circumference, the preparing and bringing the Materials, and making the Bricks, &c. is supposed to take up 130 Years more, which is in all, 300 Years. Now, from the Confusion of Languages to the Birth of *Jacob*, was but 213 Years, according to his Account; and it can hardly pass for probable, that the Confusion which that division of Languages made among them was so recover'd, that they should have advanced to any Inventions in that Time; much less to so Glorious an Improvement as this of writing down their Speech by the help of Letters, and as the poor *Indian* said, making *the Paper* or the *Tables* they wrote upon, to *Speak*. From *Jacob* then to the exhibiting of the Law on *Mount Sinai*, which was about 345 Years; was indeed no extraordinary length of Time, the Confusions and Dulness of those days considered, for introducing so noble a Part of Knowledge into the World.

BUT let us go back to this Story of the *Egyptians*, having the use of Letters before the *Israelites*; where is the probability, that GOD himself, who gave the *Israelites* the written Law, and wrote it with his Own Hand, should imitate the *Egyptian* Magicians? for this *Memnon* was a famous Sooth-sayer, or Magician, a *Negro* by Nation, born in *Ethiopia*: Or whether was more probable, namely, that it should be true that the GOD of *Heaven* should write after *Memnon's* Copy; or that *Memnon* rather hearing that the discovery of such a wonderful Knowledge was brought into the World by Inspiration from Heaven, went immediately into the Wilderness among the *Israelites*, to

learn

learn the Method from them, and carry'd it back with him into *Egypt,* from whence he was to them the firſt Inventor, and might paſs for ſuch in the Eſteem of the. future Ages of the World ; as *Cadmus* did, by going on the ſame happy Meſſage into *Greece.*

THE only Difficulty to be ſtarted here, is the Time of this *Memnon,* when he liv'd ? which they pretend, *but without any certainty,* was the 23d Century of the World's Age; ſo that he muſt probably be in his Grave, before *Moſes,* or muſt have liv'd above 250 Years. Now, as to this, we have not, I ſay, the leaſt Authority of Authors to be depended upon, for the time of *Memnon's* Life, any more than the length of it ; and therefore I do not conceive that Part to be of Force enough, to contradiᴄt the Authority I have brought for the Original of Letters; and eſpecially, becauſe we read of no Writings extant in all that time, either there, or in any other Part of the World. The great Library of *Ptolemy,* King of *Egypt,* which had in it ſo many thouſand Books, that is to ſay, Manuſcripts, *if that Story be not all Fable,* yet had it not any Books, *as we find reaſon to believe* that were written before *Moſes:* In a word, we find no certain Notice, even in *Joſephus,* or any other Author, of any Writing, of Gods or Men, before this one glorious diſcovery of Knowledge, made by the True GOD, among his Choſen People the *Jews:* So that really all Argument from Probability ſeems to be a-gainſt them.

ON the other Hand, there is the higheſt Probability, that all the other Nations, eſpecially the *Egyptians,* deriv'd their Knowledge of Letters from the *Iſraelites,* as above.

D   AGAIN,

AGAIN, the fimilitude of the Writing it felf in all thofe Ages and Countries, intimates the fame Original; the *Hebrew* Character was then, and is ftill written from the Right-Hand to the Left, and the *Egyptians* in their firft Language, wrote after the fame manner, *as we fhall fee in our next Difcourfe*, till many Ages afterwards; Then the *Greek* Tongue was fpoken in *Egypt* as the Univerfal Language, as it was alfo among the *Jews*, notwithftanding their being firft taught the *Hebrew*.

THUS, I think, it is as clear as any thing can be made, whofe Proofs are fo remote, that the Knowledge of Letters was of Divine Original, brought down from Heaven; *for fo, what was brought from GOD himfelf, might juftly be faid to be, and that it was brought to the* Ifraelites *by* Mofes, the Servant of GOD, who was divinely infpir'd, to inftruct the People in the Ufe, in the Pronunciation, in the Reading, and in the Writing of them; and this made me fay, that Writing is almoft as antient as Letters.

THIS alfo brings me to fpeak of the Nature of *Letters* themfelves, *(viz.)* That they were not only meer Figures, call'd by particular Names; for as fuch they were ftill, but Hieroglyphicks, as the Images of living Creatures were before; thofe Images were meer Independent Marks, defign'd to direct the Mind as any particular Mark might mean: *But this was quite another thing*, here was a certain ftrange and, *but by Divine Infpiration*, an incomprehenfible way of giving Diction to thofe Letters, which not only diftinguifhed them from one another, but made them capable alfo of being.

ing joined to one another, by Prolation, and Sound, by which means those Letters forming a diftinct Syllable, or Sallables, had again, a diftinct Compound Note, and those Syllables being farther join'd, compounded other diftinct Sounds, form'd from or out of several of the compound Sounds which went before; out of that far fetch'd Variety, forming the concording Sound of whatever Word or Words the Tongue could exprefs; Thefe Sounds had fuch an infinite Variety, that as the found of fix Bells may be chang'd 720 times, fo the Sounds of 24 Letters are capable of an innumerable reflux, fufficient to form Words enough, and thofe of differing Sounds, to exprefs the meaning of Mankind in all Languages now in Ufe in the World; nor would there be need to invent any more Letters, if there were ten Thoufand differing Languages more than there are.

'Tis hardly to be conceiv'd, how a Man making a certain Figure upon a Table, fhould frame his Mouth to make a Sound for that Letter or Figure; or how when he had fram'd his Mouth to form a Sound, he could fuit a Figure to exprefs that Sound by? *For Example*; Why muft an *A* reprefent fo many Things as we fee it does, being the firft beginning in Sounds, and the firft Singular in Speech? Why muft a Circle *O* exprefs our Exclamations, when we cry out for Pain and the like?

These feem to me to be Difficulties not in the Power of Human Invention; befides the innumerable Arcana that I have not Time or Room to mention here. Three Things in Nature, feem to me to Claim an immediate In-

fpiration

spiration from Heaven, as being above the reach of Human Invention, I mean meerly Human; These are (1.) MUSICK. (2.) NUMBERS. (3.) LETTERS. And these I call the *Three Infinites below*.

IF these did not come immediately from *Heaven*, Whence then did they come, and who were the Authors? To say they were Antediluvian, is to agree them to be Divine, because the consummate Knowledge of that State of the World, seems also to have been all from devine Original. But in all the Account of Things, all the Histories of Time and Persons, *taking in the sacred inspir'd World and all*, we find nothing recorded of the Original of any of these mighty T H R E E; till this of giving a written Language from *Heaven*, by which the Tables of Stone might be said to Speak, and the *Israelites* were taught to Read and Write.

OF *Numbers* I have spoken something; of *Musick* I shall say no more than this, that we have an Account of him that invented musical Instruments, and perhaps not that without divine Direction neither: But he invented only the Instrument, to improve the Knowledge, and Delight Mankind: But Harmony, and the Beauties of Sound, which are the Foundation of Musick, these are the Daughters of God; Unaccountables, beyond the reach of Human Invention; form'd in the Air, and directed by him that made that Air, in the proper divisions and proportions of Notes, for the further improvement of Sound.

NOR are these three Heads very remote from one another; they seem to be a Chain of Things of Affinity to one another, and are all

apply'd

apply'd in Conjunction on many Occasions, deriving from the same Principles, and blended one with another; there is Musick in Words, and there is Harmony in Numbers; particularly Numbers run thro',and are the Measure of Sound, which make Musick: In a Word, they are equally descended from above, and were equally above the Power of Nature to invent.

Some have been of the Opinion, *among whom I confess I am inclin'd to be one*, that all Learning, as well as all literature, as promulgated in the World, began in *Moses*; to whom all Knowledge, and Science was communicated from Heaven, either by Inspiration, or Revelation; to whom all Precept also was given, either by Tradition from the Patriarchs, or by the immediate Voice of God. Hence the History of the World was written by him, as deriv'd from *Adam*, and the Antediluvian Patriarchs to *Noah*, and from *Noah* easily transmitted to *Moses*, who was not so far remov'd from Father *Noah*, as that the Accounts transmitted from Father to Son might not easily be handed on inunalterable Truth.

Upon this Foot it was that the Scripture spake of *Moses*, that he was learn'd in all the Wisdom of the *Egyptians*; which may be understood, either *as some*, that he was learn'd above all the Wisdom of the *Egyptians*; Or, *as others*, that he had easily made himself Master of all their Traditional Knowledge, which to him was but poor trifling Stuff, *as indeed it was*; consisting chiefly in their Magick and Conjurations, things which some think they were both instructed and assisted in Personally, by the

Devil,

Devil; and in Aſtronomical Obſervations of the Motions of the Stars, which laſt they borrow'd from the *Arabians*, and they as it was ſaid from *Iſhmael* their great Anceſtor, who alſo was inſtructed by *Abraham*, and he by Divine Revelation.

OTHERS ſuggeſt that *Job* was firſt Aſtronomer, that he form'd the Stars into Conſtellations, and gave thoſe Conſtellations their Names; whence in the Book of *Job*, when GOD ſpeaks to *Job* out of the Whirlwind, he is ſaid to make uſe of the Names of the Conſtellations, and of the word *Mazzaroth*, which to this Day is not well underſtood, and leaves us doubting whether it be an unknown Conſtellation, and was then only call'd ſo, and may be known ſince by other Names; or the whole Zodaick including all the Signs put together.

AND this may be the Reaſon, why ſome think that *Job* was Contemporary with *Moſes*, in the latter part of his Life eſpecially; and that he wrote his own Hiſtory, having receiv'd the Knowledge of Letters from the *Iſraelites*, by the hand of *Moſes*.

WHEN I mention thus the Introduction of Letters by *Moſes*, I might again Quote the Words of the learn'd *Lud, Vives*, in his Commentary upon St. Auſtin, *de Civit. dei*, lib. 18. cap. 39. St. *Auguſtus*'s words are ſhort, thus, *The* Hebrew *Letters began from the Law given by* Moſes: To this *Lud, Vives*, adds thus, *The vulgar Opinion of us Chriſtians*, ſays he, *and alſo of the* Hebrews Is, *that the* Hebrew *Letters had* Moſes *for their Author, which* EUPOLEMUS, *as alſo* ATRAPANUS, *and other prophane Writers alſo do aſſert*; who deliver that *Moſes was the moſt wiſe*

Man

Man in the World, and the Inventer of Letters, *which he deliver'd over to the* Jews, *from whom the* Phenicians, *who were Neighbours to the* Jews *received them, and the* Grecians *by* Cadmus *from the* Phenicians : *The same* Artapanus *suggests that* Moses *likewise gave the Knowledge of Letters, and the Letters themselves to the* Egyptians.

This so exactly agrees with what I have already advanc'd from Reason, and the Nature of things, that I think it amounts to as much Confirmation of it, as History can yeild us. The Reverend and very learn'd Dr. *Gale*, mentions the same thing also, in his Treatise of the original of the *Heb.* Letters, where he saith that *Moses* was stiled *Mercury* by the *Ægyptians*, because he taught them Wisdom, and the Knowledge of Letters : *vid.* Dr. *Gales* Court of the *Gentiles*, pag. 56. The same learn'd Author tells us, that *Plato* in his *Phædrus* contends, that the first Invention of Letters was in *Egpyt*, by one THEUTCH, of whom it was a great doubt, whether he were a God, or a Man; and other Authors bring this THEUTCH to be the same, that the *Ægyptians* call'd *Mercury*, and that this *Mercury* was *Moses*, is affirm'd, " says he, " by *Atrapanus*, in *Eusebius Prepar. Evang.* lib. " 9. cap. 4 ". *His words are these*, " Whom the " *Hebrews* call *Moses*, and the *Greeks Musæus*, " the *Ægyptians* call'd *Mercury*; and hence " *Mercury* was said to be the God of Learn- " ing, because he was suppos'd to be the In- " venter of Letters.

Now the same learn'd Author insists that all the Oriental Languages derive from the *Hebrew*, and that therefore all the Nations, who spoke those Languages must derive their

Let-

Letters from *Moses*, who taught the *Hebrew*,
and that the Similitude, with the Manner of
Printing, and the feveral readings of the Letters
effectually acknowledge their Original. I
know Monfieur *Du Pin* is of another Opinion;
but as he touches it but in a Summary and fup-
pofitious Manner: I fhall refer what he fays
to another Place.

WHAT is faid already, fully confirms me in
the Opinion, as before, that the Exhibition of
the two Tables in the *Mount*, written, as the
Text affirms, by the Finger of God, was the
firft Specimen of Letters ever known in the
World; and why elfe could not the Coppy be
done again in the Camp, as I have obferv'd already, after the firft Tables of Stone were
broken by *Moses*, without carrying new Tables
up to have the fame Hand *at that time inimita-
ble* perform the Operation?

SOME have entertained a Notion, whether
from the old *Jews*, fruitful in Fictions, or from
fome other Brain given to Invention, that upon
the Tables of Stone before, or immediately after
the writing of the Law, was an Alphabet of
the *Hebrew* Letters, as a Key to inftruct the *Ifraelites* in the writing part for the future; but
this alfo I give the World, as indeed it is a peice
of Invention; but it intimates that the *Ifraelites*
had occafion of fuch a Direction, having probably never feen any writing before. Certain
it is, that we do not meet with any writing,
or any Alphabet in thofe Ages, before the
Hebrew; what has been advanc'd of Antidilu-
vian Alphabets, of *Noahs* Alphabet, and the
like, I fhall confider by its felf.

WE

WE are indeed told of a great variety of antient Writings, particularly *Trifmegiftus* is faid to have written 30000 Volums, and that he lived before, or was at leaft as antient as *Mofes* ; but then there is an unfurmountable Difficulty in the word Volume, how it fhould be underftood in after times, whether a Book, as it is here Suggefted, or the Leaf of a Book, as in the 40 *Pfalm* v. 7th *In the Volume of the Book, is it written, Lo, I come,* where *Volume* muft be underftood only a Leaf ; here then is a Difficulty in the word Volume, and what Tranflators muft call it in different Languages ; for we are certain there were no Books in *Mofe's* time, no, not Rolls, as we find was afterwards the ufuage in the times of the Prophets, *Ifaiah Jeremiah, Ezekiel,* &c. Either then it muft be fuppos'd that *Trifmegiftus* wrote 30000 Tables of Stone, or Leaves of the *Papyri,* or that the Tranflators mean, that he wrote as much, as was *when Coppy'd,* or Tranflated, made up into 30000 Rolls, or Volums. So we read of the five Writers in the *Apocryphal* Book of *Efdras,* Book II. cap. xiv. v. 44. *In Forty Days they wrote Two Hundred and Four Books,* what thefe Books were, is perfectly defcribed in the fame Chapter, Verfe the xiv, *Look thou prepare thee many* Box-Trees, *and take with thee* Sarea, Dabria, Selemia, Ecanus, and Afiel. *Thefe five, which are ready to write fwiftly.* In the Margin its faid, *Box-Tables to write on,* inftead of *Box-Trees* ; fo that thofe Books were only fo many *Tables* of Box-wood, of which I fhall fay more in its Place ; but as to the 30000 Volums of *Trifmegiftus,* tho' if they were written, 'tis probable they were no more than fo many Tables

Tables of Wood, yet I muſt not forget that the whole Story of the 30000 Volumns or Tables is treated by good Authors as fabulous : and indeed I think, deſerves to be ſo treated.

FOR this *Triſmegiſtus*, which ſome call *Mercury*, and the *Egyptians Thauut*, was an *Egyptian*, and at the moſt is ſuppos'd to be but Contemporary with *Moſes*, and ſo might have all his Knowledge of Letters from *Moſes*, that is to ſay, from the *Hebrew* original. He is alſo ſaid to be the Inventor of all the liberal *Arts* and *Sciences* ; *all which might be* after he had attain'd the Knowledge of Letters, and even without it, for 'tis manifeſt that the *Egyptians*, and before them the *Arabians* were Aſtronomers, Magicians and WISE MEN, *as thoſe Ages call'd them*, or to ſpeak in our Modern way, *Learn'd Men*, and yet they wrote only by *Hieroglypicks*, not by Letters ; and if *Triſmegiſtus* us'd Letters, 'tis more than probable that he had them from MOSES, *as above* ; and yet of all his 30000 Volums, which 'tis ſaid he wrote, we know of no more, than of two Dialogues, preſerv'd to the World under his Name ; One call'd *Pœmander*, and the other *Aſclepius*, that is, the Perſons ſpeaking to one another, by way of *Dialogue*, are ſo call'd. The firſt of theſe Dialogues, *is concerning the Will of God*, and the other the *Power of God* ; and theſe are Quoted by (a) ſeveral of the ancient Fathers, to prove the Truth of Religion from the Authority of ſo antient a Writer, DU PINN *Bibliothec. Patrum, or Ecc. Hiſt. of the firſt Cent.* Vol. 1. Fol. 3.

(a) By St. *Clement* in lib. 1 *Aromat.* By St. *Auguſtin* in Tract de 5 *Hareſ.* and in lib. 8. de *Civit. Dei.* By *Cyril* of *Alexandria* Contra Julianum lib. 1 By St. *Juſtin.* And by *Lanctantius*, inſt.t. lib. 4.

PART III.

IT feems needful that I fhould take a little farther Notice here, *at leaft enough to let the Reader know that I have confidered fuch a thing*, that
there have been fome Notions ftarted in the
World of the Knowledge of Letters, and the
Ufe of Writing before the Deluge ; and fome
have had Affurance enough to offer at the Manner : The firft I met with in our Nation, was one
Hepburn, a *Scotfman*, a Perfon who indeed wanted no Learning, but a little too affuming ; he
was a Student at *Vienna* ; He infifted upon *Enoch*'s
being the Father of Antediluvian Literature,
and has gone fo far, as to pretend to give an Alphabet, which he calls *Henochi literas*, and which
is to be feen in fome antient Writers, who fpent
perhaps more time in forming, than fearch-
ing after fuch a thing ; for there does not
appear, at leaft I cannot find that there
does appear any juft Authority for what they
have advanc'd.

THE utmoft Evidence, *except what feems to lye
in the Invention of thefe learned Criticks.* I fay,
the utmoft Evidence that I met with among
them, feems to amount to no more than a probability that it might be fo, which I readily
grant ; but can by no means allow that this is
a fufficient Proof of the Affirmative : They
are pleas'd to introduce their Notions of this
kind,

kind, by way of Interrogation and Inquiry, why may we not believe, *say they,* " That God " who infpir'd the Minds of the Patriarchs " in the Antediluvian Age, with all ufeful " Knowledge, fhould not be fuppos'd to have " given this Knowledge among the reft, fince " this was a thing fo many ways ufeful to " them? nay, fo abfolutely neceffary was it, to " their Converfing profitably and ufefully one " with another, that they could hardly be " faid to be able to live happily with- " out it.

I THINK all this might be granted without prejudice to any ones Opinion, or Belief, that notwithftanding all this, it really might not be fo ; and that God, who knew for how fhort a Continuance that World was intended, and how it was not to the length of full two Ages, for the Flood was in the Year 1576 of the Worlds Creation, knew very well they were cap- able of preferving the Hiftory of every Thing which was needful for them to know, by the Affiftance of their Memories ; which no Quefti- on were qualified for retaining the Knowledge, and Remembrance of Things material to be remember'd, as effectually as was needful to any of the Purpofes they cou'd require.

THE two principal Supports of this Opini- on of Antidulvian writings, and indeed the only Arguments that feem to carry Weight in them, or that requires any Anfwer, are thefe.

1. THE Words of St. *Jude,* receiv'd in the *New-Teftament,* verf. 14, 15. *And Enoch alfo, the feventh from* Adam, *Prophefied of thefe, fay- ing,* Behold, the *Lord cometh with ten Thoufands of his Saints, To execute Judgment upon all, and to convince all that are ungodly among them, of all* their

their ungodly Deeds which they have ungodly committed, and of all their hard Speeches, which ungodly Sinners have spoken against him.

FROM hence, they will have it be, that the Patriarch *Enoch* wrote these Words in a Book; to which they should add, that *Noah* must also preserve that Book, or Writing, whatever it it was, in the *Ark*, and so leave the same to his Posterity; which had it been true, would doubtless have been preserv'd to future Generations, as a valuable and precious peice of Antiquity; and if the use of Letters had been convey'd to the Post Diluvians by *Noah*, as the same Persons insinuate was done, we cannot doubt, but such a sacred Oracle would certainly have been Coppied many times, yea Thousands of times, and that it could not but have been preserv'd to the use of us his Posterity.

SINCE therefore they bring us Scripture for a Testimony, which however, if granted to be to their Purpose, is no Proof the Fact, only of the Suggestion or Probability. *I say,* since they bring Scripture, let us see what is the Opinion of the learn'd Commentators upon this Text: The Continuators of the Learned Mr. *Pool,* say thus, *Enoch* —— Prophesied. *Note,* " He doth not say *Wrote,* and there
" fore from hence it cannot be prov'd that
" there was any such Book as *Enoch's* Prophe
" sies receiv'd by the *Jews,* as Cannonical
" Scripture; but that rather, this was some
" Prophesy of *Enochs* deliver'd to them by
" Tradition, and handed down by the Patri
" archs from one to another, and which pass'd
" as a certain Truth, *that is to say,* that *Enoch*
" did so Prophesy. Vid. *Pool's Annotat.* upon the Epistle of St. *Jude.*

I D

I F *Enoch* wrote this, Why was it not said, *as it is written*, in the Prophefies of *Enoch*, the Seventh from *Adam*, &c. which is the ufage of Scripture: This Text militates nothing in favour of *Hepburn*, or any of thofe antient Writers, or of their Notion of the Knowledge of Letters in the Antediluvian World; for *E-noch* might, and certainly did Prophefy, as the Text here Quotes; but this was no other than the Words of *Enoch*, preach'd to that finful World, warning them of their approaching Deftruction; then handed down to *Noah*, and by him to his Pofterity by *Oral Tradition*, and remember'd even to that Day, when *Jude* Quotes them, *as above*.

I T is plain from the reft of the Writings of the Apoftles, and from the Words of Chrift himfelf, that when our Saviour referr'd the *Jews* in his Difcourfes to them, to any of the antient Writers, he ufually introduced it with thofe Words, *for it is Written*; particularly in his return to the Devil, when he Tempted him to caft himfelf down from the Temple; and alfo when the Devil propos'd to him to Worfhip him, and alfo when he Tempted him to command the Stones to be made Bread, *Mat.* iv. 4, 7, 10. *But he anfwer'd and faid, It is written, Man fhall not live by Bread alone, but by every Word that proceedeth out of the Mouth of God.*

Jefus faid unto him, it is written again, Thou fhall not tempt the Lord thy God.

Then faith Jefus unto him, get thee hence, Satan: For it is written, Thou fhalt Worfhip the Lord thy God, and him only fhalt thou ferve.

BUT

But seeing then, tis only said here, that *Enoch* Prophecied, it argues no more that *Enoch* wrote what he Prophecied, than that *Mose's* Relation of what *Adam* and *Eve*, said one to another was written down for the Authority of *Moses*, or that the Serpent wrote down what he said to *Eve*, when he tempted her to break God's Command, forbidding her to eat. Thus without showing any dis-regard to the Testimony of Scripture, I think 'tis Evident, that what St. *Jude* says of *Enoch's* Prohesy, is as to this Case nothing at all to the Purpose.

The Second Testimony is Quoted from *Josephus*, in his *Antiquities* of the *Jews*. lib. 1. cap. 3. Where speaking of the Sons of *Adam*, and particularly of Seth, the only succeeding Son of *Adam*, after *Cain* and *Abel*, that the Scripture makes mention of. His Words are thus render'd in *English*, in our common Edition of *Josephus*, by Sir *R. L'Strange*.

" *SETH* being brought up under the Tuiti-
" on of his Father, prov'd a wonderful Man,
" and wholly given up to the Study of Vertue,
" and his Children were the lively Image of
" so excellent a Father.

" These were the first that made their Ob-
" servations upon the Motions of the Heavens,
" the Courses, and Influences of the Stars;
" and having been foretold by *Adam* of the
" universal Deluge, and Conflagration to come,
" they erected two Pillars, one of Brick, the
" other of Stone, which they were sure would be
" off Proof against, either Fire or Water. Up-
" on those Pillars they engrav'd the Memori-
" als of their Discoveries, and Inventions, there
" to remain for the Benefit of the Ages to
" come;

" come; and leaſt the Tradition ſhould be loſt
" for want of a Record.

" THIS they did, and their Foreſight and
" Providence was not in vain, for the Stone-
" is yet ſeen in *Syria* to this very Day.

Joſephu's *Antiq.* of the *Jews.* cap. 2. fol. 6.

Now not to Enter here into the long Chain
of Argument, brought againſt this Opinion by
the Antients, and particularly by St. *Auguſtin*,
who rejects it entirely. *I ſay*, not to Enter into their Arguments, 'tis enough to Enter my
Proteſt againſt this Relation, as impoſſible to
be True by the nature of the Thing; and that
it is not Rational to Conceive, that any of the
Fabricks, Buildings or Monuments of the old
World could remain, and be viſible after the
Flood; and whether we conſider the Deluge as a
meer flux of Water collected by a ſupernatural
Power into ſuch a Poſition, as to cover the
Face of the Earth for near Elven Months, or
whether we conſider the Deluge according to
the Hypotheſis of the Learn'd *Burnet* to be an
Abſorption, or a Breaking in of the Surface of
the Earth into the great Deep, or Abyſs of
Water, which till then was Subterraneous and
unſeen. *I ſay*, whetherſoever of theſe were
the real Fact, I take it to be inconſiſtent with
the nature of the Thing, that any Column, or
Pillar could remain after the Flood. *I mean*, ſuch
as the Hand of Man, could make whoſe Dependance muſt be on the Surface of the Earth, on
which it ſtood. Seeing we all agree, that even
on the firſt Suppoſition, the Surface of the Earth
would be too much ſoften'd, and the furious
Motion of the Waters would be ſo forcible,

eſpe-

especially, at their first flux, and towards their Ebbing off, that no human built Fabrick could stand in its way; and if it be true, on the next Hypothesis, as has been the Opinion of the Learn'd, that the Face of the whole Globe of the Earth, was chang'd, and renew'd; 'tis also not likely that any Building, however firm, of the old World could remain, no, not the same Face of the Surface; but Mountains were cast up, deep Valleys made, *and the like*, and every thing overturn'd. Not so much as *Eden*, the Garden of God, was preserv'd, or the Place perfectly known where it stood, tho' describ'd so mathematically in the *Pentateuch*, as to name the Rivers, their Entrance in, and thro' and Coming out of it.

I t would seem strange then, that this Column of Antediluvian Structure should remain, and not any other thing belonging to the old World; no City or Town, no Work of the antient Inhabitants; no Monument, Altar, Temple, or Castle, however strong built, if such they had; nothing remaining in any Place of the World, to intimate that there had been Inhabitants there before them; no, not so much as the Ruins of any thing, and yet that this *Column* in *Syria* should remain, and be not only visible in *Josephus's* time, but should show the Engravement, with the History of the *Time when*, and the Reason, or, *Cause for which*, it was erected. These are Improbabilities, which argue strongly against the Authority of one single Writer, and I think may serve for a sufficient Answer.

Further, if this Pillar was remaining, the Writing, and Engravement upon it was remaining also; otherwise, How did it testify the

E

Meaning

Meaning of it ? And how did the *Jews* receive from it the History mention'd above ? and if these were remaining, How comes it to pass that so glorious a Monument of Antiquity was not preserv'd, that the Words, or at least the Characters were not copyed, and taken off, and by some artful, careful Hand, preserv'd for the Use and Information of Posterity ? Strange! that the Pillar should remain, and the Reason of it be told, and not a Word of the Inscription preserv'd, as the just Authority for Proof of the Facts, said to be, or intended to be preserv'd by that Column. But so it is, *Josephus* himself does not so much, as intimate that any Copy of the Inscription, or Engravement on the Pillar had been preserv'd, or does he so much as give us any of the Words, or Letters made use of in it.

WHAT then is the Authority of *Josephus*, to prove there was such a Column, or what the Column it self? If it had been really preserv'd as I am fully satisfy'd it was not, and could not ? *I say*, What is all this to the proving the Knowledge of Letters in the Antediluvian World ; Unless the Inscription, or any part of it, which was said to be engrav'd on the Column, had been also shown us, that we might know what Letters they used, and in what manner the Sound of Words was drawn out from them ?

IT is True, the learn'd *Fugi*, in his Treatise, entitl'd, *Exercitationum Literariarum*, Collects all that was advanc'd by those antient Writers, concerning these Letters, and gives us, or pretends rather to give, the several Alphabets of *Adam, Enoch,* and *Noah,* and his Authors, or Authority for this, which are principally,

Angelus

Angelus Boccha a Camerino, in *Bibliothcæ
Apoftolicæ Vaticanæ* Commentario, quem
Romæ, Ann. 1591, edidit.
Claudius Durretius, in Hiftoria de linguis Uni-
verfi, *Coloniæ*, 1613.
Thefeus Ambrofius, in Appendice Introductionis ad Chaldaicam linguam, Syriacam,
Armenicam, atque decem alias linguas,
quas Papiæ in Italia evulgavit, 1529.
Jacobus Bonaventura Hepburnus Scotus, Ordinis fancti Francifci de Paula, qui Pontificis *Pauli* v. privilegio & Superiorum
licentiâ confirmatus forum extruxit Romæ,
1616, & *Auream Virgam* infcripfit.

From thefe feveral Authors, are collected
the feveral Alphabets call'd by them, as in the
following Tranfcripts, from the faid learn'd
Author are to be feen, and to which I refer,
thinking it fufficient to give the Tranfcript,
with the Authority, from whence I bring it ;
without any Suggeftion of the Truth of it,
which indeed, I conceive is not to be found,
otherwife than in the fruitful Invention of thefe
Authors, which I leave the learn'd Reader to
Judge of.

QUEST. I.

*Quinam Auctores Literis Antediluvia-
nis patrocinentur, de iis teftentur, &
quibus figuris illæ exprefſæ extent ?*

ORdiemur a primi hominis, Adami, Alphabeto,
quô, fi genuinum effet, antiquius prodi aut pre-
mi nequibat, humanâ quidem induftriâ & folertiâ
elaboratum. Hujus Adamæi Characteris origi-
nem

*nem quod spectat, non heri aut hodiè nata, ante
seculum viguit, diuq; in animis credulis sedem fixit.
Veluti verò hæc* Literarum *prima stirps, ut pu-
tatur, à publicis Monumentis & nitidis Sculpto-
rum cœlis gratiam, ita ab illustri* Adami *nomine
splendorem, a diuturnitate vero temporis, quo in-
tacta & severioris examinis secura floruit, robur
ac duramentum nacta est.*

Ingrediamur modò atque contemplemur spaciosum
Literarum *Forum, quod* Jacobus Bonaventura
Hepburnus Scotus, Ordinis Francisci de Paula,
Pontificis Pauli V. *privilegiô & superiorum licentiâ confirmatus extruxit* Romæ 1616, & Auream Virgam *inscripsit : mox velut in acta pub-
lica relatum testimonium de Literis Protoplasti in-
tuentium oculis obversabitur. Nam inter Sexa-
ginta octo differentes Literarum formas magnô
quidem studio conquisitas, sed majori impendiô in
æs incisas, spectatur talis typus*

ADAMÆI ALPHABETI.

Sic vidimus Hepburni *testimonium* Literarum
Adamæarum *monumentis consignatum. Sed tantum vidimus.* Quare *à nuda* Characterum Adami *indice tabula obiter inspecta, quam* Hepburnus *Pontifici* Paulo V. *dicavit, rectà progrediemur ad lustranda* monumenta Italiæ *à*
Laurentio Schradero Halberstadiense Saxone
edita, atque inibi lustrabimus eos Adami Characteres, *quos in peregrinatione Italica viderat* Schraderus, *quosq; ex* Bibliotheca Vaticana Columna
octava

ctava in muro ad Effigiem Adami *exscriptos*
Helmstadii *ediderat,* 1592: *quibus mox aliæ*
Adamæorum Elementorum *forma ab* Hepbur-
næo Adami *charactere planè diversa nostris oculis*
subjungetur. Hæc *autem talis est,*

$$\nabla \mathcal{Z} \mathbb{N} \mathbb{E} L W \mathcal{P} P \diamond \mathcal{I} \daleth$$
$$\mathcal{F} \mathcal{X} \mathcal{I} \mathcal{H} \mathcal{G} \mathcal{I} \mathcal{J} N \mathcal{F} \aleph \mathcal{K}$$

Quoniam verò non modò in Hepburnæa Lite-
raria Tabula, *verum etiam in Schraderianis* Itali-
æ *Monumentis jam allegatis nudas tantum charac-*
terum figuras intueri licet: veniendum erit ad
alios Autores, qui non minus nonnulla fundamenta
antiquissimarum literarum ab Adamo *formatarum*
tradere conati sunt, quam nudos Characteres typis
aut Cœlis exprimere. Hos inter tres in primis
numerantur : Angelus Roccha à Camerino *in Bi-*
bliothecæ Apostolicæ Vaticanæ commentario, quem
concinnavit & Romæ, 1591, *edidit :* Claudius Duretus *in Historia de Linguis Universi, quam Gal-*
lico idiomate publicavit Coloniæ 1613; *necnon*
Theseus Ambrosius ex Comitibus Albonesii
I U D *in Appendice Introductionis in Chaldaicam*
Linguam, Syriacam, Armenicam atque decem alias
Linguas, quas Papiæ in Italia evulgavit, 1539.
Initio quidem in illud Adami Alphabetum
oculos defigemus, quod Angelus Roccha *in Com-*
mentario Bibliothecæ Vaticanæ videndum propo-
nit, pag. 79. *& verba ejus audiemus, quæ ita ha-*
bent : Supra hujus [picti Adami] caput Characteres, sive Literæ antiquiores, nunc Hebrai-
cæ dictæ, ejusmodi leguntur.

Hebrai-

Hebraicum Alphabetum Antiquius.

Ad ejuſdem verò *Adami* pedes Inſcriptio
Latina in hanc legitur verborum formam.

Adam divinitus edoctus, primus ſcientiarum &
literarum inventor. Pergit Roccha, *pag* 80. Ra-
tio ipſa perſuadet, Adamum divinius edoctum
diſciplinas, certóſq; præſertim ſcribendi Characteres adeo neceſſarios aliis præmonſtrâſſe,
ſicut inſcriptio docet. Hanc autem formam
ſcribendi hôc locô poſitam Hebraicas inter literas antiquiorem, primumque Alphabetum
fuiſſe CREDENDUM EST, quod à dex-
tro in ſiniſtrum latus legitur. *Hæc* Roccha.

Porrò nunc ad primum & principium hujus
Adamæi Alphabeti promum ac patronum pedem
promovebimus. Nobis quidem nemo hactenus viſus
eſt aut cognitus, qui publicando Literas Adamæas
Theſeum Ambroſium *anteverteret. Etenim*
Annô Chriſti, 1539, *Papiæ primus evulgavit*
Adami Characteres, *eoſq; velut è mediis, ad quas*
damnati memorantur, flammis eripuit. Qua de re
ipſum Theſeum loquentem audiamus. Sex, inquit
Theſeus in Append. variarum Literarum, p. 202,
203, relatis Hebraicarum Literarum generibus, operæ precium, me facturum arbitratus
ſum, ſi alios haudquaquam ſpernendos Hebræ-
orum Characteres, à variis non infimi nominis
autoribus excerptos in hac noſtra Appendice
adderem. Inter libros Antonii de Fantis Tar-
viſini, olim Philoſophi & Aſtrologi excellen-
tiſſimi,

tiſſimi, memini me vidiſſe opera Razielis, Pica-
tricis, Bailii, Mercurii Petri, Apponis, Salo-
monis ac Interpretis ejus Apollonii, & alio-
rum multorum, ex quibus tanquam ex virenti
& florido prato variarum Literarum flores &
Characteres diverſos collegi. Neque enim
aliam ab cauſam tam diligenter libros illos,
antequam in Vulcani poteſtatem a patribus
noſtris, in quorum manus ex teſtamento perve-
nerunt, legi; quàm ut Characteres illos, Literarum ſcilicet varias figuras, exſcriberem. In
ſecundo quippe Tractatu, in quo de lapidibus
precioſis loquitur Raziel, reprobata illorum
opinione qui dicunt viginti duas Literas, de
quibus ibi loquitur, à Samuele fuiſſe inven-
tas; Angelum Raphael in Libro, qui dicitur
Liber ignis, illas Adæ protoplaſto dediſſe ſcrip-
tas aſſeverat, & ob id filios Adami eas recuſare
non poſſe. Quarum quidem Literarum figura
& nomina ſunt infra ſcripta. *Hactenus* Theſeus.
Quia vero figuris plane conveniunt hi Angelici
Characteres Adamo *traditi cum iſto* Literarum
Adamæarum *genere, quod ſuprà primô locô viden-*
dum propoſuimus, quodq; nitido ſatis Cœlô in æs in-
cidendum, curavit Hepburnus, *nolumus Alphabe-*
tum huc denuo tranſcribere, aut idem bis cum tæ-
dio Lectoris repetere, ne actum agamus.

Veluti verò Theſei *veſtigiis preſſè inſiſtit* Hepburnus *in* Aurea Virga, *hoc eſt, ſplendida varia-*
rum Literarum Tabula, quando eaſdem quas ille A-
damæarum Literarum *Figuras attulit : ita* Claudius Duretus *ne latum quidem unguem ab ejuſ-*
dem Theſei *latere diſceſſit, niſi quòd novâ teſtimo-*
niorum Symbolâ adjectâ diligentiam ejus ſuperare
conatus ſit. Etenim Primo *allegat* Ambroſium
Theſeum *tanquam ducem, quem imitandum ſibi*
propoſuit in divulgandis biſce Adami Literis. *Hu-*

E 4

jus enim narrationem & auctoritatem velut scutum adverfantibus objicit. Deinde hunc titulum *eis prefigit :* Characteres de l' Ange Raphael, *Characteres Angeli Raphaelis.* Tertiò *plane eofdem & numero & habitu* Characteres Adamiticos, *quos* Thefeus *ante feculum excudendos curavit, ob oculos ponit,* pag. 117. Quarto & ultimo *præfcriptis Characteribus fubftruit nova fundamenta, partim petita è Cabaliftarum & Ebræorum Commentariis in* Librum Jezira, *partim ex patribus* Epiphanio & Auguftino.

Primo *quidem è fcriptis & perufchiis Rabbinices in* Librum Jezira *probare nititur, quod* patrum præceptores fuerint Angeli noti, videlicet præceptor ipfius Adami Raziel, *&c.* Secundo *afferit* Epiphanium *ad Panarium facere mentionem Libri, cujus titu'us,* Adæ Revelatio, quando Deus immifit foporem in illum. Tertio *tradit* Auguftinum *contra Fauftum Manichæum meminiffe Libri Adamæi, cujus infcriptio & argumentum fuit de* Genealogia filiorum & filiarum Adæ. Quartò *ait Librum quendam Razielis Angeli extitiffe, qui hunc prætulit titulum,* Chavæ five omnium viventium Matris admirabiles & fuper omnes doctrinas mundi fecundum evangelicam Veteris & Novi Teftamenti veritatem amplectendæ Prophetiæ, confcriptæ a Raziele Adæ primi parentis Angelo ex Libro Behn, id eft, Lucis puriffimæ excerptæ. Quintò *denique memorat* Sanctum Thomam *librô de Ente & Effentia affirmare ab* Abele *filio Adami librum fuiffe compofitum, &c. Univerfa* Dureti *Differtatio eò collimat, ut è Libris, qui* Adamo *tanquam autori affignantur,* Literarum *Libros fcribere non potuit* Adamus. *Quamobrem neutiquam fe aberrâffe putat, quando* Thefei *exemplum fequutus, tale Literarum genus, quale fuprà à nobis expreffum* *preſſum eſt, Protaplaſto* Adæ *tribuit. Sed ab* Alphabeto Adamæo, *ad Literas filiis* Seth *aſcriptas luſtrandas progrediemur.*

Alphabetum filiis Seth *ſigillatim tribui non obſervavimus niſi ab* Angelo Roccha *in Comment. Bibliothecæ Vaticanæ* p. 8, Schradero *in Monumentis Italiæ, & autore inſcriptionum, quæ viſuntur Romæ in paraſtaticis columnis Bibl. Vaticanæ, quem ducem ſequuti ſunt* Roccha *& Schraderus, ſed diſpari ſucceſſu. Hic enim Literarum ordinem confundit, ipſoſque Charaĉteres rudiùs ac impolitiùs formandos curavit :* Ille vero in celebri ſuo Commentario, *Cujus jam aliquoties neminimus, eundem plane ſitum & habitum Literarum* filiis Seth, *ut ipſe loquitur, aſſignatarum exhibet, quem ipſe in* Adamæo *Alphabeto videndum propoſuit, & quem nos cælandum ſuprà curavimus. Hoc* Alphabetum poſteris Seth *tributum nullô aliô fundamentô ſulcit* Roccha, *niſi geminîs illîs columnîs, quarum meminit* Joſephus. *lib* 1. *Antiq. Jud.* Harum una, *ait Roccha,* lateritia erat, altera ænea ſive marmorea : illa contra ignis Conflagrationes, hæc contra aquæ alluviones erecta, ut monumenta ipſa diutius conſervarentur & permanerent. His in columnis liberales artes, & eas preſertim, quæ ad obſervationem ſiderum pertinerent, conſcripſerunt. *Joſephus* autem ad ſuam uſque ætatem Columnam illam marmoream iñ Syria duraſſe teſtatur. *Hæc* Roccha, *qui porro addit opinandum eſſe, quod hæc* Alphabetum filiis Seth *præmonſtratum ſit ab* Adamo. *Tzetzes Chiliad,* 5. Hiſt. 26. Κἄν Σ᷍θ ἑϐραῖοι λέγωσιν ἐφάρετϚ γραμμάτων, quamvis *Seth* Hebræi dicant inventorem literarum : *Quô locô ipſi parenti* Setho *literarum inventum tributum obſervat. Cæterum ab* Alphabeto filiorum Seth *ad Literas* Henochæas *deſcendemus.*

Henochi

Henochi Literas, quoad *invefigare licuit,*
primus publicavit Joannes Auguftinus Panthe-
os Venetus Sacerdos. *Is Librô, quem mirô ti-*
tulô & hybridâ voce infcrifit Voarchdumi-
am contra Alchimiam, *& Venetiis edidit* 1530.
Initiô quidem ufitatas & hodiernas Ebræorum
Literas *fpetandas proponit* pag. 12. Deinde *eaf-*
dem ornatiùs excufas ob oculos ponit, atq; illos
Charateres fuiffe afferit, quos in Monte Sinai Deus
Mofi *concefferat,* pag. 13. Tertio *Figuras litera-*
rum Abrahæ *traditarum exhibet,* pag. 14. Quarto *denique* Henochæi Alphabeti *typum exprimit*
Pag. 15.

Has Literarum Henochæarum *umbras, quibus*
formidolofa fuæ Voarchdumiæ arcana (myfteriô
enim Ebraicarum Literarum, in primis quatuor,
רקבן *artis fuæ fecreta tegit) obfcuravit* Pan-
theus, *feftinus captat* Duretus pag. 127 *ci-*
tati fupra Libri, eáfq; pro veris Henochi Literarum *antiquitate venerabilium figuris orbi lite-*
rato obtrudit. Ne verò planè tacuiffe videatur,
poftquam bos Charateres ob oculos pofuit, hæc
fubjungit: Nobis, qui hôc fæculô vivimus pro-
bè innotuit extare in Æthiopiâ Librum magnæ
authoritatis & pro Canonico habitum, qui res
divinas completitur & Enocho tanquam autori tribuitur. *Cetera, quæ addit, planè funt*
ἀλλότρια, *quare ea adfcribere operæ precium haut*
putamus.

Verùm *enim verò à* Pantheo *&* Duretho *abit*
Jac. Bonaventura Hepburnus *Expreffurus* Henochi characteres, *& in fua* Aurea Virga *hodi-*
ernos Charateres Ebraicos, *fed elegantiufculè*
fculptos & puntulîs in medio inftar rhomborum
pulcherrimè cælatos pro Henochæis Literis *ag-*
nofcit. Quia verò nudas faltem Literarum Fi-
guras

guras exhibet Hepburnus *fruſtrà ab ipſo rationes
& diductiorem confirmationem* Alphabeti Henochæi *expectaveris.* Sed *miſſis* Literis Henochi,
ad Noachi *characteres veniemus.*

*Qui in colligendis ac calandis variis Litera-
rum generibus omnium induſtriam ſuperare conatus eſt* Bonaventura Hepburnus *in magna &
ſplendida octo & ſexaginta characterum Tabula,*
Virga Aurea *dicta, hiſce ſequentibus figuris ſculp-
tum exhibet*

NOACHICUM ALPHABETUM.

Heic planè ſilent Theſeus & Duretus, *auda-
ces aliàs* Antediluvianarum Literarum *promi
& patroni, ſolus* Hepburnus *loquitur; ſed quô
ſucceſſu, mox* Queſtione ſecundâ *oſtendemus. Neq;
alibi in antiquis* Monumentis Literarum *quic-
quam obſervare hactenus potuimus, quo talis* Noachi *ſcriptura confirmetur, niſi cuipiam placuerit
ad partes vocare* Noachi Librum, *quem* Cabaliſtæ
tradunt à Chamo *in arca patri ſurreptum fuiſſe:*
De quo Delrius *Diſq.* Magic. *Lib.* I. *c.* 5.
Queſt. I. *Aut ſi quis velit* Noachi Teſtamen-
tum, *ejuſq; epiſtolam huc trahere quâ ſuprema
tanti viri voluntas contineri perhibetur, quam
paucis abhinc annis è ruderibus* Volaterranis *eru-
tam cum aliis* Etruſcis Antiquitatibus *Proſper*
Italus *divulgavit. Atq; ſic etiam luſtravimus* Literas *Noachom aſcriptas.*

H A-

HAVING thus given the moſt material Arguments, and the beſt Authorities which I can find are brought to make good theſe imaginary Things, for I can look upon them as no other: I have given my Reaſons why they paſs for no other with me, and I leave it to the judicious Reader to conſider whether they have Weight in them or no.

THE ſame Author puts ſome Streſs upon the fabulous Story of the Egyptians and their early Knowledge of Letters, from the introducing of Hieroglyphical Writings by *Memnon*, of whom I have ſpoken already.

AFTER all theſe are thus conſidered, and their Suggeſtions, as far as is reaſonable, duly weigh'd, I ſee no Reaſon at all to alter, or ſo much as doubt the *Propoſition* which I have already on mature Conſideration offered to diſcourſe upon; Namely, that the firſt Knowledge of Letters was from the immediate Inſpiration of Heaven at the publiſhing the Law of God from Mount *Sinai*; and that all the Neighbouring Nations, ſuch as the *Ægyptians*, *Phœnicians*, &c. receiv'd the firſt Hints of that Knowledge which they afterwards grew ſo famous for, from the *Hebrews*, and had all their Knowledge and Uſe of Letters from them.

IT is obſerv'd by ſome Men, who are particularly critical in the literal, or conſtructive Tranſlations of the Scripture, that the Words, by which *Moſes* expreſſes the Union and Accord of the Inhabitants of the new peopled World, in the Days of *Nimrod*, in purſuing that *poor ſenſeleſs* Project of building a Tower to reach up to Heaven, &c. are wrong tranſlated, and that it ſhould not be ſaid, as in *Gen.* 11. 1. *The whole Earth was of one Language, and of one Speech,*

Speech; But thus, *that the whole Earth, that is,
all the People on the Earth*, were of *one Mind*,
and were agreed, or of one Accord in the Design, which follows, meaning the Project of
the Tower that was to be built.

IF this Suggestion is Just, as I believe it is;
it imports thus much in favour of this Proposition of mine: Namely, that having no settled
Rule of Speech, or Knowledge of Letters, and
no Alphabet; Custom and ordinary Usage,
without any other Authority, as it does to
this Day, brought them to differing Dialects,
and differing Pronunciation of Speech; such
as they being separated, and remote perhaps
from one another, tho' not at a great Distance, yet at a Distance enough to prevent
frequent Conversing together, could not easily
communicate to one another: Hence they grew
particular, and proper only to those Tribes, or
Families that had accustom'd themselves to
them, so that they might not easily and fully
understand one another: But notwithstanding
this, they might so far understand the general
Meaning of their Speech, or by some particularly be acquainted with the other, might so
interpret to each other, as to make an Agreement in the main Design: This, *I say*, however, strongly implys they had then no Knowledge of Letters, and so far tells us that the Notions *de Literatura Patriarchali*, and *Noachi-
cum Alphabetum*, mention'd above, can have
no authentick Original, nor any just Authority to suport them: This, however, as it is argued from the Opinion above named, which
is only conjectural, so it may be allow'd to be
a just Reply to that Conjecture.

HAVING

HAVING said thus much, I leave these Learned Phantasms, *for such I think they are,* just where I found them, and so proceed to speak of the Progress in the Knowledge of Letters, after they were introduc'd, and from the just Original of Literature, which we have an Account of in the Scripture, as above.

PART IV.

HAVING thus discours'd on the Original of Letters, and fix'd, *as I think, effectually* their *Epocha,* in the Year of the World 2415, there remains to enquire, In what Manner they were made Use of in the respective Ages, after their being first given out: And by what Degrees the Writing and Printing of these Letters, advanc'd to the Perfection which we see them now arriv'd to; also How, and in what Manner, and upon what Occasions the Materials, for Writing and Printing, and the Instruments and Engines for the Performance of the several Parts of it were discover'd.

IN this Enquiry, we must go back to the very Beginning; for, like the Tabernacle of GOD, the Pattern was in the Mount. There the whole Art was exhibited, the Pattern set, a Specimen work'd off, and Man had nothing to do, after he was inspir'd with the Skill of Reading it, but to get Tools and imitate it. In short, to speak in the common Usage of Men, GOD himself was the first *Writing Master* in the World, and the first Work of Man was to imitate the Materials, as well as the Manner; and this was done by Degrees too, *viz.*

on

on Stone, and by Punction, or Cutting, and Stamping, which doubtless was the first Step.

How it must be perform'd, is left to be determin'd according to the Nature of the Stone on which the Work is done. For Example, We have a Stone or blue Slate, on which, with a Piece of the same Stone, Words now, are written by Excoriation, which is but a Kind of Razing the Surface in a flight Manner, and yet the Mark will remain there for many Years, if no Wet comes upon it ; and if a greater Strength or Weight of the Hand were laid to the Pen, so that it might cut farther in, the Impression being stronger, would, no Question, remain also a longer Time.

I F we go farther than this, we come to *Mallet* and *Chisel*, when we cut Letters of any Depth and Length ; and I have seen Letters so cut in Stone for Inscriptions, and which were to stand a very great Height from the Place of Sight, which have been very near two Foot and half long, and an Inch and half deep. But we may reasonably suppose, that the written Law was given in two moderate Tables, or Slates, on which the Finger of GOD could write in what Manner he best pleas'd ; and which he, no Question, wrote so, as that *Moses* might easily repeat them, teach the People to read them, and, by reading of those, seek for farther Knowledge in the Skill of imitating either, or both ; particularly we know they were not great Stones, such as it would necessarily require to cut the Words of the Ten Commandments in, with *Hammer and Chisel* ; because 'tis plain they were no bigger than *Moses* could carry, and that in one Hand, as is evident from the same Scripture.

T H E

THE Writing on thofe Tables, we may fuppofe to be fuch as was afterwards follow'd (I will not call it imitated,) with Excoriations or Markings by a Tool, *as above*, whether a Graving Tool, *as is not improbable,* or what other Inftrument, is not very eafy to know, nor very material to the Purpofe. In examining the Manner of Writing, we muft defcend to more Particulars; it is not fufficient to fay they wrote firft upon Leaves and Barks of Trees, which was directed according to the feveral Nations in which thofe Writings were in Ufe. But I fhall enter as particularly as I can into the Degrees of Improvement, as they went on.

THE *Egyptians* being fo near to the *Ifraelites* on the one Side, as has been faid, are fuppos'd to be fome of the firft Nations that improv'd the Ufe of Letters, after their being communicated to them from the *Hebrews:* How long they wrote on Tables of Stone, I can find no Authority to determin; 'tis probable it continu'd fome Time; as it did alfo among other Nations, including the Writing on Tables of Wood, as among the Gravers of Wood; cover'd with Wax, as among the *Romans,* and the like. But after that, they found a Way to fupply themfelves with other Things. For Example:

1. THEY wrote on the Infide of the Bark of a Tree which grew on the Side of the *Red Sea,* and in this they were foon imitated by the *Latins,* who, in their Tongue, call'd that Bark *Liber* ; whence Books are call'd *Libri.*

2. ON

2. On thin Boards cut out of a folid Kind of Wood, like our Walnut-Tree, hard and firm, which bore the Impreffion of the *Stylus*, of which hereafter: And this Wood was call'd *Caudex*; whence, fay fome, the *Latins* took Occafion to call a Book *Codex*.

3. Where they found not that hard Wood to write on, as in fome Countries it could not be had, they ufed Tables, which they fpread over with fine Wax, and therein wrote very eafily what they had occafion to write; whence the Meffenger that carry'd thefe Tables as Miffives, were call'd *Tabellarii*; and a Letter-Carrier, or *Courier*, is ftill call'd *Tabellarius*: But of thofe I may fpeak again, as ufed among the *Romans*: I am now fpeaking of what was in Ufe among the *Egyptians*.

On the Bank of the *Nile*, when running in its ordinary Courfe, *not as overflowing*, there grew certain fedgy Weeds, call'd *Papyri*, fuppos'd to be the fame with which the Cradle was made, which *Mofes* was laid in when he was turn'd adrift in the River *Nile*; of thofe they made a kind of Stuff in the Stead of what we call Paper, to write on, in the following Manner, and from whence our Writing-Paper has fince taken its Name. The Leaves of thefe Weeds were very thick and fubftantial, but foft, and eafily parted into abundance of thiner Slices or Flakes; accordingly they pull'd them afunder with their Hands, fpreading them in the Sun; but as faft as the Sun dry'd them, they wetted them again, by fprinkling on them fome of the Water of the River, which, at the Seafon of gathering the

F   Leaves,

Leaves, was always thick and flimy, fome-thing like melted Glew; this thicken'd the Leaves, and made them folid and firm, as they dry'd by the Heat of the Sun : Thefe are the fame mentioned Ifaiah 19. 7. *The Paper Reeds by the Mouth of the Brooks, fhall wither, be driven away, and be no more.* My Author, for this, fays, That by Means of this Invention, *Ptolemy Philadelphus*, made up the Books which compos'd his extraordinary Library at *Alexandria*. Alfo the fame *Ptolemy* underftanding that *Attalus* King of *Pergamus*, endeavour'd to out-do him in the Magnificence of a Library, and that he began to make Collections of Books, and the Works of *Homer*, *Palamedes* and other *Greek* Authors, and to amafs an infinite Number of Volumes, which he com-pil'd of this *Egyptian* Weed, call'd *Papyrus*; and withal, that he manag'd that in a bet-ter Manner than the *Egyptians* did. *Ptolemy*, to prevent and difappoint him, prohibited the Exportation of the faid *Papyrus* out of his Dominions : And the fame Author adds, that upon this Prohibition King *Attalus* in-vented the making of *Parchment* or *Vellum* made of the Skins of Goats and Calves, on which he taught his Officers and Clerks to write and copy the *Grecian* Poets, and other Authors, as above : Thefe Skins, at firft, were call'd *Membrana*; from the Country which *Attalus* reign'd over, they were in other Places, call'd *Pergamene*, and thefe were the laft Ad-vances that I find among the *Grecians* before the Invention of Paper.

Ptolemy however compleated his Collection for the *Alexandrian* Library, with Books writ-ten on the Leaves of the *Papyri*, as above; which however durable enough otherwife, to
have

have continued to this Day, were not Proof against the Flames, being all deftroy'd in the burning of the faid Library : So that there are none to be found, at leaft, that I have hear'd of, in any of the moft antient Collections now extant in the World.

In defcribing the Inftruments, or Materials of Writing, by which the Knowledge and Ufe of Letters was propagated, We indeed fhew the Excellency of the Letters themfelves; for if they had not been capable of being copied, and imprefs'd, as above, they had been of no ufe to Mankind, any farther than God, the firft Author, fhould have communicated and exhibited new Tables, and new Writings, for the Ufe of his Creatures; which being once read, were to be recorded; as his meer Voice, and might be erected on Columns, or treafur'd up, as Records for the People to have recourfe to, that the Commands of God might never be forgotten, or the Subftance of them be loft to the People.

But the Letters being communicated, and not only made intelligible, but appearing to be imitable by Men, it was left to them to invent Methods of Imitation, and Inftruments to work by, as their firft Invention, or the art of Imitation improv'd.

Of thefe we meet with many Kinds ; as Firft, a Tool, to imprefs the Mark, or Letter, and the Subftance on which that Impreffion was to be made, as above ; and this Tool, or Inftrument, was to be ftronger, or weaker, harder, or fofter, as the faid Subftance requir'd : For Example ; While they wrote on Tables of Stone, or Slate, a piece of the fame Slate, or Stone, was ufually made ufe of, to

F 2

mark

mark the Letters, as I have already obferv'd ;
as we do to this Day in *England*, upon the ordinary blue or black Slate, which we have in
great Quanties in *Cornwall* and *Devonſhire* ;
and which they have likewife in *Germany*, and
alfo in *Egypt*, in *Greece*, and in *Italy*.

WE read of fome Writings by the bare
Finger; and perhaps for prefent reading only,
There might be much of that in ufe among
the Eaftern Nations ; and even for Duration
alfo. when Perfons might write on fuch harfh
Plaifer, or other Mixtures, as being foft to
receive the Impreffion, when they wrote,
grew hard afterwards (in the Weather) as
Stone ; many Kinds of which are yet found ;
and fome, in particular, in *England* ; of which,
in *Nottingham-ſhire*, *Leiceſterſhire*, and other
Places, where they make not Walls only, but
Floors of Houfes of it, as alfo Threfhing-
floors, and the like.

OF thefe Sorts of Writings two are mentioned in Scripture ; One is the Hand-writing upon the Wall at *Belſhazzar*'s Feaft, and the
other, when our Saviour ftoop'd down and
wrote on the Ground, in the Cafe of the Woman taken in *Adultery*; but as thefe are both
extraordinary, they only intimate, that it
was not ufual to write in that manner ; for
the Hand upon the Wall was miraculous, and
'tis probable our Saviour only ftoop'd down as
feeming to write, to put the *Phariſees* to a
Trial, and give the guilty Part of them leave
to obey their own Confciences, and make off.

WHEN they came to write on the Barks and
Rinds of Trees, and efpecially when they
wrote on folid Tables of Wood, fuch as principally Box, Walnut, Ebony, *Lignum Vitæ*,
and

and the like hard durable Subſtances, or Sorts
of Wood, the Inſtruments which they wrote
with were then made either of Bone, of Ivory,
or of Iron, and afterwards of Steel; and
hence it was called *Stylus:* An Account of
which is very accurately given, as well of its
Antiquity as of its Uſefulneſs, by the learned
and ingenious Mr. *Clark* of *Pennycook* in *Scotland*; a Gentleman, by his Studies and Travels, furniſh'd with many Kinds of uſeful
Learning; and who is ſince, by his real Merit, advanc'd to be one of the Barons of the
Exchequer in that Kingdom; to whoſe Book I
refer.

IT is to be obſerv'd withal, that during
theſe firſt Ages of Literature, Invention was
continually at work, to find out ſome more
convenient Method of Writing, as well relating to what they wrote upon, as what they
wrote with. Tho' they knew ſomething of
Letters, they were yet ſenſible, that farther
Improvements might be made, and that they
might ſtill underſtand one another better, if
they thought fit to ſearch into the Nature of
Writing, and the Method of performing it:
The *Egyptians* had long before fill'd the World
with their Manner of Writing, (*viz.*) by the
Figures of Things, and Shapes of living Creatures; theſe the *Greeks* call'd Ἱερογλυφικά;
and theſe were to give the like Sound to Words
as they bore in Speech by their uſual Forms,
and theſe before the Uſe of the *Papyri*, which
I have given an Account of, were engraven, or
cut in Stone; from whence *Lucan* expreſſes
himſelf thus;

——— Saxis tantum Volucre/q; feraque
Sculptáque fervabant magicas animalia linguas.

IT was, it feems, by thefe Figures, that
their Magicians and Sooth-fayers, or Wife
Men, *as they were called*, gave out their Conjurations, fomething like the Oracles which followed, by which they amufed the People, and
referv'd a *double Entendre* in all they faid, to
preferve the Reputation of their Skill if their
Interpretations of Things failed, or their Predictions did not come to pafs. This Way of
Writing, I fay, continued in the World a great
while after the Ufe of Letters was firft known;
and thofe Figures were for fome Time alfo
mingled with the Letters and Words which
they firft learn'd, and fo helped out one another.

IN like manner the *Greeks*, and the *Latins*
alfo, ufed Characters, or Marks, which they
call'd *Notæ*; and they were, as a farther Defcription of them called *Notæ Horopollinis Ni-
liaci*; of which the Inventor, or chief Artift,
at leaft, liv'd in the Time of *Theodofius*: Whether this was firft brought out of *Egypt*, or not,
as fome write that the whole Body of Gramma-
tick Learning was, is not to my purpofe now;
but that the *Greeks*, and *Romans* alfo, made
ufe of thefe *Notæ* in their firft Writings is manifeft; and we have many of them yet remaining in their Writings, the Signification of
which is known and remember'd; and they
were of two Kinds;

1. Meer invented Marks, fuch as this or
that eminent Writer of that Time legitimated

mated the Ufe of, as in *Tyro* and *Seneca pag.*
8. where a particular Mark is made ufe
of to fignify the Word *Rempublicam.* Alfo, according to that fame Author, another
for *Eo eft.*

2. Initial Letters placed for whole Words
were at firft ufed in private Writing, but
gradually appeared in Publick, being legitimated by Cuftom ; fuch as *E. Q. R.*
for *Eques Romanus. S. P. Q. R.* for *Sena-
tus Populufque Romanus.*

E N N I U S tells us, they invented, or introduc'd Eleven hundred fuch Marks as thefe
in his Time, into ufe in common Writing, befides many invented by Others; as by *Tyro,
Cicero, Libertus,* and the feveral Writers of
thofe Times, as *Eufebius* tells us; till the
Number of Inventors were fo many, that it
would be troublefome to the Reader to repeat
their Names, and till the Number of their
Marks amounted to above 5000, and grew
burthenfom to the World. A fuller Account
of this, and a fufficient Authority for what I
have faid of it, is included in a Speech, or
Prologue rather, of *Petrus Diaconus* to the Emperor *Conrad.*

" Nunc quis primus Notas inftituerit fcriba-
" mus. Vulgares notas Ennius primus mille
" ducentum invenit ; ad hunc fcilicet ufum, ut
" quicquid per contentionem præfentium di-
" ceretur, liberarii fcriberent complures fimul
" adftantes, divifis inter fé partibus, quæs
" quifque verba, & quo ordine exciperet. De-
" hinc Tullius Tyro, Ciceronis libertus, notas
" præpofitionum commentus eft. Poft hunc
" Philargyrus Samius, & aliqui (lego Aquila)

Mœcenatis

" Mœcenatis alias addiderunt. Deinde Luci-
" us Annæus Seneca, contractis omnibus, di-
" gesto & aucto numero, opus in quinque mil-
" lia extendit. " *Voſſius de Arte Grammatica,*
pag. 148, line 9.

HAVING thus mentioned the Marks and
Stamps uſed in Writing among ſeveral Perſons, and in particular Countries, I come to
ſpeak of the publick Marks or Stamps uſed
alſo, which were not particular to this or
that Country, or Language, but that were
univerſal, or common to all Languages in the
World, and theſe were of ſeveral Sorts; as,

1. The Figures uſed in Arithmetick, which
   are commonly call'd Cyphers, and are
   the ſame in moſt of the Languages in
   Europe.
2. The Marks of Aſtronomers, which are
   alſo univerſal in all Languages; ſuch as
   ♄ ♃ ♂ ☉ ♀ ☿ ☽ ; alſo the twelve Signs
   of the Zodiack ♈ ♉ ♊ ♋ ♌ and the reſt.
3. The ſeveral Marks in Muſick, directing
   the Meaſure of Notes, and the Tune, or,
   Conſonance, and Diſſonance of Sounds,
   which are likewiſe eſteem'd univerſal.

ALL theſe Modes of Writing are ſuppos'd
to reſpect the Infant Days of Letters, before
the Invention of Men carry'd thoſe Arts on
to the Perfection to which they are ſince arriv'd.

AFTER the Uſe of thoſe *Notæ,* or Marks,
which were uſual in the firſt Ages of Letters,
and which ſignify'd diſtinct Words, there were
Marks impreſs'd in the ſame Age, importing
whole Sentences; but thoſe were not ſo frequent, becauſe they laid too much Weight on
the

the Memory, and young Scholars did not so
easily understand them ; tho' it is true, it was
an easy Way in one respect ; because, like Figures, they were capable of being understood
alike in all, or in sundry Languages : Nor
was there more difficulty in making or inventing so many Marks, or *Notæ*, as above, than
there has been since of inventing Words in
every Language, to know them by ; the Number and Variety of which is incredible, and
which is a much greater load on the Memory
to those who learn other Languages, than in
reading their own. I say also, it was much
greater than that of charging the Head with
such a Number of Marks, which, as before,
were never above 5000 : Nay, if we may Credit *Nocholaus Trigaultius*, Hist. *Sinensis*, lib. 1.
cap. v. he says thus, *Non. pauciores Sinensibus
literas esse quam voces numerantur, eas tamen ita
inter se componere, ut* lxx *aut* lxxx *millia non ex-
cedant.* This indeed refers to the *Japoneses*, as
well as to the other ; but 'tis so that they perfectly understand one another both in Writing
and Reading.

I F it be true also, as *Paciano Barcellonensi*
says, That at the Confusion of Languages they
were from one universal Speech or Dialect,
divided into 120 ; or into lxxxii, as *Eusebius's*
Opinion delivers it, and Abundance of other
Authors ; then the Variety of Writings, and
the Number of Words, Stamps, Marks and
Characters among them all, when the Knowledge of Letters and of Writing came to spread
it self among them also, must be infinitely
great.

I might proceed from this to that Part
of the Art of Writing which the Learned
call

call the ορθογραφια, that is to say, of right placing the Letters, whether separate or in Syllables, and joining them as they ought to be joyned; this we call in a more vulgar way of expression, *Spelling*; but of this hereafter.

IT would be necessary now, to mention some of the various Characters, that is to say, forms of the Letters of the Alphabet, or of the various Alphabets which are in use in the several Languages, and the manner of their Writing them: There were at first, *generally speaking*, three ways of Writing, and no more, I mean, that were practis'd when the Knowledge of Letters came to spread it self in the World, for at first, 'tis certain, there was but one Method, and one Language.

THE first of these, and the most antient, is from the Right-hand to the Left; and this very Thing strongly confirms what I said before, namely, That the *Israelites* were the first who had the Knowledge of Letters, seeing we find none of those Languages which would be supposed to be of Antiquity, writing any other way but in a plain Imitation of the Hebrews, reading all from the Right to the Left, except the Hieroglyphicks of the *Egyptians*, which are said originally to stand promiscuous, and to be read in the Position which they were to be found in, without Order, or without any Sequence, except as the Nature of the Creature (describ'd,) intimated to them. For Example, if a Bird was painted flying upwards, then they read from the Head of the said Bird, to the Tail of the Creature which was next above him; and so if it were a Beast, or a Fish,

whether

whether walking or Swimming and the like: This, however Cuftom might have made it familiar to them, was in it felf very confufed, and intimated in the plaineft manner imaginable, that they were infinitely at a lofs for a Rule to make the Marks or Figures they ufed more intelligible.

THUS in their manner of Accounting, of which I have made mention before, and which, as I faid, was by Sticks or Reeds bundled up, it feem'd perfectly indifferent to the Perfon accounting, whether he reckon'd from the left to the right, or from the right Hand to the left, according to which Hand he laid out the Numbers of Reeds which he made his reckoning by.

BUT after the *Hebrews* had receiv'd the Knowledge of Letters from Heaven, as I have obferv'd, the *Egyptians* who not only convers'd with them more intimately than any other Nation, but even among whom a great many profelyted *Egyptians* liv'd, and others that went with them as Servants, for it is not to be doubted but that the great Wonders wrought by *Mofes* and *Aaron*, in the Name of God, in the *Egyptian* Court, and among the whole Nation, muft make a greater Impreffion upon fome of the People of the Country, than it did upon *Pharaob* and his Courtiers; and that many of them were fo convinc'd that the God of the *Hebrews* was the only true God, by thofe terrible Judgements, that they became Believers, and embrac'd the Religion and the God of the *Hebrews*, and followed them, or rather went with them, into and thro' the *Red Sea*; as we fee afterwards, the *Kenites*, the Pofterity

fterity of *Jethro Moſes* Father in Law, were found in the Camp of *Iſrael*, and had their Portion and Inheritance with them in the promis'd Land.

Thus the *Egyptians*, who, being proſelyted as above, went with the *Iſraelites* into the *Wilderneſs*, ſoon with the reſt learned the Knowledge of Letters at Mount *Sinai*; and by the ſame Rule correſponding afterwards with the *Egyptian* Country communicated that Knowledge to them in the firſt Place; and therefore we find the *Egyptians* were the firſt, who following the Example of *Iſrael*, tho' they might corrupt the Pattern, as without doubt they did, ſoon had an Alphabet and Letters of their own; from which afterwards the *Syriack* no doubt is derived.

There are, beſides thoſe, ſeveral barbarous Nations, who are ſaid alſo to be very antient, and whoſe Writings, if themſelves may be believ'd, are much more antient than in our Account the World it ſelf is ſuppoſed to be, and theſe write in a perpendicular Line from the Top of the Leaf to the Bottom, or as ſome ſay, from the Bottom of the Leaf to the Top.

These I do not find were ever receiv'd, either in *Europe*, or in that Part of *Aſia* which was within the Reach of the *Grecian* or *Roman* Empires, but is heard of chiefly among the *Chineſes*, and *Japoneſes*, who had no known Correſpondence with any Part of the civiliz'd Nations, 'till within a few Ages paſt, when Commerce ſeemed to have acquainted them a little with one another, and that not much neither.

And

AND yet even among thefe *Chinefes* and the *Barbarians* of the *Eaft*, there is to be found fome Affinity between the *Chaldee* Letters and theirs, fo much as that we may eafily perfwade our felves to believe, that the one were originally but a Corruption of the other; what might occafion the Alteration of the Progreffion in Writing, that we cannot account for, neither is it material.

THE Subjects of the Great *Mogul*, that is to fay, in that Part of the World we call more properly *India*, and feveral Nations of the flitting or moveable *Tartars*, make ufe of this manner of Writing, as alfo the Natives of *Siam*, *Pegu*, and *Sumatra*; if the latter have any Writing, or Ufe of Letters at all, which I do not find any good Authority for.

BUT to go back to the *Ifraelites*, while they continued in their wandering State, and poffibly had very little, if any, Correfpondence with the World, the *Egyptians* excepted, *with whom I doubt not they not only correfponded, but even traffick'd for neceffaries while they were in the Neighbourhood of them*; I fuppofe they kept the Knowledge of Letters among themfelves: But when they came into *Canaan*, and had an immediate, nay, a too intimate Correfpondence with the *Phenicians*, that is to fay, the *Canaanites*, they, in like manner learn'd from the *Ifraelites* the Knowledge of Letters.

HENCE, as I obferv'd at firft, the *Phenicians* fo early obtain'd the Knowledge of Letters, and fo mightily improv'd upon them, that *Cadmus*, a *Phenecian* Prince, travelling afterwards into *Greece*, and carrying with him a new form'd Alphabet of his own, but drawn from the general Theory of Letters, obtain'd

in

in his own Country from the *Hebrews*, obtain'd the Honour of being call'd the Inventor,
of all Letters in general; tho' as I have prov'd
before, the Tables of Stone at Mount *Sinai*,
were written by the Finger of God, some
Ages before *Cadmus* was Born.

HOWEVER, that we may give *Cadmus* and
his *Phenicians* their Due, they certainly were
the Inventors of a differing Method of writing, and forming the *Greek* Alphabet out of
the Corruption of the *Hebrew*, inverting the
Method; and thus the World came to Write
from the left Hand to the right, which is the
third Method of Writing.

CADMUS, indeed, carryed but 19 Letters
into *Greece*, the Rest were brought in a long
Time after, as I have noted already, several Years after the Destruction of *Troy*.
But the first and fundamental Letters of the
Greeks, were thus brought from the *Phenicians*,
and by them most certainly from the *Israelites*,
who over-ran the Country of *Canaan*, in so furious a Manner.

AND thus I think I have accounted for the
Original of Letters, in a manner consonant to
Reason and to History; nor do I meet with
any Thing material that is offered against my
Opinion: All that the Writers of a different
Opinion have yet said against it, amounts to
no more than this; that they do not think it
probable, that the World was for so many
Ages without so useful, and indeed so necessary an Art; and that the *Antediluvian* World,
who had such a Perfection of Knowledge, as
that some think we are not yet arriv'd to an
equal Degree of Improvement with them to
this Day, could not be suppos'd to be Ignorant to such a Degree as this.   BUT

B u t this is all begging the Queſtion. The Patriarchs of the *Antediluvian* State, were without Queſtion Maſters of Science, and had great Diſcoveries made to them, or were in-ſpir'd, let us call it what we will, with great Knowledge and Underſtanding; but this only proves that perhaps they might be, and 'tis poſſible they were bleſt with the Knowledge of Letters; but it does by no means prove that they really were ſo, and therefore we are but ſtill where we were, in all they can ſay for the Fathers of the old World.

I t is ſufficient, after all, that we have an Original, *a Pattern in the Mount*, which we know was handed to *Moſes*, from the Finger of God, and that no Hiſtory gives any Account that can be depended upon, or is more ratio-nal than this, that all the pretended Know-ledge of Letters before it, is without Ground, or ſo much as Probability; and ſo far were they from having left any Remains behind them, of that Knowledge, that their Poſterity valued themſelves infinitely upon, that dull un-performing, and as we may call it, Dumb Lan-guage of *Hieroglyphicks*, and Images of Crea-tures, making the Brutes Speak for them, when at the ſame Time they knew not how to form any proper Character for Words, or to which the Sound of Words might be appropiated.

A n d if this was not the Caſe, how came it to paſs, that whereas before this great Diſco-very from *Heaven*, they were driven to ſuch Shifts for want of an Alphabet, and for want of the Knowledge of Letters, on the contrary as ſoon as the *Hebrew* was once dictated, and the Children of *Iſrael* were taught to write, immediately all the World follow'd the Ex-ample,

ample, and every Nation borrowing the general Syſtem, or the Idea of Writing from the
Hebrews, began to Write, and tho' they proceeded to forming different Alphabets to themfelves, as if they were for improving after that
the Invention, and had every one their differing way of Writing, yet the Thing it felf it was
apparent came all from this happy Original.

AND as the very fiſft Thought came from
hence, fo did the Method of it, (*viz.*) the Prolation and joyning the Letters to form Syllables,
and then rejoyning thoſe Syllables to form
Words of many Syllables, alſo the Manner of
Writing or Impreſſing thoſe Letters and Words
to make them legible to others, (*viz.*) by Excoriation, or Inciſion, or Impreſſion, which
we come next to conſider.

PART VI.

HAVING thus ſpoken of the Original of
Letters and of the Method of Writing,
it comes of Courſe to ſay ſomething of the Materials of Writing and Printing, not as they
were us'd in the Infancy of the Art only, for
that has been mention'd, but as they have
been uſed ſince Men came to an ordinary Skill
and Improvement in the Art of Managing,
Placing, Coupling and Spelling the Letters,
call'd as I have ſaid above

FROM the *Papyri*, a Weed growing as I
have ſaid on the Banks of the *Nile*, came the
Word *Paper* in our Language, not that this
was

was really made into Paper, such as we now use, as some think; for the Leaves were at least a Cubit or a Cubit and half in Length, and of unequal shape and Substance, and were as I have shewn, pull'd in Pieces, and several Operations about them perform'd before they were fitted for Use: But as from hence, *for ought we know*, the true Method of Paper-making was deriv'd, which is it self very antient; so from hence all Compositions of any kind made to form any Thing to write upon, were, when finish'd, call'd *Paper*.

BUT let me examine then, by what Methods, and by what slow Degrees, the Knowledge and Use of Paper to write upon came into the World: From Tables of Stone, and from the Leaves and Barks of Trees, *as I have noted above*, they came to the Use of Tables of Wood, that is to say, thin Boards cut out of the Body of a Tree; these were either *Tabellæ Nudæ*, plain naked Boards, or Boards cover'd or polish'd over with Wax or Rosin, or such other Substance as they usually cover'd them with, in those Days. There were many Sorts of these Tables also, some very thick and coarse, upon which the Boys at the Schools usually wrote or learned their Lessons.

OTHERS they made thin and fine, and polish'd them, to be the fitter for receiving the Impression of the Stylus or Pen.

Secta nisi in tenues essemus ligna tabellas.
                    Mart. lib. xiv.

This is fully explain'd, in that memorable Text of apocryphal Scripture,

G   2 Esdras

2 Efdras, chap. xiv. ver. 24, 25, 26. *But look thou prepare thee many box-trees, and take with thee* Sarea, Dabria, Selemia, Ecanus, *and* Afiel, *thefe five which are ready to write fwiftly ; and come hither, and I fhall light a candle of underftanding in thine heart, which fhall not be put out, till the things be performed which thou fhalt begin to write. And when thou haft done, fome things fhalt thou publifh, and fome things fhalt thou fhew fecretly to the wife : to morrow this hour fhalt thou begin to write.* Ver. 42, 44. *The Higheft gave underftanding unto the five men, and they wrote the wonderful vifions of the night that were told, which they knew not : and they fat forty days, and they wrote in the day, and at night they eat bread. In forty days they wrote two hundred and four Books.* By this it appears, there were Writers in thofe Days who wrote fwifter, by which I underftand alfo fhorter, than others : What Books they wrote is evident from the 24th Verfe, where he is bid to bring many Box-Trees with him, as well as Writers ; this in the Margin of fome of our Bibles, is explain'd in direct Words to be Box-Tables to write on, or Tables made of Box-Wood, which confirms alfo what has been faid of thofe Tables in the former Part of this Work : What the Books were, of which two Hundred and Four, our Margin fays nine Hundred and Four, could be written in forty Days by five Men, is not fo eafy to determine.

THERE were alfo fmall Pieces of Boards fmooth'd and polifh'd for Bills, or other fuch fmaller Occafions, which did not require whole Tables, thefe were call'd *Codices*, and fmaller yet *Codicils*, as we at this Day call a fmall Piece of Parchment annext to a Will ; and
thefe

thefe were call'd fo becaufe made out of the Body or Stump of a Tree ; and hence from *Caudex* a Book was call'd *Codex*, and the Collection of Laws by *Theodofius*, *Juftinian*, and others are call'd *Codes*.

The *Danes*, in Confirmation of this, call Books in their Language *Boger*, which indeed is the Original of the Word Boke or Book, and which fignifies in *High-Dutch*, a *Eeech-Tree*, becaufe the publick Acts were imprefs'd, or ftamp'd, or mark'd, or written, *call it which we will*, upon Boards made of Beech and polifh'd very fmooth: See *Olaus Wormius, in Faftis Danicis*, lib. 1. cap. 6. Thefe were call'd Wax'd-Tables, becaufe the Beechen Boards were crufted over or polifh'd with Wax, and to this Day our Faniering Artifts or Cabinet-Makers, polifh over the Olive-Wood, Ebony, and Walnut-Tree, which covers and adorns their Work ; I fay, they polifh it over with Wax, and the fame may be written on very legibly and well.

Next to Books and Tables thus made of the Wood or Bark of Trees, the Antients came to write upon Linnen, and rather before that upon the Skins of Beafts, which we now call *Vellum* and *Parchment*; but this laft was a kind of Accident, and never came into general ufe for the making of Books. This Linnen was called *Lintcum* from *Linum*, the Flax, of which it was made ; this Linnen *Pliny* tells us, was put into, or dipt in Oil, as the Cloths are which the Limner or Painter now prepares to draw a fine Picture on, *Pliny* lib. xiii. cap. xi. Of thefe, when they were very fine, fev al large Volumes of Books were made, on which the *Oracula Sibyllina* were written, *Symmachus*, lib. iv. Epift. xxxiv.

ALSO

ALSO the publick Leagues between Princes and States, were written in this Manner, that is to fay, upon that Linnen Cloth dipt in Oil, fee *Tit. Livius* lib. xxxi. Alfo, *Conftantine* caufed the Laws of the Empire to be thus written; as alfo Epiftles of private Princes one to another, *Flav. Vopifcus in Aureliano*; his Words are, *Inveni Nuper in Ulpia bibliotheca, inter linteos libros epiftolam D. Valeriani.*

OTHERS wrote upon a Paper made of a Subftance like a Caul taken from the Bowels, or Gut of any Beaft; they were call'd *Elephantinos Libros*, which alfo fome took to be Leaves of Ivory; but it was taken both ways; for it was a Book or Paper made of the Skin of a Beaft, whether Sheep, Goat, or Calf; or of a Gut, or other thick glutinous Subftance, fuch as the Caul was, and which being dried by the Heat of the Sun became hard and folid, and on thefe they frequently wrote; and fuch were thofe Manufcripts in the *Hebrew* Tongue, which *Eleazer*, the High Prieft of the *Jews*, fent to *Ptolemy Philadelphus*, and which were curioufly written on Parchment or Vellum, as *Jofephus* fays expreffly, *lib.* xii. *Antiq. Judaic.* And yet *Pliny* fays, as I have obferv'd before, which is a little ftrange, that the King of *Pergamos* invented Parchment to write upon, becaufe *Ptolemy Philadelphus* prohibited the Carrying the *Papyri* out of his Dominions.

BUT to leave that, let *Jofephus* anfwer for the Inconfiftency *if there is any*; for 'tis equally ftrange which we read in *Varro*, that the Battles of *Alexander* were written on Paper and carried to the Egyptian *Alexandria*; and this Paper was in Ufe long before thofe Times; but then it was the Paper only which was

made

made of the Egyptian Weed *Papyrus*, that is to say, it had the name *Paper*, but was nothing of the Kind now in Use, or so much as like it.

FROM these Times, therefore, when Parchment came to be in full Use, Writing encreased and improved exceedingly: and then they soon came from the linnen Cloth, to make Paper of the Substance of the linnen Cloth, (*viz.*) the Lint or Flax itself, pressed, and bruised, and beaten fine in an Engine or Mill, and then mixed up again with Gums, and such glutinous Substance, as brought it to be a *firm Leaf* as we see at this Day. For tho' much of our Paper, in this Country, is made of the Rags of old Linnen beaten to Pumice; so the Paper also now, *that is to say the greatest Quantity of it*, is made of Flax, which is one of the first Principles in the making Linnen, and this Flax is esteemed to make better Paper than that of Rags.

FROM the Paper, we come next to speak of the liquid Substance which we call Ink ; and with which those, who make Use of Paper, Parchment, or linnen Cloth, write upon them ; of this there has not been much Variety. The first Ink we find in Story, was made of the Blood or Juice which was found in the Fish called *Loligo*, which some call a *Calamary*, others more vulgarly the *Cuttle-Fish*, and whose Blood casts a fix'd Black Colour, tingeing the Paper or Parchment with a durable Black; this is by some call'd *Niger Succus*, a Black Juice; by others the Blood of a Fish ; and this was used instead of Ink, whence the *Germans* call this Creature in the old *Gothick* Language d'INTENFISCH, or in English, the *Ink-Fish*. *Pliny* tells us also of a Fish call'd

the

the *Sepia*, whose Blood is as Black as Ink; but he does not say it will tinge or dye any Thing Black as the *Loligo* does. *Perseus* mentions this in his 3 Sat.

——— ——— *Sepia lympha*
Dilutas querimur geminet quod fistula guttas.

THIS *Sepia*, or *Ink-Fish*, is found on the Coast of *Lancashire* in *England*, and formerly was more frequent there than it is now; of which the learned Dr. *Leigh*, in his natural History of *Lancashire* and *Cheshire*, gives the following Account.

‘ The next remarkable Fish, says he, is the
‘ *Sepia*, or *Ink-Fish*, of which I have seen se-
‘ veral upon these Shores. It has ten Horns,
‘ not much unlike those of a Snail, and with
‘ these, as with Oars, it rowes it self for-
‘ ward in the Water: It has two full Eyes.
‘ Its Substance seems to be a Kind of Pulp,
‘ and one Half of it is invested with a Mem-
‘ brane like a Leg within a Stocking; and
‘ therefore by some it is call’d the *Hose* or
‘ *Stocking-Fish*. It has only one Bone, and
‘ that upon its Back, thin, flat, and pellu-
‘ cid. From its Mouth descends two pellucid
‘ Ducts, which terminate in a *Vesica* which
‘ contains its Ink; by pressing this, the Ink
‘ quickly ascends, and as some Naturalists af-
‘ firm, when they are in Danger of being Ta-
‘ ken, by contracting this, they discharge
‘ such a Quantity of Ink as blackens the Wa-
‘ ter and secures them from Discovery. I have
‘ a Letter by me, written with this Ink about
‘ ten Years ago, which still continues. This
‘ Liquor was the Ink of the Ancients; hence
came

' came that Expreſſion of the Poet, *Nigro diſ-*
' *tillans Sepia nodo.* It has no remarkable
' Taſte, and by Reaſon that the Whole ſeems to
' be a Kind of Pulp, it is hard to determine
' whether this Liquor is its *Chyle,* or perhaps
' the Juice of ſome Sea Plant which it lives
' upon, or elſe a Liquor ſeparated from its nu-
' tritive Juices ; for what elſe to term it I
' know not, ſince I could not obſerve in it ei-
' ther Veins or Arteries ; yet doubtleſs there
' are other Veſſels adequate to thoſe. This
' Fiſh, ſometimes, the People eat ; and it is
' obſervable that it will mildly Purge them
' like *Caſſia,* or ſome ſuch *Lenitive.* '

To go back from thoſe, farther to the com-
mon People, theſe, as alſo the ordinary School-
Maſters and Students made their uſual com-
mon Ink of the Soot out of the Chimneys ; but
States Men, and Men of better Sort, uſed the
Blood of the *Sepia* as above.

Again, the Ink with which they often
wrote Books, but eſpecially the Titles and
capital Letters in Books, was of another Sort,
and was of a Red colour inſtead of Black, but
this was leſs uſed than the Black. Theſe
Things they made ſhift with, for ought I can
find in any ancient Writings, 'till they found
out the proper Ingredients for Ink as we now
uſe it. As for Printing Ink, which is a Thing
by it ſelf, and quite differing from the write-
ing Ink, as it was a modern Invention, and
arriv'd to with, or ſince the Knowledge of
Printing it ſelf, which is much more modern
than the Times we are now ſpeaking of, I
leave that to be mentioned again in its Place.

Before the Uſe of Ink, they wrote by
Way of Racing, or Cutting, or Scratching,

the

the Substance which they wrote upon, which I mentioned before, where I term'd it an Excoriation; and this as it was done in various Forms or Methods, so by several and very differing Instruments.

WHILE they wrote upon the Barks of Trees, and upon Tables, and especially on the wax'd or polish'd Tables; as also while they wrote on the *Tilia* they used the *Stilus*, a Pen or Instrument made first of Iron, sometimes of Bone, sometimes of Ivory; this was used I say in Writing on such hard Substances as requir'd an Incision or Cutting, and was called *Graphium*, and as afterwards the Writings on Stone or Tables of Wood required it, this *Stylus* or *Graphium* was the only Instrument But there follow'd great Inconveniencies upon this, for the *Stylus* being made of Iron, and some of them being fork'd and having divers sharp Points, the Boys who learned to Write would often quarrel and wound one another with them, and even Men also, for they were really very dangerous Weapons.

THE Accidents which happened on this Occasion, were so many, and some of them so fatal, that the *Romans* were oblig'd to forbid the Use of them, that is to say of Iron; after which others were invented made of the Teeth of Fishes and of the Bones of Beasts, and lastly, as above, of Ivory.

As to the Authority given for the Report of Mischief done with the *Stylus*, the Persons writing with them having frequently Wounded others with them, *Plutarch* expresses it fully in *Gracchis*, and among the *Romans*, *Martial*, and several other Writers of those Times.

Hàc

Hàc tibi erant armata suo Graphiaria ferro.
Si puero dones, non leve munus erit.

Mart. Epig. xxi.

But beyond all this, *Suetonius* and *Plutarch*
also in several of their Writings say, that
Casca wounded *Cæsar* in the Senate House, not
with a Dagger but with a *Stylus* or Roman
Pen of Iron, or perhaps of Steel.

Plut. *in Appianum.*
Cassi Brachium arreptum graphio Cæsar trajecit.
Suetonius *in vit.* Jul. Cæs. 82.

It was a Felicity to the People of *Rome*,
that these Instruments for Writing grew useless in a few Years, by the Improvement of
the Age, and the better Materials they had to
write upon ; for in a few Years they wrote no
more by Incision or Impressing, by Raceings
and Excoriations, but by moist Juices tin-
ging the Materials, and on proper smooth Substances fit to receive the Tincture, such as
those I have mentioned, (*viz.*) the Blood of
Fishes, and Decoctions of Soot and other Ingredients.

As the Use of Parchments, and of the *Papyri*, and of the *Tilia*, which some have mistaken for *Tilea*, but was only a thin Substance, or a Kind of Skin lying between the
outer Bark and the Body of a certain Tree ; I
say, as the Use of these came into the World,
the *Stylus*, and all other Instruments which
work'd by Incision or Impression were laid by,
and in a little more Time became useless ; and
how many Kings and Emperors soever have
been

been ftab'd by the Pen, a dangerous Inftrument in its kind; yet none more will ever be ftabb'd by it, as an offenfive Weapon, as it feems had been the Cafe before.

SOME think it was of this Manner of Writing, by Incifion, and of the *Stylus* of Iron which *Job* Speaks, Chap. xix. *Oh that my words were now written! Oh that they were printed in a Book! That they were graven with an iron pen and lead, in the rock for ever!* But I think that thefe were only tranflated according to the Author that wrote the Book; for as to the beft Account we have of *Job* himfelf, he lived and died before the Knowledge of Letters was in the World, and the Pen-Man of his Hiftory might be allow'd to Exprefs the Senfe of the Good Man in the Manner of the Age in which he then wrote.

From this Time, the ingenious Part of the World, having found feveral Ways for the Writing of Books upon Materials foft and fmooth, which required no Incifion, the Ufe of thefe Inftuments grew obfolete and fit to be forgotten; and they now ferve for no more than to be remembred among the Monuments of Antiquity, as we now fpeak of them.

PART VII.

HAVING thus given an Account, or rather fome Account of the Writings of the Ancients, and brought them out of the Infant Days of this Art, it will not be amifs to fpeak

a little of the general Ufage of the World,
from the Time that they came to the plain
Ufe of Pen, Ink and Paper, to the Time when
the Invention of the Printing Prefs, and the
Ufe of Types for impreffing the Letters *as
Written*, was found out in the World, taking
up an Interval of above 1500 Years at leaft ;
for the Writing with Pen and Ink was faid to
be known the latter End of the Reign of *Auguftus*, tho' not in Perfection 'till fome Years
after ; (for in St. *Luke*, we find *Zacharias* cal-
ling for *a writing Table*) whereas the Art of
Printing was invented in the Year 1420, by
one *Lawrence Cofter* a Soldier of *Harlem*, who
after he had found the firft Font or Foundiary
of Types or Letters, and had not fully put
them in Ufe, had them ftollen from him by
his Servant, who carried them into *Germany*,
and there claimed to be the Inventor of them,
and having fet up a Prefs, *Tully's Offices* was
the firft Book that ever was Printed in the
World. But this by the way.

ALL Intelligence, Commerce, and Correfpondence in the World, was now managed by
the *Pen*, *Ink*, and *Paper* ; the Works of the Ancients were all written by their own Hands, or
by the help of Clerks and Amanuenfes ; infinite Numbers of thefe People we now call
copying Clerks, were employ'd to make Coppies of valuable Books ; and if it be True,
that there were 12000 Copies of *Virgil's*
Æneid, made in *Auguftus's* Days, and twice as
many of *Ovid's* Metamorphofis, what innumerable numbers of Hands had been employ'd in
thofe daily Works, and of what Labours, and
what multitudes muft that *Alexandrian* Library be Compofed, if there really was fuch a
Thing ;

Thing; for the doubt is far from being refolv'd
to this Day.

THE Regifters and Records of Nations muft
be all written in the fame Manner ; all the
Works of the Ancients, and all the Copiers
of thofe valuable Works which were in themfelves innumerable, muft have been made in
the fame manner. It would be endlefs to reckon them up, but let us Name a few. The
Works of *Homer*, *Hefiod*, *Herodotus*, of *Livy*,
of *Jofephus*, of the feveral *Plutarchs*, of *Cicero*,
Julius Cæfar's Commentaries, of the Poets,
Ovid, *Tibullus*, *Perfins*, *Juvenal*, *Lucan* and
Virgil, with innumerable more : Among the
Hebrews, the *Bible*, the *Talmuds*, as well the
Babylonian as the *Jerufalem Talmud*. To what
purpofe fhould we enumerate the Particulars,
ancient Hiftory is full of their Names and
Works; how voluminous they are, and yet how
often were they written over.

IN the Exercife of fo much Writing, it is no
Wonder if fome were very dextrous, and were
as much Mafters of the Pen as their Authors
were of the Tongue. And as we have feen
fome Things moft accurately done in the Art
of Writing, within Five or Six hundred Years
back from the prefent Time, there can be no
Room to doubt, but that there was the like in
the World many Years before that. And it
muft be acknowledg'd, that 'tho the Manner
is much different, and there are very fine
Things done with the Pen in this Age, yet
that in the former Ages they greatly excell'd
us. But I fhall have occafion to fpeak of this
Part again more fully in its Courfe.

NEXT to the Manner of Writing, and the
Materials, it becomes neceffary to enquire a
little

little into the Meafure of Words, which we call Prolation, the giving proper Sounds and Quantities to the Letters, either joyned together or apart.

This certainly came from Heaven with the Letters themfelves, and the Power which infpir'd Mankind with the Knowledge of the Letters neceffarily adapted them to their Sounds, and empowered thofe Sounds to carry with them the Signification of the Letters. Hence came the Diftinction of Letters into Vowels and Confonants, which are fo married together in the Art of Reading, that no Man can feparate them: The Vowel like the Husband to the Wife, giving Cadence of Sound, Diction and Expreffion to the Confonant; and the Confonant being Capable of no Sound without the Conjunction of the Vowel to govern the Voice and make a Harmony, and is therefore call'd *Confonant* or agreeing, joyning and affifting to the Sound of the Word.

It is fomething furprizing, to think how this Cadence of Sounds, and how the Joyning of Syllables, in compounded Words, came to be formed in the Underftandings of Men; nothing but the being fatisfy'd that it was form'd above and came down from Heaven, could reconcile us to the Wonder of it.

The writing Words, in all Languages, agreeable to the Idiom of every refpective Tongue, joining them in Monofyllables, joining the Monofyllables again into compounded Words, and giving every Letter its right Place, with its Accent or Emphafis, is a furprifing Thing in the Nature of it, and if fully and ferioufly confidered, carries us beyond

yond Nature it felf, ending only in Aftonifh-
ment and an unrefolv'd Wonder. This is what
the *Greeks* underftand by the Word 'Ορθογραφια,
and which from them we call to this Day
Orthography.

To enter far into this Part, would be to enquire into the Grammar of every Tongue,
and with *Voffius*, to write *de Arte Grammatica,*
which is not my Bufinefs here ; but to fpeak
of correct Writing feems abfolutely neceffary,
feeing if there was cxx feveral Languages into
which the firft univerfal Way of Speaking
was divided ; there are for ought we fee now,
cxx thoufand Ways of Speaking, (*viz.*) fo many differing Idioms and Dialects of Speech
which Men now make Ufe of in the World ;
fome Languages, nay moft Languages being
again fubdivided into many differing Ways of
Expreffion ; in all which, 'tis Evident, that
long living in any one Country, generally
naturalizes the Speech of that Country fo to
our Ear, that we foon make it our own, and
even forget that which was formerly our Mother Tongue.

But we have in *Great-Britain,* Befides
the real and folid Variety of Tongues, fuch as
the *Welch* or ancient *Britains,* the *Cornifh,* the
Highland Scots and the like ; I fay we have
fuch a Variety in the Expreffion of cur own
Mother Tongue, as that in fome Counties of
England, they can very ill underftand one a-
nother ; how the Orthographifts can manage
this in all Languages is not very eafy to def-
cribe.

On the other Hand, many Tongues, as the
Englifh we now fpeak for Example, having
no Grammatical Syntax, no Rule for the Meafures

ſures or Quantities of Words or Letters, by Conſequence have no Authorities for the Uſages of their Speech; but all is Aſſumption, legitimated only by Cuſtom, which is Judge of the Orthography, as it is of the Propriety of Speech; and were it not that this Cuſtom does as it were legitimate the Orthography, we ſhould be confounded in writing many Words in the *Engliſh* Tongue, where Words bearing the ſame Sound, ſignify various Things; as particularly in the Words, *Two, Tow, Too, To, Then, Than, Bow, Bow, Bough,* and many others.

Two, Signifying 2 in Number.

Tow,   *Flax* or *Tow,* made of *Flax.*

Too,   Too much or too long.

To,   To go to any Place, or give any Thing to a Perſon.

Bow,   To Bow in Compliment, or make a Bow, or to bend any ſtraight Thing into a Curve or Arch, differing its Poſture from what it was before.

Bow,   A Bow to ſhoot an Arrow.

Bough,   The Bough of a Tree.

Bough,   The Barking of a Dog.

Right,   The right Hand.

Right,   Juſt or to do Right.

Right,   Oppoſite to, or over againſt.

Wright, A Wheel Wright, or a Ship (*viz.*) a Carpenter.   *Wright,*

Write,   To write a Letter.

Then,   Time, as *then it was ſo.*

Than,   A compariſon (*viz.*) *better than another.*

A s

As these are the Usages of Speech, and that no Rule is to be found for the Direction of the Speaker, other than that so it is accustom'd to be, a Stranger has nothing to trust to for the Learning these Things, or how to write them, but by the Strength of his Memory.

The more Grammatical Languages, such as the *Latin*, the *Greek*, and other *Eastern* Languages, having establish'd Rules by which these are all regulated, the Difficulty is not so great, and they have no more to do than to place those Rules before them.

But, as I said, it is possible for People to forget even their own native Speech, and likewise to forget the Manner of Writing it. They tell us that the *Hebrews* who were captivated by the *Chaldeans*, and continued so Seventy Years, lost so much of the Original *Hebrew*, that except the Priests and learned Men whom they call'd Rabbies, the common People never recover'd the Use of it ; and therefore the *Hebrew* which the *Rabbies* retain'd in its Purity, is call'd, by Way of Distinction, the *Rabbinical Hebrew* ; and this is taught to the Children of the *Levites* and others at their Schools, whereas the *Jews* in common used the *Chaldaic* or *Syriac* Tongues, and at last the *Greek* ; and to this Day the *Rabbinical Hebrew* is no where found but in the Writings of their *Rabbies*, and in some ancient Manuscripts of their Law ; and whether any of those are now extant, which if they are, must be above 2200 Year old is very hard to determine. The Orthography then of every Language, as the Tongues in Use now are governed by received Custom, is so uncertain, that nothing can instruct the

Writing

Writing of thofe Languages, but a thorough learning and acquainting themfelves with the Languages themfelves, and the Cuftoms and Ufages which are allow'd in them.

IN this Difficulty we find the Writings or MSS. of divers Languages in *Europe*, not only written after a different Manner, but that the feveral Inhabitants fpell thofe Languages, or feveral Words in them, after a different Manner from one another ; and this I mean not of the unlearned Common People, for they feldom are able to fpell their own Country Language, and oftentimes not to pronounce theWords of it, which is the Reafon of fo many different Brogues upon their Tongues, and of fo many different Dialects in one and the fame Speech, and even in one and the fame Country: For Example,

THE *Normans* and *Walloons* in *France*, and the *Gafcoigns*, between *France* and *Spain*, the People of *Bearn*, and the People of *Bretaign* ; all of them have a different Way of Speaking, and fome fo different from the other, or from all the Reft, as not eafily to underftand one another, tho' the Language is ftill all of it call'd *French*.

THE like it is in *Spain*, the *Bifcayners* fpeak one Dialect, the *Caftilians* another, the *Catalans* a third, and the *Navarrois* a fourth, the *Audalufians* a fifth, and yet all is call'd *Spanifh*.

Even in *Italy* itfelf, as the *Italian* is a grofs Mixture of Tongues, as well as a Corruption of the *Latin*, fo what a Mixture of Dialects is there among them ? The *Calabrians* fpeak one Kind of *Italian*, the *Genoefes* another, the *Savoyards* a third, and the *Venetians* a fourth.

Nor is this all, but the Writing of thefe Languages differs in itfelf from what it was in former Years: The Authors in *French* in the Time of *Charlemaigne*, or in *Englifh* in *Edward* the Confeffor's Time, nay, and even to the Time of *Henry* the VII are fcarce to be underftood now, and their Words are called *old French* and *old Englifh*. I might give Inftances of the like Changes in all the Languages in *Europe*, they being all refin'd, and render'd more polite fince thofe Times than they were then.

With all thefe Improvements the Orthography of the Languages has alfo taken its fhare, to the bettering of the Speech, and perhaps may be like to do the fame in the Ages that are to come, Speech being ftill capable of farther Embellifhments.

It remains then, in order to clofe this Difcourfe, that we only enter a little upon the Manner of Pen and Ink Writing, and its feveral Ufages, Improvements, and Excellencies in the World; the Beauties of it, and the Perfection it was brought to, till it received a fatal Baulk in the ftill more exquifite, tho lefs difficult, Art of Printing: And tho' this will not require fo laborious a Search into Antiquity, nor fhall I have an occafion to quote fo many, or indeed any, Authors for the Enquiry; yet there will be found a certain fecret Excellence in the Art of Penmanfhip, which will never fail to recommend it to the Ingenious part of the World, and caufe the Artifts in it to be valued in all Countries, and in all Ages; of which in its Place.

PART

PART VIII.

BEING now come to the Manner of Writing, and the Ufe and Improvement of
it as an Art, I muft, according to the Method
of the Learned *Voffius*, obferve, that there
were antiently two Sorts of Writing, *Apertus*
and *Opertus* ; *Apertus*, or common and apparent,
or *Opertus*, that is hidden and occult, or fecret:
I mention this to *Note*, that the latter of thefe,
which fome pretend to, as a rare or a new Dif-
covery, as if it was born with them, and had
no other Parent but in their ingenious Brain,
as they would have it be thought, was yet as
antient as the firft Ages of Paper Writing ;
which I fhall fhew prefently.

THIS occult Writing was at firft ufed upon
the Occafion of Publick Difpatches, and Bufinefs of Moment in the State only, and was
called *Steganography*, being kept as a Secret
among fome particular Perfons, and this was
of two Sorts. (1) *Vifible*, but written in unknown Figures or Charaéters ; or new made
Words, contrived on purpofe for the Occafion ;
this *Steganography* we now call *Cypher*, of which
all the Perfons to or from whom fuch Writings
are fent, muft have the Counterpart, which in
fome Cafes is call'd the *Key*, to write by, or read
it by ; This is as antient as Writing itfelf, and
more antient than the Ufe of Paper. (2) The
other Sort of occult or fecret Writing, is *Invifible*,
or unfeen at firft, being written with certain

Liquids

Liquids compounded for that Purpofe, and which, tho' not to be feen at firft, yet by a certain Art to be known to, and ufed by the Perfon to whom it is written, fhall be made to fhew itfelf afterwards, as plain and vifible as other Writings.

Of thefe Kinds there were feveral differing Sorts, as (1) Some that could not be feen by Daylight, being written with Water diftill'd from *Nitre*, and putrified or rotten *Willows*; the Words written with which, would caft a Kind of light like the Phofphorus, and were only to be read in the dark: Others could not be read unlefs they were held up againft a Candle, or againft the Stars, and then were eafily feen: Others might indeed be feen by Day, the Ink they were written with not requiring the Air to illuminate it; but then firft it was neceffary to ufe fome other Preparation to joyn with, and fetch out to Sight, the Tinge or Colour of the firft Writing, that is to fay Earth, or Water, or Fire, or perhaps fome of all thefe artfully mixt together.

Some have written in this Manner with the milky Juice of the Herb *Tithymalus*, or *Sea-Thiftle*, which is alfo by our Simplers call'd the *Milk-Thiftle*, of which *Pliny* fpeaks in his *Natural Hiftory*, lib. xxvi. cap. viii. Others have found the Milk of fome living Creatures that would perform the fame Operation; others with the Fat or Oil of Bodies of Animals; others with Urine, or with fome Gums, which mixt with the Tallow or Fat of the Creatures would do the fame thing: All which Kinds of Writings were not vifible when plain and unmixt, the Subftance of them lay on the Surface of the Paper, but were thus difcover'd:

viz.

viz. The Perſon who was to read them was to ſprinkle ſome fine Duſt or Sand upon them, colour'd or ting'd with black or red, and that Duſt lodging upon the Writing, which was ſoft and glutinous, but not on the Intervals of the Paper, which were clean and dry, would thereby diſcover the Writing to the Eye.

OTHERS of theſe ſecret Writings were done with *Allom*, or with *Vitriol*, and theſe had another particular Quality, namely, that being at firſt perfectly conceal'd and inviſible, they were to be dipt in Water, or in Wine prepared by Art for that purpoſe, before they could be read ; and ſome again of theſe could not be read unleſs dipt in Water prepar'd with *Quickſilver* or *Mercury*.

FOR ſome of theſe Compoſitions Fire was neceſſary to be uſed to make the Letters appear, and make them legible ; as when the Ink or Liquid they wrote with was made of the Juices drawn from *Lemons* or *Citrons*, *Onions*, *Cherries*, the Herb *Cyclamen*, or other acid Fruits or Plants ; which tinge or contact the Surface of the Paper, and which by the help of Fire are made apparent; of all theſe artificial Ways of Writing, and of many other, we have a full Account, *Apud Jo. Baptiſtam Portam Neapolitanum*, lib. xvi. *Mag. Nat.*

THE viſible Writing requires no Art to deſcribe the Subject of it ; ſufficient has been ſaid already : It conſiſts either of Letters or Marks call'd *Notæ* ; of the laſt I have ſpoken already, what remains relates to the various Kinds of Letters. The Kinds which we beſt know are the *Hebrew*, the *Chaldee*, or *Syriack*, or *Arabick*, which differ little from one another ; the *Greek*, which differs from all the reſt.

and

and the *Latin* or *European :* This *Latin* or *European*, which is beſt known to us, is divided in its ſeveral Characters, tho' with very little Difference in the *Alphabet*, ſuch as the *Roman*, the *Italick*, and the *Gothick*; theſe (ſince Printing was invented) are more particularly diſtinguiſh'd, but were, even when all Things were written by the Pen, diſtinguiſh'd into the *Roman*, and the *Italian*, and the *Text-hand*, of which we ſhall ſpeak again in their Places.

THERE were other Characters in former Times, in Uſe in this very Country, and ſome are ſtill remaining, which are ſcarce legible to us, and yet are eſtabliſh'd upon the *Roman* Alphabet, ſuch as the *Saxon* and the *Iriſh*; the laſt is ſtill in uſe among the Highlanders of *Scotland*, and the *Bible* is printed in that Character, which none but themſelves can read. But it would be endleſs to enter here into the ſeveral Characters which have been written in *England*, and which have been written in other Countries alſo, which are now obſolete and almoſt forgotten ; 'tis enough to obſerve that there were excellent Writers in all theſe Times, who wrote thoſe Characters in a manner ſo fine and ſo exact, that no Writers can be found in our Time that can equal them, much leſs outdo them; and ſome antient Manuſcripts ſhow ſtill the Remains of the excellent Writers of thoſe Ages.

ESPECIALLY in the Text-writing or *Gothick*, of which ſome ancient Manuſcripts are ſtill to be ſeen, done with ſuch Exactneſs, and with ſuch exquiſite Art, as nothing can come up to them (that I can meet with) in this Age; and tho' there are ſome very good Artiſts ſtill in the World, and who are great Maſters of of Penmanſhip, eſpecially in other Hands, *as we call them*, yet nothing excels them: There is alſo Writing by Engravement, performed by a Tool. This is an Inciſion upon braſs or copper Plates, and is an Art of another Kind, and will come under our Conſideration when we ſpeak of Printing, Stamping, or Impreſſing, which is a Work by itſelf.

As we have ſeveral Kinds of Writing the ſame Characters in our ordinary Way, ſo we have a ſingular Way of expreſſing the Difference by the Word *Hand*; it is true that Writing is an Art or Operation more particularly perform'd by the Hand; but to call it by that as a Sirname, and to make the Word Hand be a Term of Art, as it is ungrammatical, ſo it muſt be confeſs'd 'tis without Example or Authority: The Abſurdity is apparent from the following Accident in Story, which there are many living Witneſſes at this Time to prove the Truth of.

' There was a famous Fellow went about
' this Iſland to ſhew himſelf for Money, who
' was a *German*, or rather a *Swiſs* by Birth,
' named *Buchinger*, who not only had no
' Hands, but no Arms, and was born ſo, his
' Body being entirely ſmooth in the Places
' where ordinarily the Arms of Children may
' be ſaid to grow; now this Man had by many
' Years Practice, and I ſuppoſe a very early
' Application, brought the Joynt of his Knees
' to be ſo ſupple, that, contrary to the Uſage
' natural to our Bodies, he could turn them any
' way, and could as eaſily turn his Leg to a
' perpendicular Poſition upwards, as we all
' turn our Legs downwards to bear the Weight

' of

' of our Bodies when we walk, at the same
' time preferving the ordinary Situation alfo
' for the immediate Ufe of his Feet, to ftep,
' walk, leap, run, or other Exercifes proper
' for the Leg to perform.

' By this Ufage of the Joynts of his Knees,
' he could without any Difficulty turn up his
' Foot, and by the help of his Toes, which
' were alfo become as tractable as Fingers, I
' had almoft faid as handy as Fingers, he
' would pull off his Hat, fcratch or comb his
' Head, wafh his Face, take any Thing out of
' his Pockets, ufe a Sword, (handle a Sword I
' was going to fay) fire a Gun, nay fence and
' fight, and we were told he kill'd a Man with
' a Sword, and by what they call fair Fencing
' or Fighting, tho' that I do not believe ; a-
' mong the reft of his Performances he wrote
' very well, and that in feveral Languages,
' and feveral Characters: Now as this was
' perform'd with the Foot, it would be a grofs
' Impropriety to fay he wrote a very good
' *Foot*, and yet 'twas as abfur'd to fay he
' wrote a good HAND.

BUT Cuftom has legitimated this Way of
Speaking in *Englifh*, tho' it is not fo exprefs'd
in any other Language, as I meet with, in the
World: However I muft be allow'd to follow
the Ufage of our Country in Speech, and after
this Account given of my Thoughts about it,
I can bear no Part of the blame, or be quoted
as an Authority to any one elfe.

PART

PART IX.

IN speaking of the Manner of Writing in a stricter Sense, I confine my self to the *European* Writing; for of the Writing in the *Hebrew, Greek,* or *Arabick* Tongues, there is now no Room so much as to speak, except it be to note the miserable Degeneracy of the Writers in those Countrys; occasioned, principally, by their Discouragements in all Science, and Arts in the Parts of the World which are now over-run by the *Turks:* But of that, in its Place. I say, I am now confin'd to discourse of the several Usages of the Pen in the Christian World, and more especially in *England,* where the Art of Writing is carried to the highest Perfection of any Part of the Globe; not the *Dutch* excepted, tho' the *Dutch* really write very well too.

In *England* we divide our Manner of Writing into several Hands, and these we give several Names to, all with the Addition of the Word HAND, as a general Term of Art; such as Text-Hand, Court-Hand, Italian-Hand, Round-Hand, Running-Hand, and the like: Mixt with these are a Text Italian-Hand, and the Lawyers Hand; add the Ingrossing Hand, which is, indeed, but a kind of Text, and that, in General is a Kind of *Gothick,* which had its Original from the *German,* or *High Dutch* Way of Writing, who, to this Day, print all their Books in that Character.

BEFORE

BEFORE I come to speak of the ordinary Writing, or the Writing the ordinary Hands used in *England*, I must mention Two Extraordinary: One is particular to the Lawyers, and has its Usage only in the Proceedings in our Courts of Justice, and from thence is called *Court-Hand*. As our Laws, since the Conquest, were usually written in the *French* Tongue; some would have it, that the Court-hand was also introduc'd by the *French*; but as we have no Authority for saying so, and do not find that the *French*, or, indeed, any other Nation use any such Writing, so I shall not do it the Honour of so much Antiquity; and if the Gentlemen of the Long Robe would bear with me for using so much Freedom with them, I should rather say it was a Kind of Cant in Writing, such as the Gypsies and Thieves are said to use in Speaking to amuse; and tho' I do by no means compare the Gentlemen of the Law with those People I last mentioned, yet the Reason of the Thing might be just the same.

THE Lawyers, perhaps, found it necessary that their Clients should not always be too knowing in their Proceedings, and in the Particulars of the Methods they took in Solliciting; also the Law Terms, used in their Indictments and Declarations, were Things, which for sundry and various Reasons, the Lawyers were unwilling their Clients should so well understand as themselves. There may be other Reasons given also why this Hand was made use of, but who invented it at first we have no Account of.

As for Tachygraphy, or Short Writing, it has been suppos'd to be a modern Invention, and first found out by our *Sermon Writers*, a few Years since, when Writing Sermons from the

Mouths

Mouths of the Preachers was firſt in Uſe in *England*: But there are good Reaſons to be-lieve, that this Way of Writing was in uſe a-mong the *Romans* alſo, and that the Speeches of their Orators, their funeral Orations, and their Pleadings at their Tribunals were often, if not always, taken in Writing from their Mouths by the Artiſts in this way of Writing, which was then call'd Writing by Notes or Marks, and probably this may be underſtood in the Scrip-ture by what is call'd, *The Pen of a ready Wri-ter*. We have, indeed, no Remains of the Characters which they made Uſe of in thoſe Times, nor do we ſee any ſuch Writing as that we call *Short Hand* among the Nations round us; and thoſe who firſt invented the preſent *Short Hand* which we now practiſe, doubt-leſs are to be eſteemed as Men of Merit, be-cauſe they firſt formed it into a perfect Syſtem of Art, and placing the Vowels in a Circular, or rather a Semicircular Poſition about the Conſonants, made the Connexion ſo exact, that they could not only write Short, but read what one another Wrote, which in other Short Hands could not be done.

By this Art the Tongue has indeed been out-ſtript by the Hand, and I have ſeen ſome who have been able to write faſter than Men ordina-rily ſpeak; by which means Speeches in publick Auditories, Pleadings on Eminent Trials, Speeches at the Places of Execution, and ma-ny valuable Things which would otherwiſe have been loſt to the World, have been pre-ſerved, even unknown to the Speakers them-ſelves.

This Invention, as it is in moſt ſuch Caſes, has been followed with many others, pretend-ing

ing to improve it; but it may be faid, what is
not often faid of any Inventors, or Inventions,
(*viz.*) that the firft has been the beft, and. that
no Improver has gone beyond them or perhaps ever will.

THERE feems, indeed, to be lefs Occafion
now for this Art than ever was in *England*, and
the Occafion leffens every Day, for as to *Sermon Writing*, that is quite laid afide, (*as Sermon
Hearing indeed feems alfo likely to be in a little
more Time ;*) and as to Trials in extraordinary
Cafes, and Speeches, People have fo often been
reproved for Writing on fuch Occafions, and
put out of the Courts and Places where they
have attempted it, that this alfo feems to be
left of ; and as to Dying Speeches, Dying Men
have been fo often injured by the false and
imperfect Accounts given from thofe that have
pretended to write from their Mouths, that
fuch People generally give (what they defign
to fay) in Writing to the Sheriff or Officer, appointed to attend the Execution, and defire it
may be made Publick; leaving Coppies with
fome of their Relations, in order to be fure
that nothing fhould be added, or omitted, and
fo that no Wrong be done them.

THESE Things, I fay, make this Art of
Short Writing, or as tis commonly call'd writing *Short Hand*, grow out of Ufe in *England*,
and as for *Scotland*, I fcarce ever met with any
that underftood it there, neither in *France* nor
in *Spain*.

THERE is another Art or Method of Writing which has been of very antient Ufage,
and tho' it is not now much in ufe, yet we have
the Equivalent to it now, which we call a Cypher, and they are indeed the fame thing that
the

the Antients call'd *Steganography*, as above. I shall
give a brief Account of this Way of Writing here,
and difmifs it at once, for it has no great matter in it to make it worth while to dwell on,
for any long time.

STEGANOGRAPHY is the Art of writing Secrets, fo as that none but the Party, to whom
they are addrefs'd, fhall be able to read or
underftand them, the Word it felf fignifying
Writing that is to be cover'd or concealed : and
though this Art were known amongft the Antients, yet it feems that *Trithemius* was the firft
that fet down the Rules of it, which he hath
perform'd, not only in his fix Books of *Poly-
graphy*, but more efpecially, in his famous
Treatife of *Steganography* which has made fo
much Noife in the World. Now though his
Defign was, in part, to reveal this ufeful Secret,
yet was he not willing to make it indifferently intelligible to all Sorts of Perfons; his End
being only to inftruct the Learned, and the
Minifters of State ; and, therefore, to deter
the common People from reading his Books,
he pretended to a Familiarity with evil Spirits,
and made ufe of fome ftrange Baftard *Hebrew*
Names; fuch as *Pamerfiel*, *Camuel*, &c. which
though he only ufed to illuftrate the Method of this Art, yet was the good Abbot, upon
this Account, fufpected to be a Magician; and
notwithftanding all the Endeavours that *Trithemius* ufed to vindicate himfelf, his Slanderers
have endeavoured, and that with fome Succefs, to make his *Steganography* pafs in the World
for a Piece full of Superftition and unlaw-
ful Magick : However there have not been
wanting many learned Men who have under-
taken to defend *Trithemius*, and to improve the

Art

Art he had publish'd. The most Illustrious of
these Apologists was the Duke of *Lunenburgh*,
who caused a Book on this Subject to be printed, call'd *Cryptography, i. e.* A hidden Way of
Writing, in 1624. The famous *Caramuel* also
publish'd his *Steganography* at *Bruxels*, afterwards at *Collen*, in 1635, which is nothing
else but an Explication of *Trithemius* his *Steganography*, and of the *Clavicula* of *Solomon* the
German: Father *Gaspar Schottus*, a Jesuit, publish'd also, in 1665, his *Schola Steganographica*,
wherein he defends the good Abbot ; and last
of all, about twenty five Years ago, one *Wolf-
gangus Ernestus Heidelius* hath written a Commentary upon *Trithemius* his *Steganography*,
where he sets down many new Ways of disgui-
sing one's Meaning in a Letter, by the means
of Variety of Characters, with many ingenious Principles for the improving of this Art,
*Vid. G. Caramuel in Cursu liberali. Baillet Juge-
mens Des scavans.*

I COME next to speak of the Art of Writing as it is now practised in *England* ; and
here, I must confess, it is a terrible Satyr upon our Nation, to reflect how sorrily, not to
say sordidly, most People, in our Country,
write their own Mother-tongue, and especially
how they spell it : And 'tis a little hard, that
before I mention any Thing of the good Writing among us, in which our Artists, at this
Time, excel most of the Nations in *Europe*, we
must speak a little too of the scandalous Negligence of almost all our People, and especi-
ly the Gentry and People out of Trade, in
teaching their Children to write ; Insomuch
that, in some, the greater and higher the Quality of Persons be, the worse, generally speaking
they.

they may be found to write ; as if Writing, which
is one of the moſt eſſential Parts of Education,
was grown uſeleſs or obſolete, and out of faſhion,
and that it was no Scandal to be Ignorant of it.

I HAVE not, indeed, critically examin'd
how it is in other Countries, having, however,
ſeen the miſſive Letters and publick Acts of
many Nations ; and this I ſpeak upon the
Foot of what I have ſo ſeen of the other Kind
from abroad : Namely, that many Nations
write worſe than the *Engliſh*, but none ſpell
worſe or ſo ill. I have ſeen ſome publick
Writings in the *French* and in the *Spaniſh*
Tongues very curiouſly written ; and the *Biſ-
cayners* in *Spain* are accounted excellent Pen-
men : And though both theſe Nations, eſpecially the *French*, have more difficult Spelling,
though not more difficult Pronouncing than
the *Engliſh* ; yet none of them that I have met
with, ſpell their Words ſo Ill, or are, in general, ſo Ignorant in the Orthography of their
Speech as the *Engliſh*.

IT would be too much a Satyr upon our Education in *England* to enter into the Reaſon of
this, or examine why our Gentry ſo generally,
(and the Women univerſally) ſpell our Language ſo ill, or as it rather ſhould be ſaid, can
not ſpell it at all.

BUT to come back to the Work of Writing,
(as now in uſe) it is perform'd (1.) by the Hand,
Writing with the Inſtrument call'd a Pen, and
upon Paper, or Parchment, and Vellum ; or
(2.) by a Graving or Carving Tool, or Inſtrument: This indeed follows the Pen, and perfcrms
very curious Things, by Engraving in Copper or
Braſs, which is afterwards made capable o Impreſſing the Letters on Paper by an Engine,

which

which some call Printing, tho' perform'd after a different Manner from the ordinary Way of Printing; the Engine it is wrought with is called the *Rolling-Press*.

Now in these several Methods of Writing, the Ingenious Masters of this Art, have invented several shaped Characters, or rather Methods of making the Characters by which they write, these are, as I observ'd before, ordinarily, but very improperly, call'd HANDS; from whence Men are said to write such or such a Hand: And our Writing Masters generally write over their Doors, *Here are Taught all the Hands used in* England: These several Hands are ordinarily call'd, as follows,

Round Hand,
Italian Hand,
Text Hand Small,
Court Hand,
Text Italian,
Running Hand,
Large Text,
Short Hand.

THESE, in the Printing Art, are call'd by differing Names, and those Names again multiplied according to the Size of the Letters, o Types, in which each of them are expressed, and with some particular modern Names also occasion'd by the extraordinary Performance of some modern Founders of Letters, which have made finer and more curious *Types* or Letters than what had been made before. The geneal Names are thus,

Roman

Roman and under this Denomination. {
Capital Roman,
Great Primmer,
Englifh,
Pica,
Small Pica,
Small Primmer,
Long Primmer,
Brevier,
Non Parreil,
Elziver.
}

Italick anfwerable to all the feveral Sizes of the Roman Types abovementioned, and bearing the Addition of their Names, as Italick Capitals, Englifh Italick, and the like.

Gothick, among which the Roman is ufed in proper Names, as the Italicks are among the Roman Letters.

In writing the feveral Hands, mentioned above, there is certainly requir'd different Art; and feveral Mafters are particularly skilful, and excel in one, more than another Way of Writing ; as fome excel in one Hand, fome in another.

It is needlefs to give Specimens here of the feveral Hands now in Ufe, and mentioned as above : The ordinary Copy-books, publifh'd for the Teaching the Art of Writing, are compleat Directions in this Cafe ; and fome of them are Teftimonies of the moft exquifite Performances of the Mafters concern'd ; to which I refer.

But as, fince the Art of Printing has been invented, the laborious part of Writing is ta-

ken

ken off, and the Copying or Writing of
Books is at an End; fo neither is the Writing
itfelf fo embellifh'd by Art as in former Times,
nor are the Artifts fo innumerably many as before: But the *Printing Art* has out-run the
Pen, and may pafs for the greateft Improvement of its Kind in the World.

LEARNING, in particular, is infinitely be-
holding to it by the fpreading of ufeful Knowledge in the World, and making the Acceffion
to it cheap and eafy: For not to fpeak of the
Difficulty of Writing, and the Number of
Hands that muft be employ'd about it, 'tis
moft certain the Price of Books muft infinitely
have exceeded what it is now; and as in
Trade it is a received Maxim, that Cheapnefs
caufes Confumption, fo here Cheapnefs cauf-
ing now the fpreading and extending of Books,
its contrary (Dearnefs) muft have leffen'd and
reftrain'd it ; confequently Knowledge, without it had been under greater Limitations and
Reftrictions, and the moft ufeful Branches of
Science had been much more hid and conceal'd;
the Knowledge of Hiftory and Geography (to
launch out into no more Particulars) to how
few Ears wou'd it have reach'd, and how few
People wou'd have known what had been
done in the World ?

How little a Way wou'd the Fame of the
greateft Heroe have reach'd ? The Noife of a
Victory would have fcarce been heard farther
than the Noife of the Cannon ; much lefs could
Things have continued in Time, longer than
the Memory of the Perfons concern'd wou'd
preferve them, or that moft corrupting multi-
plying Ufage of Tradition have convey'd
them ;

them; of which already we see so many fatal Effects, and by which Things of the greatest Moment done as it were but Yesterday, that is to say, within the Compass of two or three Ages, turn into Fable and Romance: Scoundrels are made Heroes, and Heroes are made Gods; for so no doubt the Deifying the first Tyrants of the World, such as *Saturn*, *Jupiter*, *Bacchus*, and *Mercury*, and *Belus* (or *Baal*) came about. Thus again the Memory of Wise Men has been handed down to Posterity, as of Monsters; and of Learned Men, as of Wizards, and afterwards as of Devils: Thus *Atlas*, said to carry the World on his Shoulders, is made a Giant carrying that load (the *Globe*) upon his Back; and *Prometheus*, a Giant, chain'd down upon Mount *Caucasus*, with a Vulture gnawing his Liver, and condemn'd to that Fate by *Jupiter* for stealing Fire from the Sun to put Life into his Man of Clay which he had made; all which was no more than this, That *Atlas* by his Wisdom and Knowledge instructed the whole World in the Knowledge of Things, and gave them just Rules for Government, whereby he might be said to bear the Weight of the World's management upon his Shoulders; and that *Prometheus* was so studious for the general Good of Mankind, that he brought Light and Life from Heaven into their Souls; and was so intent upon his Studies of the heavenly Bodies, that lying on the Ground whole Nights together upon Mount *Caucasus* (where he liv'd) the better to observe the Motions of the Stars, he contracted Diseases which eat into his Vitals, and brought him into a Consumption, prey-

ing

ing upon his Liver, and deſtroy'd him. The like of *Dædalus* and *Icarus*, and his making Wings to fly in the Air, which was no more than his inventing Sails for Boats and Ships to ſail upon the Sea ; and the like.

THESE Things have been the Effect of the Want of Letters, and of the Art of Writing; and the like wou'd be the Effect, and that notwithſtanding the Knowledge of both, if the Art of Printing had not follow'd, to make what was written diffuſive, by the Multitude and Cheapneſs of Books.

THE Effect of the Want of this is plain, in the Difficulty it has been to the World to preſerve authentick Copies of the Hiſtories of Things done in former Ages, and of Aſſertaining the Integrity of thoſe Copies we have.

HOW few, and thoſe how uncertain, are the Accounts left us of Antiquity, and how little do we know compar'd to what might have been known, of the Hiſtory of the early Ages of the World ? What an ineſtimable Loſs was the burning of the Library of *Ptolemy Philadelphus*, at *Alexandria?* wherein, if the whole Story be not fabulous, was 700,000 Volums, that is to ſay Rolls, or Tables, or Bundles of Papirij Manuſcripts.

NAY ſuch was the Fate of Things, that, if we are not miſinform'd, in the Reign of good *Joſiah*, there was but one Copy of God's Law left in the whole World, and it was next to a Miracle, that the ſame Calamity, namely, the idolatrous wicked Doings of *Manaſſeh* his Father had not deſtroy'd that one ; ſo that, in ſhort, if that one Copy had not been extant, the whole *Levitical* Inſtitution had been loſt,

and

and we had never known what the Laws of *Mofes* were to this Day.

B U T to come nearer; How many noble Works have fince that time been loft, as particularly feveral Books of *Livy*'s *Roman* Hiftory are not found; and how ill are they fupply'd? And how few Hiftorians are there that record the great Actions of the Heroes of that Age? Not a Man that has given any particular Relation of the greateft Actions of *Julius Cæfar*, but his own Commentaries, which are fhort to a Fault; the Beginning of the greateft Battles are fcarce told, but the End follows, they began to fight *fo* and *fo*, and then the Enemy were beaten, &c.

O F all the Wars of *Alexander*, *Quintus Curtius*'s Abridgements conclude the whole; the Siege of *Troy*, were it unfung by *Homer*, what fhou'd we have known of it? And even now we fcarce know whether it is a Hiftory, or that Ballad-Singers Fable to get a Penny.

H o w are the Books of the *Sibyls* loft, and the Hiftories of all the reft of the World, after the Declining of the *Roman* Empire? How imperfect is Antiquity in all thofe Things?

H A D Printing been in Ufe in the flourifhing Times of *Auguftus Cæfar*, when the World was full of the politeft Writers; and in the Times of the other Emperors, when Learning had all poffible Encouragement; how many noble Authors fhou'd we have had recording the particular Hiftories, and fome the Annals and Chronicles of thofe Ages, befides a *Livy* and a *Saluft*, and two or three more, upon whom we are left to depend for all that we can learn of thofe Times?

How

How many *Virgils*, and *Juvenals*, and *Lucans*, and *Ovids*, fhou'd we have feen inftead of thefe few, in a Time when Poetry was arriv'd to fo correct, and fo juftly admir'd a Perfection? Inftead of which, how few are all the Writers of thofe Ages? not a Moralift among the *Greeks* but *Plutarch*, or among the *Latines* but *Seneca* and *Cicero*, and two or three more.

AGAIN, Since the Times of Chriftianity, How many of the Writings of the moft antient Fathers have been loft? Whence is it become a Doubt among us, Whether St. *Peter* was at *Rome* or no, and who, and who were the real Succeffors in the Papal Chair? Can it be conceiv'd, that if Printing had been in Ufe, the Writings of thofe Times, would not have been preferv'd? Manufcripts were eafily fupprefs'd, and once loft never recover'd; Where are the Journals of all the famous Councils and the Speeches of orthodox Heroes of the Church in the primitive Times? Among the Collections we have, how often is it faid with a Note of Lamentation, *Such and fuch Things are loft?*

NAY to this Day, How valued, rather, how invaluable is an antient Manufcript efteem'd; and what Rarities do we count them for preferving Hiftory and Chronology? Much of the Hiftory and Chronology of the World, is only preferved in old Coins and Medals, Bufto's and Infcriptions, Altars and Monuments, dug out of the Earth, and pickt up in the ruinous Heaps of demolifh'd Towns and Caftles.

BUT, in one Word, when the Writings of the Moderns have not one thoufandth

Part

Part of the Weight in them, no not even the beſt of them, we have a Method, by which a Work once printed is ſcarce ever loſt.

I T is true, that Books printed ſometimes become ſcarce, and as we call it, out of Print, and ſometimes are quite loſt; and we think many ſuch were loſt (with reſpect to our *Britiſh* Affairs) in the Deſtruction of Abbeys and Monaſtries in *England* and *Scotland*, alſo in the firſt Heats of the Reformation, and per-haps in our Civil Wars; no doubt ſome very valuable Manuſcripts were loſt; and in par-ticular thoſe relating to Antiquity, and the firſt Times of Chriſtianity in this Nation; for Example, the ſeveral Tranſlations of the Bible, and Writings of the firſt Reformers were loſt in the Perſecutions which follow'd; we ſee nothing of *Wicklif*'s Writings, or any of the Fathers of the Reformation, except a few of old *Latimer*'s Sermons left among us, tho' we are aſſur'd they wrote and printed many Thouſands; even *Tindal*'s Tranſlation of the Bible is not to be had, except in ſome extraordinary Libraries.

I C o u l d run this Remark out into many Particulars reaching even to the holy Scrip-tures and the ſacred Writings of the Apoſtles themſelves, many of which, 'tis believ'd, are entirely loſt in the World.

B u t to bring it down to the Caſe, Such is the excellency of the Art of Printing, that every Thing worth recording in the World, is now ſo ſecur'd, that it may almoſt be ſaid, it cannot be loſt, and perhaps may never till the general Conflagration,

T h e

T h e Eafinefs of the Performance makes the Books printed now fo cheap, that the meaneft and pooreft People that have any Thing more than juft to fubfift them, may purchafe Books for needful Ufe; fo that whether Sacred or Prophane, the Knowledge of Things fpreads, as far as the World is inhabited with Creatures that can read.

T h i s Art of Printing was faid to be found out at *Harlem* in *Holland*, but was either carry'd from thence to, or firft invented at *Mentz* in *Germany*: They fpeak of it as fomething wonderful, that Printing was invented by a Man of Arms, [*Soldier*,] and Gunpowder by a Man of Letters, [*Monk*;] all that is to be faid of that, is, that was a learned Soldier, and this a Chymift, or chymical Fryer, or Monk; neither of which hath any Thing wonderful in it.

I t is not to my Purpofe here, to enter into a large Hiftory of the Art of Printing, or into the particular Improvements of it in the feveral Ages fince its Invention; But the following Abridgement of both I think needful to the prefent Purpofe, and agreeable to the Defign.

I t was invented by *Lawrenzs Janzs Cofter* a Soldier at *Harlem*: This I find recorded in the Town Regifter there, in the Year 1430. The firft Operation, it feems, was perform'd by Pieces of Wood, on which the Words to be imprefs'd were firft cut with a carving Tool, and the Impreffion was eafily made, by laying ir hard on upon the Paper, juft in the fame manner as our Callico Printers practife at this Day; and by this Means he printed not one

Letter

Letter or one Word at a time, but a Line, or Paragraph; nay at laſt he came ſo far as to print a whole Page at a ſtroke.

B U T finding this not to anſwer, except in ſmall Things, which contain'd no more than what one of his Pieces of Wood cou'd likewiſe contain, he ſet his Invention at work, and found out a Way to cut the Mould of a Letter in Steel, and by that caſt the *Type*, or Letter itſelf, in the ſame manner as is now practis'd by the Letter Founders; nor has any better Method been ever found out ſince, or I believe can be.

J O H N Guttenburgh was Comrade to this *Coſter*, and having ſeen all his Methods, and made himſelf Maſter of the Performance, ſtole away his Tools, and went with them to *Mentz* in *Germany*; where having nothing to do, but to ſet them up and go to work, whereas *Coſter* had every Thing to make over again, he (*Guttenburgh*) got to work a great while before *Coſter* could be ready, and ſo obtain'd the Fame of being the firſt Inventor.

T o prove this they tell us, That one *Rabbi Joſeph*, a Jew, in a Chronicle (of his Writing) of *Germany*, mentions a printed Book which he ſaw in the Year of the World 5288, that is of our reckoning 1428, as may be ſeen in *Scriverius*: Upon the whole *Guttenburgh* carry'd the Honour of the firſt Inventor in *Germany*, and *Coſter* in *Holland*, each Country contending for their Countryman. Both it ſeems agree, that *Tully*'s Offices was the firſt Book ever printed by this Art, printed in the Year 1465; this is ſaid to be printed

b

by one *John Fauſtus* aſſiſtant to *Guttenburgh*, as is mention'd by a *N. B.* in that Copy of *Tully* of the firſt Impreſſion, which is now to be ſeen in the *Bodleian* Library in *Oxon*.

B E it which it will, *Coſter*, or *Guttenburgh*, about thatTime the Way of Printing began in theWorld,which is not full 300Years ago; how wonderfully it is improv'd and encreas'd ſince that Time we are all Witneſſes ; it ſeems it came very early to be practis'd in *England* ; for *Henry* VI. or *Boucher* Archbiſhop of *Canterbury* rather, in *Henry* VI's Time, ſent over two Men to *Harlem* to learn this Art ; The Men ſent were *William Turner*, Maſter of the King's Robes, and *William Caxton*, Merchant ; Theſe managed ſo well that they privately prevail'd with *Fredrick Corſelies*, one of *Coſter*'s Workmen, to whom he had taught the Art, to come over with them to *England*, having, it ſeems, brib'd him with a good Sum of Money : Having ſucceeded thus happily, they brought him to *Oxford*, where he ſet up a Printing-houſe; and this they tell us was in the Year 1467 ; and there is a Treatiſe of *Ruſſinus* now to be ſeen, printed on a broad un-ſhapen Octavo, in the Year 1458, about three Years after the *German* Edition of *Tully's Offices* mention'd above.

T H E firſt Book ever printed, as *Tully* in particular, is on Vellum, but the Book of *Ruſſinus* is upon Paper; for about the ſame Time, namely, in the Year 1417, the Making of Paper was invented, and firſt found out at *Bazle* in *Switzerland*, by *Anthony* and *Michael Galicion*, two *Greeks*, and this ſoon ſpread every

every where, the Art itfelf not being fo difficult as that of Printing had been.

FROM *Oxford* the Printing-Prefs came to *London, Anno* 1471, tho' *Moxon* in his Art of Printing fays, the firft Book printed in *London* was in 1480, when alfo it began to be practis'd in *France, Germany,* and other remote Countries.

IN the Library at *Bennet's* College, *Cambridge,* is a very antient printed Book, faid to be done the moft antient of any, and to be the Work of *Cofter,* at *Harlem* : It is printed but on one Side of the Leaf; the Letters are plainly cut in Wood, not fet and compos'd by Letters caft in Metal, as is now perform'd; and it is wrought not with Printing-Ink, but with the ordinary Writing Ink, tho' very good; but there is no Imprimatur, fo that we neither know the Time when, or the Place where it was performed.

BUT there are many Proofs for the Priority of *Cofter* to *Guttenburgh*; and that in particular, that we have no Book printed by the latter before *Tully's Offices,* which were not printed till the Year 1465; whereas *Fauftus,* who was firft a Servant to *Cofter,* printed a Pfalter, and another Book entitul'd, *Alexandri Doctrinale cum* Petri Hifpani *Tractatibus,* dated 1442.

THIS Art was fo great a Surprize to the World, at its firft being publifh'd, that this *John Fauftus* coming to *Paris,* and offering to fell fome printed Teftaments, or Pfalters there, as if they had been Manufcripts; fome of the learned Men, viewing the exact conformity of them one with another, even to a

Line,

Line, a Word, a Letter, nay to a Speck; and not able to imagine which Way it was poffible, and that none of their Scribes could do the like; took up *Fauftus*, declar'd he was a Wizard, and a Magician, and that he dealt with the Devil, and order'd him to be profecuted as fuch; thus putting him in Fear of his Life, they got the Art out of him; and this it feems is the Original of that fo famous Story of Dr. *John Fauftus*, or *Fofter*, a *High-German* Conjurer.

About the fame Time, very happily for the propagating the Invention of Printing, the Invention of Paper-making ftarted into the World, as it were on purpofe to go hand in hand with the Prefs; it was invented, as I have faid, at *Bazil*, in the Year 1417, by *Michael* and *Anthony Galicion*, and was prefently improv'd to a great Perfection.

Some think that this Paper, made at *Bafil*, was made of Flax, not of Linen Rags: The two Brothers, who contriv'd it, were *Greeks*, who fled out of their Country after *Conftantinople* was befieg'd by the *Turks*: But this does not agree with the Year, it feems it was an Imitation of the Cotton Paper ufed in the *Levant*.

Certain it is, That Cotton Paper has been of very antient Ufe in the *Eaft*, there being in the *Bodleian* Library an *Arabick* Manufcript among thofe the Univerfity bought of Dr. *Huntingdon*, written in the four hundred and twenty feventh Year of the *Hegira*, which is *Anno. Dom*. 1c49, on this Paper, and fome there are without Dates, which feem older.

And

AND as for the Linnen Rag Paper, it muſt be much older than 1425; for in the Archieves of the Library of the Dean and Chapter of *Canterbury*, there is an Inventory on our Paper of the Goods of *Henry Prior*, of *Chriſt's-Church* there; that is dated in the twentieth Year of *Edward* the Third, which is *Anno Dom.* 1346; and in the *Cotton* Library are ſeveral Writings on our Paper, as high, at leaſt, as the fifteenth Year of *Edward* the Third.

SOME think the Rolling Preſs was invented by *Lipſius.* But there is a printed Book in the *Bodleian* Library, placed *Laud*, page 138, being a *Miſſale ſecundum uſum Eccleſ. Herbipolenſis*, that is, *Wurtzburgh* in *Germany* : At the Beginning of this Book is an Inſtrument of *Rodulfus* the Archbiſhop of this Church, containing the Reaſon of the Publication of this *Miſſale*; and inſtead of a Seal there is annexed a Print, Engraven, of the Arms of the See, *&c.* very finely done (for that Time, for it was before *Purer)* and on which are evident Marks of the Preſſure by the Plate, with ſome Touches of Ink at the Edges, which they that have ſeen it judge to be the plain Marks of its being done, or wrought off in a Rolling Preſs, and there are ſufficient Reaſons to prove that this Book is as antient as 1481.

THE next Form of Printing at *Harlem*, was by cutting whole Forms of Wood from Manuſcripts exactly written, and without Pictures; ſuch perhaps was the *Donatus*; which might bear Date about 1450, ſome
ſay

ſay 1440; *This appears plain* (ſaith Mr. *Bagford*) *from Copy Books which we have ſeen printed at* Rome, Venice, Switzerland, *and* England, *as high as* 1500.

THE third Way of Printing was with ſingle Types made of Wood, but who invented this is not known: It was at firſt eſteemed ſo great a Rarity, that the Printers carried about their Letters in Bags at their Backs, and got Money at great Mens Houſes, by Printing the Names of the Family, Epitaphs, Songs, and other ſmall Pamphlets.

THE fourth Improvement of this noble Art was the Invention of ſingle Types made of Metal, which is owing to *Peter Scheffer*, above mentioned, firſt Servant, and then Son-in-Law to *Fauſtus*, who worked at *Mentz*; ſometimes you have the Names of theſe two Men printed at the End of their Books, and ſometimes not, ſometimes with Dates as high as the Year 1457, and as low as 1490.

BUT to return to the Subject of Writing, with which I ſhall conclude.

HAD Writing only been the Way of Publiſhing in this Learned bookiſh Age, I believe I may venture to ſay, that Writing wou'd neceſſarily employ as many Hands as the Woollen Manufacture, and would as much have deſerv'd the Name of a Manufacture; that is to ſay, upon a Suppoſition, that the Number of Books ſhou'd be as great, and the Itch of writing
ing

ing Books as ſtrong as it is now. Of the Manner, Excellencies, and Improvement, of this excellent Art, and what it may yet be farther capable of with mathematical Rules for exact Writing; having no room to enter upon it here, I may diſcourſe of at large hereafter in a Work by it-ſelf.

F   I   N   I   S.